MOONLIGHT FLYER

MOONLIGHT FLYER

DIARY OF A SECOND WORLD WAR NAVIGATOR

JOHN GELLNER
EDITED BY PAVEL VANČATA

FONTHILL

Fonthill Media Language Policy

Fonthill Media publishes in the international English language market. One language edition is published worldwide. As there are minor differences in spelling and presentation, especially with regards to American English and British English, a policy is necessary to define which form of English to use. Both John Gellner and Pavel Vančata are of Czechoslovak origin, so British English has been adopted for this publication.

Fonthill Media Limited
Fonthill Media LLC
www.fonthillmedia.com
office@fonthillmedia.com

First published in the United Kingdom and the United States of America 2016

British Library Cataloguing in Publication Data:
A catalogue record for this book is available from the British Library

Copyright © Pavel Vančata 2016

ISBN 978-1-78155-509-5

The right of Pavel Vančata to be identified as the author of this work has been asserted by him in accordance with the Copyright, Designs and Patents Act 1988.

All rights reserved. No part of this publication may be reproduced, stored in a retrieval system or transmitted in any form or by any means, electronic, mechanical, photocopying, recording or otherwise, without prior permission in writing from Fonthill Media Limited

Typeset in 11pt on 13pt MinionPro
Printed and bound by CPI Group (UK) Ltd, Croydon, CR0 4YY

Foreword

During the Second World War, there were more than 2,400 airmen serving in the Royal Air Force who proudly wore the shoulder insignia that read 'Czechoslovakia'.

Only a small number of them kept a personal diary, and even fewer of these diaries have survived to this day. One of those who had documented his day-to-day experiences in considerable detail was a navigator by the name of John Gellner. He was a member of the Royal Canadian Air Force who had flown with No. 311 'Czechoslovak' (B) Squadron RAF.

Gellner characterised himself in one of his contributions about No. 311 (B) Squadron in the book *Wings in Exile*, first published in London in 1942:

> The aircraft which landed safely, fourth out of the seven sent out, has, for its navigator, an officer who keeps a diary. Not too many members of the Squadron do this; your average airman is a light-hearted soul, who prefers to forget the vicissitudes of his profession as quickly as possible. The navigator, however, is an exception, and it is his great delight to live over again in spirit the events of which he has been a witness.

Gellner settled down in Canada after the Second World War and embarked on a lifetime of literary activity. Some entries from his war diary were used in a number of articles, and further extracts reflect a modest attitude to his war service:

> My wartime career was a very ordinary one. I served as an air observer, then after re-training, as a pilot, and in the end as a staff officer—by VE day, I was a Squadron Leader with the Distinguished Flying Cross, like so many other air crew who by good luck had survived in a service in which the number of casualties was outright appalling; in our group of thirty-seven, for instance, the first of BCATP graduates to go overseas, only eight were left when it was all over.

Gellner's comparatively brief memoirs were published posthumously by his cousin Ernest Zucker. They described his wide-ranging, colourful, and dangerous life experiences, and were appropriately titled *A Life That Might Seem Like One Long Adventure Holiday*. John Gellner was truly a vibrant and interesting character, and his unique wartime diary from 1940–41 can now be shared with the reader.

This book was first published in 2009 in the Czech language. The enthusiastic acceptance among Czech readers, and the disappointment of my English-speaking friends all around the world, inspired me to prepare an English edition of the book. The decision was an obvious one; John Gellner spent more than half of his life in Canada, where he became a world-renowned journalist and military expert.

I hope that this English edition of John's diary will have a strong appeal to those who are interested in accounts of the brave men who fought and died in the Second World War to secure ultimate victory for the Allies.

Pavel Vančata
Prague, July 2015

And those navigators! Imagine hitting a little island in the middle of a big body of water. I can't even find the soap in the bathtub. But a navigator can find anything. He just takes out some maps, shoots the sun, draws a circle on his map, trisects the circle, figures the number of degrees in each angle against his compass reading, cut the cards, and before you know it he's located the only blonde in town.

Bob Hope (1903–2003), American comedian and actor who performed in countless programmes for American soldiers and their Allies between 1941 and 1991

Preface

I am honoured to be asked to write a few words about John Gellner on behalf of many of us who knew, served, and worked with him during his years of service as an RCAF officer and, for many years after, as a defence thinker, journalist, and editor.

John was already well-known throughout the RCAF when I met him in Ottawa as he joined the Directorate of Air Training in 1942. He had just returned to Canada following the completion of his first tour of operational flying over enemy territory. John had successfully completed his tour as a navigator with a Czech squadron during a period of the war when casualty rates among bomber crews were very high. When he finished sharing his operational experience with young trainees in Canada, he requested to be trained as a pilot himself.

I next learned about John when I arrived in England. I had been posted to an Operations Training Unit at RAF Honeybourne, where he had successfully completed his own training. He had subsequently joined No. 429 'Bison' (B) Squadron for a further operational tour. However, the Air Force soon determined that John's best contribution to the cause would be probably through his other skills.

It was John's unique background, education, and experience growing up in Europe, plus skills acquired in operations during the Second World War and first-hand experience with eager young pilots in training, that made him an outstanding candidate to serve as the first Chief Administrative Officer of No. 3 (F) Wing, RCAF, in Zweibrücken, Germany. Through his command of languages, his knowledge of Europe and its ways, his diplomatic skills, and his war-time experience, John made an outstanding contribution to the launching and effective operation of the base, all the while working to support Canadian involvement with the local community.

When we first arrived at the new Canadian base in Zweibrücken in early 1953, construction on the base was not yet completed. I recall that there was only one chair in what was to become my office in the headquarters building, and the civilian contractors had not yet completed our accommodation on the base. For a time, therefore, we took up residence at the Adler Hotel in downtown Zweibrücken.

The Zweibrücken base was formally turned over from France to Canada on 27 April 1953. This was a memorable ceremonial event as diplomacy was much more formal then than now. Not long after, on the Whitsun weekend of 1953, an expedition of Gellners (John and Herta) and Hulls (Jane, my wife, Diana, my oldest daughter, and me), along with Helen Claxton (daughter of the Defence Minister), all set off for a holiday in the mountains. We stayed in Oberammergau, south Bavaria, visited the Black Forest and Kandersteg in Switzerland, and had a memorable lunch in the garden of a restaurant at Spiez. This is just one such adventure that serves to illustrate how fun could be inserted into the demands of what was a very active military life.

But all was far from play. With all three squadrons of Canadian-built F-86 Sabres safely arrived, the pilots got into their busy routines of training and preparation. During these years in Europe, the complement of Canadians in uniform was relatively small compared to the civilian staff employed on the base. Managing the civilian staff in the light of the recent war, in which many of the German men had served and who thus came from a very different military culture than Canada's, was in great measure accomplished through John's understanding.

John was also very aware of the need to build good relations with the civil authorities in Zweibrücken. He advised me that before we began to participate in local formal festivities, we needed to have formal introductions to the town mayor and his colleagues. We also established good relations with the authorities of the villages around Zweibrücken, and we took some pains in following their politics as a precaution in defence of critical fuel pipelines that ran through villages adjacent to the base.

John's skills were also instrumental, at every stage, in the creation of the Zweibrücken-based-and-launched hockey team—the RCAF Flyers. The Flyers travelled and played all over Europe—on arenas larger than the NHL standard and to rules and customs more courteous than those observed in the NHL at the time.

My family's first home in a Zweibrücken suburb was a duplex, with each floor having a self-contained unit. We were on the ground floor, and the Gellners the floor above. The house had a small garden at the back and a little lawn where the Hull and Gellner families first met for a Canadian-style picnic and barbecue. The families got to know one another, and discussions among Hulls and Gellners about the 'ways of the world' began at this moment and continued until shortly before John's death. Diana was particularly close to Herta and John, and my son Brian agreed that John was his 'honorary' uncle. I am grateful to say that John was able to provide Brian with some good advice and help at key moments in his life.

There is not too much that I can add to John's remarkable post-RCAF career. He retired in 1958, wrote for *The Globe and Mail*, and travelled widely as a correspondent to the world's trouble spots. He contributed immensely to elevating the thoughtful attention given in Canada to strategic affairs, both from the military and political dimensions. The country is richer and more effective in the world for the intellectual roots that he helped nourish.

Through all of this, Hulls and Gellners met from time to time for trips to Stratford, visits to John's home in the Caledon Hills, north of Toronto, and other family occasions. In the spring of 1993, Brian was able to share his delight with John on the occasion of Brian's first visit to Prague.

John's mentoring touched the lives of many young officers, their wives and girlfriends, and their children, and provided understanding support to many couples at important turning points in their lives. In short, John was a great contributor to his adopted country and many people—military and civilian, young and old—in their professional careers and in their lives. As I hope the readers will learn from this, the first complete telling of his story, he was a truly remarkable man, with many-sided talents and a great human spirit.

Lieutenant General Allan Chester Hull CMM DFC CD
Belleville, Ontario, Canada
8 May 2009

Acknowledgements

The author would like to express his gratitude to all who contributed by providing all of the information, documents, and photos for this book, as their assistance was vital. In alphabetical order, they were: Jan Bobek, Steve Brew, David Briggs, James Ernest Buckland, Dennis Burke, Peter Clare, Alan Clark, Robert J. Collis, Karel Čvančara, Otakar Černý, Steve Darke, Josef Doubek, David Duxbury, Eddie Fell, Ben Fisher, John Foreman, Jaromír Foretník, Thomas Fuller, Norman Franks, Thomas Grothkopp, Franek Grabowski, Håkan Gustavsson, Randal Hankla, Hugh A. Halliday, Jürgen Haus, Ian Herbert, Bertrand Hugot, Ian Hunt, Božena Husáková-Vellová, Remco Immerzeel, Iveta Irvingová, William R. Chorley, Mirko Janeček, Armin Karcher, Václav Kolesa, Clara Koser, David Krakow, Marie Lambourne, Joss Leclercq, Ken MacLean, Stephen Liska, Norman Malayney, Francis Marshall, Errol Martyn, Simon Muggleton, Eric Murray, Miloslav Pajer, Colin Pateman, Jane Pilling-Cormick, Sakpinit Promthep, Jan Rail, Ondrej Repka, Christoph Regel, Jim Robinson, Laurent Rizzotti, Jaroslava Rozumová, D. P. Sheerin MBE, Steve Smith, Robert M. Stitt, Petr Stachura, Boris Súdny, Herkiran Toor, Pavel Türk, Milan Vacek, Petr Vacek, Dušan Vávra, R.W. Walker, Larry Westin, Henk Welting, and Vladimír Zimola.

The staff of the following institutes and organisations are to be also thanked for their contributions: 264 Squadron Association—Geoff Faulkner; *Archiv Masarykovy univerzity v Brně*—PhDr Jiří Pulec; *Bundespolizeidirektion Wien, Referat 7—Bibliothek und Archiv*—Michael Winter; City of Peterborough—Lynn Clark; *Slovanské gymnázium Olomouc*—Zicháček Vladimír; *Česká advokátní komora, pobočka Brno*—Mgr. Lenka Danilišin; McMaster University, Mills Memorial Library, Hamilton—Kim Scott; *Národní archiv*—Bc. David Hubený; National Defence Imagery Library—Janet Lacroix; *Österreichisches Staatsarchiv, Abteilung Archiv der Republik*—Rudolf Jerabek; *Památník Terezín*—Eva Němcová, Miroslava Langhamerová; RAF Museum Hendon—Peter Elliott, Mary Jane Millare-Adolfo; The Royal Archives—Pamela Clark; Veterans Affairs Canada—

Cynthia Ford; *Vojenský ústřední archiv (VÚA)*—Ing. Alena Hrnčířová, Mgr. Zuzana Pivcová; *Židovské muzeum v Praze*—Mgr. Monika Sedláková.

The author's special thanks go to Lilo Gellner, who agreed with the author's intention to publish her late husband's diary and who kindly provided long-term and truly broad support. Ernest Zucker, John Gellner's cousin, is to be thanked for providing useful information and also a copy of John Gellner's autobiography. The author is grateful to Morris Gates, who dragged him into the story of John Gellner, provided him with a copy of Gellner's diary and other personal documents, and also provided the original idea that this story should be published. Lt-Gen. Allan Chester Hull, John Gellner's friend, is thanked for the foreword and personal memories. His son, Brian Hull, and nephew Allan Hull contributed reminiscences and photos from family albums. Jan J. Šafařík is thanked for obtaining documents from the Masaryk University archive in Brno, and for materials from the estate of Flt Lt Karel Vildomec. The author is grateful to his father, Milan Vančata, for his unsparing efforts in transcribing the original manuscript into electronic form. David Bruce is thanked for his numerous valuable suggestions.

Last but not least, the author's gratitude is extended to Chris Charland, as without his support and precise proofreading, this edition would never have been published.

CONTENTS

Foreword   5
Preface   7
Acknowledgements   10
List of Abbreviations   15
Notes on the Diary   19

Part I: War Diary

1	Canada to England, 15–24 November 1940	23
2	Liverpool, 24–25 November 1940	26
3	Uxbridge, 25–29 November 1940	28
4	Journey to East Wretham, 30 November–3 December 1940	31
5	Beginning at No. 311 (B) Squadron, 3–21 December 1940	33
6	Course at Manby, 21 December 1940–5 January 1941	38
7	Back with No. 311 (B) Squadron, 6 January–2 February 1941	41
8	Leave in London, 2–6 February 1941	48
9	Third Stage at East Wretham, 6 February–2 May 1941	51
10	Nottingham and London, 2–9 May 1941	78
11	Back with No. 311 (B) Squadron, 9 May–3 June 1941	82
12	London and Kemble, 4–11 June 1941	90
13	Back in Wretham, 11–23 June 1941	95
14	Third Leave, 24–30 June 1941	101
15	No. 311 (B) Squadron, 1 July–11 August 1941	105

Part II: Biography

16 John Gellner: Solicitor, Mountaineer, Airman, Journalist   126

Appendix I: Decorations Awarded to John Gellner   154
*Appendix II: Correspondence Regarding the Award of
    Czechoslovak Decorations to John Gellner*   162
*Appendix III: Air Raid on the Cruiser Prinz Eugen in Brest Harbour,
    Night of 1–2 July 1941*   171
Appendix IV: Aircraft Flown by John Gellner   179
*Appendix V: Graduates of the British Commonwealth Air
    Training Plan's First Air Observers Course*   184
Appendix VI: Pilot Officer Sydney 'Timbertoes' Carlin MC DFC DCM   200

Endnotes   203
Bibliography and References   222

List of Abbreviations

2Lt	Second Lieutenant
A/C	Aircraft
AC2	Aircraftman 2nd Class
ACM	Air Chief Marshal
ADC	Aide-de-camp
AFC	Air Force Cross
AFRO	Air Force Routine Orders
AG	*Aktiengesellschaft*—the German term for a corporation owned by shareholders
AM	Air Ministry
ANS	Air Navigation School
Anschluss	The German term for 'annexation'—used as a term for the unification of Austria by Nazi Germany in March 1938
AOC	Air Officer Commanding
AOS	Air Observer School
AP	Armour-piercing
ARP	Air Raid Precautions
ATA	Air Transport Auxiliary
AVM	Air Vice-Marshal
B	Bomber
B&GS	Bombing & Gunnery School
BCATP	British Commonwealth Air Training Plan
Blitz	Shortened form of the German term '*Blitzkrieg*', meaning 'Lightning War'
BR	Bomber Reconnaissance
Capt.	Captain
CB	Companion of the Most Honourable Order of the Bath
CBE	Commander of the Most Excellent Order of the British Empire

CD	Canadian Forces Decoration
CET	Central European Time
CF	Coastal Fighter
CM	Member of the Order of Canada
CMC	Czechoslovak Military Cross 1939
CMG	Companion of the Order of St Michael and St George
CMM	Commander of the Order of Military Merit (Canada)
CO	Commanding Officer
Cpl	Corporal
CSI	Companion of the Most Exalted Order of the Star of India
CVSM	Canadian Volunteer Service Medal 1939-1947
D/F	Direction Finding
DCM	Distinguished Conduct Medal
DFC	Distinguished Flying Cross
DFM	Distinguished Flying Medal
DMS	Doctor of Military Science
DSO	Distinguished Service Order
EFTS	Elementary Flying Training School
ETA	Estimated time of arrival
F	Fighter
FE	Flight Engineer
Fg Off.	Flying Officer
Flak	Short form of the German term '*FlugabwehrKanone*', meaning anti-aircraft gun
Flt Lt	Flight Lieutenant
FS	Flight Sergeant
Gen.	General
GP	'General Purpose', a bomb type with an explosive capacity of 30–35 per cent
GR	General Recconaissance
Grp Capt.	Group Captain
H/F	High Frequency, indicating a range of 3–30 MHz
H2S	The first British ground-scanning radar system, mostly used on the Short Stirling, Handley Page Halifax, and Avro Lancaster bombers from 1943
HCU	Heavy Conversion Unit
HE	High-explosive
HMS	His/Her Majesty's Ship
HMSO	His/Her Majesty's Stationery Office
HQ	Headquarters
HT	Heavy Transport
I	Intruder

Ing.	Master's degree (Czech)
ITS	Initial Training School
JG	*Jagdgeschwader*—'Fighter wing' (German)
JUDr	*iuris utriusque doctor*—doctor of both laws, civil and church law (Latin)
KCB	Knight Commander of the Most Honourable Order of the Bath
KCIE	Knight Commander of the Most Eminent Order of the Indian Empire
Kriegsmarine	Military Navy in the Second World War (German)
L/Cpl	Lance Corporal
LAC	Leading Aircraftman
LAC	Library and Archives Canada (used for sources in endnotes)
LG	Landing Ground—a temporary airfield. Mainly used in northern Africa and western Europe after the Allied invasion
LMS	London Midland & Scottish Railway
LNER	London & North Eastern Railway
Lt	Lieutenant
Maj.	Major
MBE	Member of the Order of the British Empire
MC	'Medium Capacity', a bomb type with an explosive capacity of 40–50 per cent
MC	Military Cross
MP	Member of Parliament
MU	Maintenance Unit
MUDr	*medicinae universae doctor*—Doctor of Medicine (Latin)
NAAFI	Navy, Army & Air Force Institutes
NCO	Non-commissioned officer
NF	Night Fighter
NHL	National Hockey League
NJG	*Nachtjagdgeschwader*—'Night-fighter wing' (German)
OBE	Officer of the Order of the British Empire
OC	Officer Commanding
ON	Designator for Allied ship convoys from United Kingdom (Liverpool) to Canada (Halifax) from July 1941
ORB	Operations Record Book
OTF	Operational Training Flight
OTU	Operational Training Unit
Plt Off.	Pilot Officer
PRC	Personnel Reception Centre
PRU	Photographic Reconnaissance Unit
psi	Pounds per square inch
R/T	Radio/Telephony
RAF	Royal Air Force

RAFR	Royal Air Force Regiment
RAAF	Royal Australian Air Force
RCAF	Royal Canadian Air Force
RD	Repatriation Depot
RMS	Royal Mail Ship
RNDr	*rerum naturalium doctor*—Doctor of Natural Sciences (Latin)
RNZAF	Royal New Zealand Air Force
rpm	Revolutions per minute
RTO	Railway Traffic Officer
SAP	Semi-Armour Piercing
SBA	Standard Beam Approach
SBC	Small Bomb Container
SD	Special Duties
SDVN	*Sborník důvěrných výnosů a nařízení*—Volume of Confidential Issues and Orders (Czech)
SEMO	Self-Evident Military Objectives
SFP	Service Ferry Pools
SFTS	Service Flying Training School
Sgt	Sergeant
Sqn	Squadron
Sqn Ldr	Squadron Leader
SS	Steamship
T	Transport
T/Maj.	Temporary Major
TB	Torpedo Bomber
TC	Training Command
TNA	The National Archives, Kew, London, United Kingdom
U/C	Undercarriage
USAAC	United States Army Air Corps (2 July 1926–20 June 1941)
USAAF	United States Army Air Forces (20 June 1941–18 September 1947)
USSR	Union of Soviet Socialist Republics (1922–1991), now the Russian Federation
VC	Victoria Cross
VIP	Very Important Person
VÚA	*Vojenský ústřední archiv*—Central Military Archive (Czech)
W/T	Wireless Telephony
WAAF	Women's Auxiliary Air Force
Wg Cdr	Wing Commander
WO	Warrant Officer

Notes on the Diary

The diary contains personal and subjective opinions that were recorded at the time the events occurred, so there may be inaccurate, partially distorted, incomplete, or totally invalid facts. To preserve the diary's authenticity, the original text is used, and only serious discrepancies receive comments in the endnotes.

The diarist's criticism of the achievements and behaviour of some of the members of No. 311 (B) Squadron are based on his personal experiences; however, these do not diminish the contribution to the war effort by the unit. They only show how many different characters served with the Squadron, and how their professionalism in taking the fight to the enemy was unequalled.

PART I
WAR DIARY

1

Canada to England, 15–24 November 1940

We embarked from Montreal, Quebec, around 11 a.m. on the transport ship E 81, which is actually the 20,000-ton Canadian Pacific Railway Company steamer *Duchess of Richmond*.[1] I shared cabin M.3 together with Happy Hill. Just above our cabin is the sun deck. The ship is conservatively luxurious, but shows signs of damage from its previous use as a troop transport. The food is very good, but there isn't much of a choice. The menu card in First Class can't be compared with that of tourist class on the SS *Champlain*, a ship I crossed the Atlantic on some sixteen months ago.[2] There aren't very many passengers: staff of the 6th Canadian Infantry Brigade including Brigadier Sargent; RAF officers who had been on assignments in the United States and Canada; a great London solicitor; and even a few ladies with children.[3] One of them, Mrs Barclay, knows Jan Masaryk, who had been her guest in her country-house on Lago di Como, Italy.[4] I think that there were some 400 passengers on the boat.

We set sail the next day in the early morning hours of Saturday 16 November. I was on the sun deck soon after we had left our berth and got a last glimpse of the docks of Montreal. It was a grey morning with a hint of sunlight breaking through. In the afternoon, we passed underneath the railway bridge. I would have never believed that our mast tops, some 150 feet above the water, would clear the bridge prior to stopping opposite of Quebec City. A pilot boat was tied to our ship and mail loaded. We drifted slowly down the river and sailed past the Plaines d'Abraham with its old fortifications. Then it was by the Château Frontenac, towering above the old part of Quebec City, as we moved down stream past the imposing harbour.

Next morning we were well out into the Strait of Belle Isle. We passed an iceberg, supposedly a very unusual sight at this time of the year. To the left we had the desolate coast of Labrador, just a reddish stormy plateau, and to the right, the coast of Newfoundland. You could only see some rocky islands. By night time, the ship was out in the open Atlantic.

We were sailing without being attached to a convoy and on a route well off the established normal peacetime shipping lanes. The course is being kept secret, but I was on the bridge so often that I was able to make out where we were going. We were steaming first north-northeast to north-east up to about 57 to 58 degrees north. We then went straight east on this latitude. Then it was south-east, from the early morning of 23 November, during the eighth day of the voyage, to hit the furthest northern tip of Ireland. We were zigzagging at a moderate speed of some 16 knots. The armament of the ship consisted of a 6-inch gun and a 3-inch anti-aircraft gun mounted on a platform on the stern. An American-designed .303-calibre Lewis Aircraft Machine Gun Model 1918 was located on the bridge.

I was entrusted with the organisation of watches on the sun deck. We had to provide three aerial observers. Another two men formed the crew of the Lewis gun on the bridge. My party consisted of twelve officers and twenty-five sergeants. I rounded up more officers and sixteen other ranks from the Army. Everybody had one two-hour night watch or one three-hour day watch during a twenty-four-hour period, followed by twenty-four hours off. Certainly not too much to do.

The constant opposition by Acland and Mather, with their whining about anything and everything, caused all kinds of problems. The response of the others was very good. I myself rather enjoyed the watches, although they were very cold and wet. The weather was extremely rough throughout the whole of the passage. The ship was pitching and rolling badly. It was rather difficult to sleep as one was continuously tossed around in the bunk. In any case: the North Atlantic in November is far from being a comfortable place. I even had a slight accident. On one particularly bad night, a 60-mph gale was blowing and the decks were covered with sleet. I went up to the sun deck to withdraw our three guards, as no plane could fly or submarine hold the sea in such a night anyway. I opened the door to the deck and stepped outside. At that moment, the ship listed heavily. I slipped on the frozen deck, falling while bumping the railing. As a matter of fact, I almost fell over the railing; as it was, I didn't get more than a few bloodied scrapes on both legs. There isn't very much to be said about the trip itself. I had rather unusual luck playing bingo. I won three times and left with some $18. Otherwise, I had to straighten out some of our Sergeants in Tourist Class. They were minor things, like swearing and excessive drinking, accompanied by very loud singing.

We didn't see any other ships until the morning of Saturday 23 November. I was on the bridge, when soon after 9 a.m., an aircraft carrier with four or five destroyers appeared on the horizon. They must have been over 10 miles away in the mist and heading in a southerly direction. I didn't see more than the bulky hull of the carrier and the flashes of their signals. They were speeding southward to look for a convoy.[5] Two hours later, two destroyers appeared quite near, emerging and disappearing between the waves. After lunch we got the first and only bit of excitement during our uneventful trip. We heard the roar of aircraft engines and then a plane emerged from the clouds coming head-on toward the ship. Action stations were sounded and we manned the machine gun. Alexander was supposed to shoot while I passed and reloaded the three drums of ammunition we had. The plane turned out to be an Avro Anson. It was soon followed by a Bristol Blenheim. Both planes circled above the ship until twilight. Later in the afternoon, the hilly coast of Ireland appeared. At approximately 5 p.m., we went around Rathlin Island and entered the Irish Sea. We then steamed between the blacked-out coasts of Northern Ireland and England before anchoring after midnight just outside the mouth of the Mersey River. The night was quiet; apparently, Liverpool hadn't been raided.

2

Liverpool, 24–25 November 1940

We moved on around 9 a.m. There is a channel up the Mersey, which is probably swept from mines every morning before any ship is allowed to steam up the river. We saw several sunken ships that may have hit our own or German magnetic mines. One passenger ship had broken in two parts. Liverpool appeared against the sunlit eastern sky. The balloon barrage floating in the sky is a very impressive sight. We steamed alongside the docks for about half an hour, but I wasn't able to see the minor damage around the extremely busy harbour.

We were met by an Air Vice-Marshal who gave a speech and by Air Commodore Leigh Forbes Stevenson, Officer Commanding the RCAF in the United Kingdom. Then two very business-like and efficient disembarkation officers, Mr Bridges and Mr Allen, got hold of us and took us off the boat to the Overseas League Club. The president is Mrs Ross, an overweight and very nice widow of a surgeon. We were given tea and food and then I made arrangements for our billeting with Mr Bridges.

We were all lodged with local families. Our job was to put the right boys together and then assign them to the right families. Some choices worked out rather well. We put Martin with Mr Martin, the wild Scott and Noble with a local nabob, our two snobs, Acland and Mather, to Lady Kelly, and our noteworthy black sheep, Herbie Easton, to the Right Reverend Albert Augustus David, Lord Bishop of Liverpool. I myself, as leader of the party, am a guest of Mrs Ross herself. Gilmore and Florence went to Dr Ross, son of Mrs Ross, who resides across the street but dines in Mrs Ross's home. The whole of the Ross family seem to be concerned with the improvement of human health. Her daughter is nurse in a hospital. I received a marvellous reception and meals contradict all rumours about strict rationing in England. Miss Ross drove us also around the town and through the Mersey Tunnel to Birkenhead. The tunnel is really remarkable, much bigger than those under the Hudson River, with crossroads traffic lights etc. The new town is unremarkable if one doesn't consider the enormous Adelphi Hotel or the unfinished cathedral, which will eventually be worthy of a visit. Although Liverpool was bombed every night for the last two or three months, one doesn't see much in the way of bomb damage.

In the afternoon, we went over to see Dr Ross, who lives in a very nice old house. He is an antique collector and an expert on the subject. The doctor especially likes to collect cast-iron back pieces for fireplaces. He showed us art treasures with the same calm demeanour as the hole in his garden caused by an incendiary bomb that landed there, 20 yards from his house. There were still remainders of white phosphorous around. There was no air raid this night, the first quiet night for Liverpool since the *Blitz* started.[1]

3

Uxbridge, 25–29 November 1940

We arrived at London's Euston railway station at 3.15 p.m. on Monday and went straight by bus to the RAF depot at Uxbridge, located some 20 miles west of the city. During the one-hour drive through the streets of London, we witnessed for the first time the real, serious devastation caused by bombing. Our route took us through the residential area of the west and non-industrial suburbs around Acton and Hammersmith. We could see for ourselves that the German bombing is really indiscriminate. Royan said to me, 'We are getting hard, John.' This was our first exposure to war.

Uxbridge is an immense camp, having roughly the same function as Toronto's Manning Pool.[1] Recruits get their kit while the Personal Dispatch Centre provides stations with personnel.[2] The Commanding Officer, Grp Capt. Jackson, gave us another speech. After dinner we went out, guided by Plt Off. Wyse, a Canadian air gunner now laid off and employed with the station defence. Like most of grounded former aircrew, he is very sarcastic about the way things are run. We felt our way through the blackout for the first time. We visited two pubs; the second, named the Old Mill, located some distance out of the village, is very nice. An Air Force band was playing and after a few drinks I even ventured to dance with one of the many pretty girls in the place.

I went downtown the next evening to meet Karel Česaný in the Cumberland on Marble Arch. I hadn't seen him since the occupation. He looks well, although a little changed by the bushy moustache he has grown. Karel lives in the cellar of a house destroyed by a bomb with the janitor, who is also a Czech. He stays mostly in the flat on Upper Berkeley Street belonging to Miss Věra Uhlířová, the former girlfriend of the younger Miki Skorkovský. I think she is now his girlfriend. It was there that I spent the night (or the few remaining hours of it after having talked until after midnight). I had to be up at six o'clock to get back to Uxbridge by 8 a.m. I went by tube from Marble Arch. Stairways, gangways and platforms are filled with people who are going in at 3 p.m. to get a good place when they are admitted at 4 p.m.

They will spend the next some sixteen hours in the unhealthy subterranean tubes, with the warm draught, dust, and dirt, sleeping intermittently, half-sitting, half-laying, people stepping over them and under the drone of incoming and outgoing trains. These people have the dishevelled appearances of convicts whose faces bear the expression of hopelessness. There may be people amongst them whose homes in the East End have been destroyed by bombs, but I doubt it. People who have really been bombed out are looked after by the government. The majority of the people down there seem to be simply afraid of bombing, seeking the safest place to hide.[3] There are many down there who are refugees from the continent.

Wednesday 27 November 1940 will be always a memorable day for me as I had tea with the Queen and the Princesses. We were merely told at Uxbridge that an excursion had been organised for us to Windsor Castle and that Lady Hardinge would act as the hostess.[4] We were told that we were to be in her home for tea, at which time we may meet some interesting personalities.

Our bus took us to Windsor Castle, where we were met at Henri VIII's Portal by Lady Hardinge and her daughter, who is fourteen years old or so. Our group was shown through the magnificent castle. At about 4.30 p.m., we were taken into the part inhabited by the Royal Family. Standing in a sort of gallery, we suddenly found ourselves in front of the Queen and the two Princesses. I was introduced first and welcomed by Her Majesty.[5] I then made formal introductions of my friends to a court official, Lord Kirkdenny, if I understood the name correctly, who introduced them in turn to the Queen. She is awfully nice, simple and charming. Then we went in a marvellous gallery to have tea. I was at Her Majesty's table, together with Princess Margaret, Rose, Grp Capt. Jackson, the CO of Uxbridge, Snell, Flaherty, Gilmore and Mather.[6] Three other tables were presided over by Princess Elizabeth, Lady Hardinge and another very beautiful young lady in waiting respectively.[7] The Queen poured the tea and was like any other normal lady entertaining guests. We all spoke freely with her, with no waiting to be addressed, no etiquette whatsoever. She and the Princesses spent more than one hour with us. I thanked Her Majesty afterwards on behalf of all of us for an afternoon we wouldn't forget. All the boys were very excited and very proud. After dinner, everybody was busy to write home to Canada, describing the big event in great detail. Alexander compiled a letter of some twenty pages!

I saw Lojza Pražák the next afternoon. He too is quite unchanged. It is a pity that he is wasting his energy trying to fight the Czechoslovak military authorities after they treated him very badly. They have used a frivolous matter to try and get back at him. While in France, Pražák gave Dr Hartmann a travel warrant to allow him exit the country before others did. The authorities wanted to replace Pražák with someone else, so disciplinary action was taken against him as a result. There are too many officers for the small Czechoslovak force in England. The professional soldiers are trying to put Permanent Force personnel everywhere they can. I had my own bad experiences while in Canada. One is helpless against official intrigue. Lojza will find that out eventually. He went with me to talk to the former director of National Bank, Ing. Malík. He too was not at all happy with what was going on. I slept at Lojza's place near Finsbury Park. He stays with a family of Slovakian refugees. Lojza got up the next morning, cooked breakfast and went with me by tube to Uxbridge and finally the camp's entrance. In the camp, I learned of my posting to No. 311 'Czechoslovak' (B) Squadron at Honington in Suffolk, and that I had to report there the next day. So I went to London again, saw Torelli and went to our old Embassy at Grosvenor Place.[8] I saw Gen. Antonín Nižborský (whose real surname is Hasal), Chief of the Military Cabinet of Dr Beneš. I met also Eda Wichta, who works at the Czechoslovak Ministry of Finance. His wife resides in London.

I forgot to mention that we were filmed on (I think) Tuesday morning. Flaherty and Jepson had the speeches. I saw myself some three weeks later on the screen at Thetford.

4

Journey to East Wretham, 30 November–3 December 1940

Members of our party have been posted out to seven different stations: Acland and Gilmore to No. 2 School of Army Co-operation, Andover; Alexander, Waldron, Webb, Webber and Williams to No. 11 OTU, Bassingbourn; Pidduck, Noble, Roberts and Rose to No. 20 OTU, Lossiemouth; Florence, Mather, Purser, Easton, Heywood, Jeffrey, Jepson, King and Mavor to No. 17 OTU, Upwood; Bezaire, Hill, Leboldus, Leishman, MacKenzie, Martin, Mansell and Moris to No. 42 (TB) Squadron, Wick; Flaherty, Snell, Carter, Craik, Cleaver, Royan, Scott and Smith to No. 22 (TB) Squadron, North Coates; and myself to No. 311 (B) Squadron. I got a warrant to Honington via Grantham, which proved to be a tragic mistake. I departed around 1 p.m. from King's Cross. After changing at Grantham, I arrived at Donington, Lincolnshire, just before nightfall. There was neither No. 311 (B) Squadron nor an airfield to be found. The only people there were an RAF Fitting Party with a Flight Sergeant in charge of a group of sheds. I was told that I had been misdirected, that 'my' Honington was somewhere in Suffolk, near Bury St Edmunds. The same screw up had happened to quite a number of personnel previously. An RAF truck took me to the nearest RAF facility, which turned out to be No. 12 Service Flying Training School at Grantham. I could spend the night here. I had a quiet evening, and I spent the whole of the following day there because there wasn't a scheduled Sunday train to Bury St Edmunds. I felt uneasy as I thought that I'd be losing God-knows-what by not being on time at my station.

Something struck me at Grantham; the upper class of pupils (LACs, as we were in Canada) ate in the Officers' Mess. I couldn't help but to recall that in Canada we were treated as ordinary Aircraftmen up to the very day of our commissioning.

I left at 10.22 a.m. on Monday, and then had to change in Peterborough. I used the couple of hours I had there to get a haircut and to tour the town, with its marvellous cathedral. I didn't get to Bury St Edmunds until evening. After waiting there for hours at the RTO, I was picked up by a station transport and brought to RAF Station Honington. Honington is home to two bomber squadrons—Nos 9 and

311 (Czech). The operational flight of No. 311 (B) Squadron is on a satellite airfield 14 miles away, at East Wretham in Norfolk.

The first thing that struck me in the mess at Honington was the fact that British officers were kept apart in the ante room, while the Czechs occupied the writing room. There I saw a dozen of them—nice, mostly very young boys, but very different from the British, with their open tunics, dishevelled hair, and loud and cheerful conversation. They complained bitterly about the restraint of the British toward them. There may be some justification for the complaints on both sides; the British were not being very tolerant and the Czechs were drinking too much and being very boisterous and over-cheerful. They had some fun telling every Czech newcomer that I was English, and having him struggle desperately to speak English with me. I was made aware of lots of complaints about the deficiencies of our Czech military command. These were familiar stories, and I heard them from almost every Czech in uniform. The next morning, I heard that I was posted to the operational flight, East Wretham. I went there by station transport, along with a group of Czech NCOs.

5

Beginning at No. 311 (B) Squadron, 3–21 December 1940

When I arrived at Wretham, the operational flight of No. 311 (B) Squadron was equipped with the Vickers Wellington Mk ICs. The 'Wimpy' (as the Wellington is affectionately known) is powered by a pair of Bristol Pegasus XVIII engines. The Squadron was manned by eleven crews of six each. The British Commanding Officer was Wg Cdr Simonds. His Czech counterpart was Wg Cdr Toman, a well-known pilot whose real last name is Mareš. The British Adjutant, Flt Lt Earle, was soon to be replaced by Plt Off. MacNicol. Our Czech Adjutant was Flt Lt Provazník. The British Flight Commander was Sqn Ldr Pickard DFC. His Czech equivalent is Flt Lt Ocelka. Plt Off. Pekárek is acting as a sort of technical translator. Plt Off. Fantl is our Operations Officer. Some two weeks later, Plt Off. Schneider joined us as general interpreter. There are two Medical Officers—MUDr Novák and MUDr Krůta. There are five more British officers on squadron strength: Sqn Ldr Powell, Administrative Officer; Plt Off. Morisson, in charge of Gunnery; Fg Off. Lucky, Intelligence Officer; Plt Off. Robinson, in charge of mess and supplies; and Plt Off. Menassia, a quiet fellow of Turkish descent, who is doing all kinds of odd jobs.

The aerodrome is just a fairly large field with a dozen planes dispersed widely under bushes and trees, alongside a few scattered tents and wooden barracks. It must be almost impossible to inflict any appreciable damage to such a satellite field. The Officers' Mess is in Wretham Hall, a castle built in 1914 and owned by Mrs Claire Rich. Her husband was killed in the last war on 11 November 1918, just two hours before the Armistice.[1] She is now living in a cottage nearby, and we have her castle all for ourselves. Mrs Rich has been wise enough to remove all the furniture (except for bathtubs and an unmovable billiards table), so we are sleeping on field cots in empty staterooms. I slept on the floor for two nights, and then I used Wg Cdr Simond's field cot and ended up breaking it after a few nights. I got another one and it has held up well after spending another two nights on the floor.

I am sharing my room with Fg Off. Lucky, a recipient of the Military Cross in the First World War and two rows of other decorations. He had previously been in the civil service in Egypt. Lucky certainly had a very colourful past. He speaks a number of languages flawlessly, which made him ideal to serve as an Intelligence Officer. He first served with the RAF in Iceland, and he was then posted to our squadron. Fg Off. Lucky is certainly brilliant and well-mannered, but I take him for an opportunist and he doesn't know very much about his staff. Despite this, he gets along, using all kind of technical expressions rather indiscriminately and letting Fantl do most of his work. I like him though. Last, but not least—food is good, although much simpler than that at Uxbridge or what I later experienced at Manby.

At first, I had almost nothing to do. I was posted as a navigation instructor and all I did was teach the eleven navigators astro for two or three hours every day. It was rather difficult to teach as the station only had one book of navigation tables (for latitude 50–54 degrees north) and three Air Almanacs. There were plenty of sextants though. I gained some additional equipment by making a nuisance of myself—Mercators, notebooks, an A. P. 1234 etc.[2] When I left for Manby on 21 December 1940, the situation was like this—our only Navigation Tables had been destroyed with Křivda's plane on 16 December, and there weren't any others. It is a pity, as almost all the navigators had been very keen on astro and had picked it up surprisingly quickly (considering the circumstances). However, with Křivda's accident, astro instruction came to an end. By then, I had taken over the duties of Squadron Navigation Officer in a new and improved Operations Room, and I was rather busy—although not as much as one should be in an operational squadron.[3]

I asked both COs, Sqn Ldr Pickard, and finally even the Group Navigation Officer, Flt Lt Freeman, to let me go as an observer on raids. I was first told that this was altogether impossible as my services on the ground were so valuable that they wouldn't risk my precious life. When I insisted, they promised to let me go on shorter trips over the Channel ports or so. They haven't kept their promise so far. Otherwise, I am helping Wg Cdr Toman (who doesn't speak English) with the preparation of raids and briefings. On the whole, I am certainly far from being overworked.

We had a dance in the mess on Saturday, 7 December 1940. Our common rooms were decorated by Mrs Simonds. We had a lot of guests. There were two bands— the regular RAF band from Honington and another formed by Czech officers who played all kinds of well-known Czech tunes. I was keeping to myself by the bar when Lucky broke his way through the crowd with a young girl. He introduced her to me as Dorine Lucy. Dorine (better known as 'Dordie') has regular features, including a pretty face, but she is a little too small to impress me. She is twenty-one and a companion of Mrs Williams, the twenty-two-year-old wife of Grp Capt. Williams, CO of RAF Station Watton.[4] He must be almost twenty-five years older than his wife, who is really beautiful. Dordie and I remained together throughout the whole party, and we ended up having a very enjoyable evening. I think that I have loved only two girls in my life—Micinka and then Herta. I don't think that I'll ever fall in love again, but I am apparently too young to give up the idea of being in the company of young and pretty girls. I therefore kissed Dordie a few times and promised to come over to Watton to see her at the first convenient opportunity.

On 12 December 1940, our squadron was inspected by President Dr Beneš. We were lined up on a parade square; there was the typical rousing speech that only a politician can deliver, but with no real content. He then pinned Czech Military Crosses on the tunic breast pockets of three British officers and four Czechs—Flt Lt Šnajdr, Plt Off. Fikrle, and two Sergeants.[5] Dr Beneš stayed for lunch at the Officers' Mess, followed by an inspection of quarters and working rooms, then departed about four hours later. The President was well-liked and held in high esteem. This was reflected in the very enthusiastic reception given to him. The same could not be said of the military brass-hats, including Gen. Ingr, the Minister of National Defence, Gen. Nižborský, Chief of the Military Cabinet, Gen. Slezák, Chief of the Air Force, and some more whom our men have a hearty disliking for. This hatred of our military leaders is common to every member in the Czech armed forces I have seen so far. It may be beneficial to address this problem more thoroughly. As far as I was able to make out, the main grievances are as these: most of our airmen had fled our country before the outbreak of the war, guided by sheer determination. They reached France and were forced to join the Foreign Legion as privates at 50 centimes per day, serving under very bad conditions. The generals left after the outbreak of war. They arrived in Paris, where they presented tremendous travel claims and for which they received payment. One colonel supposedly charged for a newspaper he had bought at the railway station in Budapest! The officers were instantly enrolled, maintaining their previous Czech ranks. They received 10,000 francs per month or more for organisation work, which was generally considered superfluous and badly done. Moreover, these generals somehow forgot that they were refugees themselves and tried to run things in an unpleasant, official manner.

I got first-hand proof of that myself. Gen. Slezák once called up our squadron around lunchtime, and I happened to take his message on the telephone. I simply introduced myself as Pilot Officer Gellner, and as he didn't seem to understand, he barked in the phone, 'Report properly. Are you an Officer or a Sergeant or what?' A British senior ranking officer would hardly use this sort of overbearing tone toward anybody in an operational squadron. Our boys won't stand for this after coming back from Berlin or Mannheim. Such arrogance from a man waging war from behind his office desk. There are more serious grievances; our fliers hardly flew over France, nor did they do much night flying training. After arriving in England, what they really needed was a period of intense training at an OTU. Our leaders were misleading probably because they had to base their claim for recognition as Allies on something, but there was not anything to substantiate the claims about the readiness of our airmen. They stated that our crews were fully capable of going on operations straight away. Only after the Squadron had lost three crews in one October night due to inexperience was the Squadron stood down for six weeks of training. Our men are calling this procedure by our leaders 'murder'. The discontent has brought serious results. Before I arrived, three officers—the Kozák brothers, sons of a famous professor, and Úlehla—had refused to fly. They were subsequently discharged from the Air Force. In the nineteen days I was with the Squadron, two Sergeant Pilots—Fák in Wretham and Novotný in Honington—did the same. I heard that the Kozáks were just bad characters, and I don't know Úlehla and Novotný, but I know Fák, and I can vouch for him. He has been on operations and is no coward but rather just fed up, downhearted and doesn't want to go any more.[6] We have a marvellous bunch of men in Wretham. They are brave, loyal and would do anything for a bit of recognition (acts, of course—not words) and sincere sympathy. As it is, our men are dissatisfied and grumbling—a state of affairs that may eventually prove dangerous.

On the afternoon of Sunday, 15 December, I went on Flt Lt Šnajdr's bike to Watton to visit Dordie. It was somebody's birthday that day, and we had quite a few drinks after lunch. My legs were like lead and it would be dark before I could cover the 12 miles back to Wretham. I decided to stay overnight in the Officers' Mess, and I was put in the room of one Flt Lt Gautier, a French Canadian. Then I went to the CO's residence and had dinner with the Grp Capt. and Mrs Williams and Dordie. I left Watton in the early morning of the next day, and I was back in Wretham for breakfast.

That was on Monday 16 December, the day we lost Wellington T2577/KX-G with three men. It was the night of the big reprisal raid on Mannheim, Germany, when 300 bombers plastered the town for some seven hours.[7] Our squadron was supposed to send four aircraft, which started to take off from 6 p.m. onwards. The third plane to leave had Sgt Křivda as skipper, Sgt Pavelka as second pilot, Plt Off. Nedvěd as navigator, Plt Off. Doubrava as W/T operator, Sgt Janoušek as front gunner, and Plt Off. Toul as rear gunner. About five minutes after the take-off, we saw a glow from a big fire somewhere between the aerodrome and Wretham Hall. We knew instantly that one of our planes must have crashed. Flt Lt Earle and I dashed in Earle's car through the village and into the adjacent wood, where we calculated the plane had crashed.

We were some 150 yards away when the 500-lb bombs in the plane went off. There were two tremendous explosions; I think the second was when two bombs exploded simultaneously, lighting the sky bright pink. We thought that nobody could have survived and turned around. As a matter of fact, by some miracle four crew members were alive. I'd better give a reconstruction of the accident instead of relating the events in chronological order. Sgt Křivda had started with partially lowered flaps at 10–15 degrees, in order to shorten the run of his heavily loaded plane. He got off normally and soon built up his speed to 100 mph, which is the normal initial climb speed. He raised the flaps, but he didn't set them in the neutral position; they were raised to a point just below the locking groove.[8] In such a case, the flaps will start to rise but then slowly drop to a fully lowered position. That's what probably happened. Křivda had circled the field and saw his airspeed drop despite the engines running at full power. He didn't understand the reason and made the decision to return to the flare path, which ran roughly in a north to south direction. Sgt Křivda carried on northwards to set up for a landing approach. As he made the final turn, he rapidly lost airspeed and altitude. The left wing tip of the Wellington clipped a tree and they crashed onto a small field. The front of the aircraft caught fire instantly. Janoušek and Křivda must have been burned at once. Nedvěd escaped through the astro-hatch and then dragged Pavelka, who had somehow managed to exit the aircraft and make his way a short distance from the flaming wreckage. Nedvěd next tried to extricate Toul from the rear turret. By this time, Doubrava had jumped out of the plane and was running toward the wood for cover. Nedvěd, who behaved like a hero throughout, was with Toul when the 500-pounders exploded. The aircraft was severed into two sections. Nedvěd remained unhurt, and he eventually succeeded in dragging Toul from underneath the turret with the help of others who reached the spot from the airfield. Toul was still alive, but he died on the way to hospital. Nedvěd is all right, and Doubrava and Pavelka were only slightly injured and are recovering quickly in hospital.[9]

I have mixed up things again, forgetting to relate an event that occurred on Monday, 9 December. When I arrived in Wretham, Plt Off. Konštacký was up for a general court martial. He had been drunk while on duty and insulted Sqn Ldr Pickard. Konštacký was supposed to appear before the AOC of No. 3 (B) Group, AVM Baldwin, who I would accompany as interpreter. We went to Group HQ in Exning, near Newmarket, by car. The whole procedure was a very unpleasant affair, but Konštacký got away with only a verbal reprimand. Wg Cdr Toman had recommended giving him another chance. Konštacký promised to stop drinking. Sqn Ldr Pickard, who is a good chap, shook hands with him, and a sad story had a happy end.

On Thursday I was told that I had been sent on a Bombing Leaders Course in Manby, near Louth, Lincolnshire, which was to begin on 21 December 1940. The next night (from Friday to Saturday) four aircraft from our squadron were supposed to raid Ostend. The start was delayed again and again due to bad weather, but it was finally set at four o'clock on Saturday morning. As the briefing had been done in the afternoon and I have nothing to do with operations after that, I went to bed. Wg Cdr Toman, Sqn Ldr Pickard, Flt Lt Earle and Plt Off. Fantl went to a country inn to pass the time before the start. At about 3.30 a.m. I was awoken by the batman, who brought me Sqn Ldr Pickard's message to come to the Operations Room immediately. There I saw Fantl, the man in charge of operations, completely drunk and apparently 'unserviceable'. I sent him to bed and took over his work, despite the fact that MSIs, coordinates, colours of the day, forms G and Q etc. were, up to then, more or less a mystery to me.[10] I was up until 9 a.m. and saw our crews go. I followed their progress during the flight on the map, and I listened to their reports when they came safely back. In the afternoon I was taken by plane to Manby, where I arrived at around 4 p.m.

6

Course at Manby, 21 December 1940–5 January 1941

The idea of a Bombing Leaders Course, of which twelve have already been run, is to put one observer in a squadron or flight in charge of the bomb aimers, and it should instruct and supervise as to help improve the bombing. There are fourteen of us on the course. Two are from OTUs—Plt Off. Holden is from No. 14, Cottesmore, Rutland, and Sgt Thomas is from No. 16, Upper Heyford, Oxfordshire. The rest are from operational squadrons (Plt Offs Eperon, No. 102 at Topcliffe, Yorkshire; Proudlock, No. 114, Aylsham, Norfolk; Caunter-Jackson, No. 61, Hemswell, Lincolnshire; Winder, No. 21, Watton, Norfolk; Shaw, No. 103, Newton, Nottinghamshire; and Henslop, No. 77, Topcliffe, Yorkshire; Sgts Gilmour, No. 9, Honington, Suffolk; Martin, No. 101, West Raynham, Norfolk; Sobieszczuk, No. 300, (Polish) Swinderby, Lincolnshire; Walmsley, No. 99, Newmarket, Suffolk; and Redgrave, No. 44, Waddington, Lincolnshire).

We are gaining lots of knowledge about new equipment and doing some refresher training on older systems. The class involves public speaking and instruction practice. The RAF Station is very beautiful, with the mess almost being a palace. The food is so sumptuous that I am getting fatter and fatter. There are negatives too; it is a school, and the spirit is much more subdued than on operational squadrons. The mess is as stiff as the Court of Spain. There is lots of school work—some days we go from 8 a.m. to 7 p.m., with two one-hour breaks for lunch and tea. Then there's homework on top of it. No other entertainment is available other than a cabaret in the NAAFI every Saturday night.

We started in the morning of Monday 23 December, and we were told the next day that we would get the afternoon of Christmas Eve off in addition to Christmas Day. I decided to go to Bradford. Departure was at 1 p.m., and (after the usual delays and changing trains at Grimsby Town and Doncaster) I reached Bradford after 7 p.m. Apparently, Kurt hadn't got my cable as it only arrived at 10 p.m., so no one was at the station to meet me. I could not get a taxi either. A lady took me along some pitch-dark streets to a bus. The bus driver had me get out in front of Oak

Course at Manby, 21 December 1940–5 January 1941

Villas, a huge park with a number of named homes. I went into about half a dozen of them to find out where Kurt's place (Oak Mansions) was. I finally got there and was greeted with sincere joy. Kurt, Vally and Tomy haven't changed since 23 June 1939, when I last saw them in London. There is another lady with them whose name I can't remember. I had met her in May 1939 in Trieste, after having spent some three months incarcerated in the Rossauer Lände—a Viennese police jail. So, at one time or another, the three of us had all enjoyed the hospitality of a Vienna jail. Kurt is the manager of a textile factory in Dewsbury and serves with the ARP.[1] Vally manages to cook (which she never did before), and Tomy goes to grammar school. The outward appearance of this family is a very bright one, considering that they are refugees. I got a different impression the next morning, when Vally came in to ask me for advice. She told me that she couldn't go along with Kurt any longer. There are no real issues (except some fooling around with other girls, and she seems to have gotten back at him in a similar way), but they don't like one another and virtually stopped living together as a married couple several months ago. She now has a male acquaintance by the name of Paul Hecht, who visits her when Kurt is in his factory. Paul would marry her if she divorced Kurt. He is impatient, and she fears that she may lose him if she waits too long. I think Vally is around thirty-four. A woman can't let go of opportunities like this without feeling sorry later on. As can be imagined, I advised her to stick with Kurt. He is well off and a good chap, and they have a child. I feel sorry that it has come to this with their marriage.

On Christmas Day I inquired at the station about a train back to Louth, and I was told that one was leaving Bradford at 8.30 p.m. and would arrive in Sheffield at 11.16 p.m., where I would have to wait until 3.05 a.m. for my connection to Louth. I decided to take the train, arriving in Sheffield around midnight. As I was feeling my way from one station to the other through the pitch-black night, I heard that the 3.05 a.m. train was cancelled. There were quite a number of Air Force and Army chaps milling around the station. We decided to try to reach our respective stations by other means. First we asked for a special train, which was refused. Then we tried to get a taxi. Sheffield has 500,000 inhabitants, but it had been very heavily bombed recently, leaving 36,000 people homeless. We couldn't get any phone connection with a number of the taxi companies (which had probably been bombed out of their premises), and the one we heard from said that their cars had been destroyed in the raid or were commandeered. Eventually, I rang up the Balloon Barrage and asked for one of their tenders; I got a polite refusal there too. I had to wait for the 6.50 a.m. train, which brought me to Louth at 11 a.m. I missed the morning's lectures and had a rather bad conscience. As a matter of fact, nothing happened, as Flt Lt Rivers (who was in charge of the course) said to just forget it. This event taught me the difference between an officer of an operational squadron and a student officer. On New Year's Day, one Acting Pilot Officer on Probation Chevron, attending Air Gunnery School, had not turned out for the morning's lectures after a rather wild New Years' Eve celebration. He was dragged before the Chief Instructor, confined to camp until further orders, and threatened with being kicked out of the Air Force if his academic results didn't show a marked improvement in the near future. He had done less than I did, as I had left the camp for Christmas without asking for permission and therefore had no excuse for being late.

I spent New Year's Eve in bed. On the last day of the course, Saturday 4 January 1941, I walked to Louth with Sgt Havlík, who had been living in Paris, where he owned a perfumes factory, for the last seven years.[2] Now he is in charge of a course of forty-two Czech Armourers in Manby.[3] I heard the customary talk about the deficiencies of the Czech military leadership. He had been recommended for a commission by the British and thinks that our own people had barred him from getting it.

I have very little to say about Manby otherwise, except that it was an extremely interesting course and that the CO of Test Flight is a very famous man; Wg Cdr George Hendley Stainforth AFC was the Schneider Trophy winner in 1931.[4] I left Manby by train on the morning of Sunday 5 January, reaching Wretham in the late evening only to find everything as I had left it—with the exception of Flt Lt Earle and Fg Off. Lucky, who have left for Honington.

7

Back with No. 311 (B) Squadron, 6 January–2 February 1941

There have been a few changes in our squadron after all. Fg Off. Lucky has been replaced by Flt Lt Borman, a serious and very active Intelligence Officer, and Plt Off. Morrison has been replaced by Plt Off. Stratton, who as a Gunnery Leader finds himself with nothing to do, so busies himself as Mess Secretary. Plt Off. Cígler and Plt Off. Fikrle have been sent temporarily to Honington as instructors. The Adjutant, MacNicol, has become a Flying Officer, while Plt Off. Robinson expects to be posted away. We have a new assistant in the Operations Room, Sgt Robb from No. 99 (B) Squadron. He is a very good man. On Sunday 12 January 1941, I went to Cosford with our dual-controlled plane to fetch a new Wellington.[1] We flew close to the balloon barrage of Birmingham–Wolverhampton, and the view of the balloons, floating above the ground mist, was very impressive. Cosford is an enormous maintenance station with scores of planes on the ground and in turf-covered hangars that look like hills from above. I had no collection order and therefore some difficulty trying to get the new plane. While flying back, Sgt Anderle, the pilot gave me a demonstration of low flying. This was rather exciting. In the afternoon I went to Thetford and spent four quiet hours in the home of Mr Mock, the manager of Lloyds Bank in Thetford. On Monday we were supposed to send two crews to Milan, Italy, to bomb the Pirelli works. I was slated to go in Wg Cdr Toman's plane with Sgt Rozum as second pilot, Sgt Slánský as W/T operator and Plt Offs Šimon and Študent as air gunners. The start was postponed from 6 to 9.30 p.m. We were in the plane, with the engines running, when the flight was cancelled practically at the last minute before take-off due to bad weather over southern Europe.[2]

We were very annoyed as we had made very detailed preparations and hoped for a very interesting trip. Pretty much the same thing happened the next day, when we had to raid Bordeaux (with me again in Wg Cdr Toman's plane). This time, at least operations were cancelled around noon, so we were off until the next morning at 9 a.m. I went with Plt Off. Partyk in his car to Watton and saw Dordie. We had a little walk in the countryside and then tea with Grp Capt. Williams and Mrs Williams, along with Sqn Ldr Harris, the Padre of Watton. I was back for dinner and took two aspirins and a quart of hot tea, then went to bed early to get rid of a cold that has been bothering me now for ten days.

On Thursday, 16 January, we were supposed to send five crews to bomb the synthetic oil works at Police, on the outskirts of Stettin, Germany. This was later changed to Wilhelmshaven, Germany, with Emden as secondary target. I flew on Wellington T2553/KX-B, with Sgt Bufka as skipper, Plt Off. Breitcetl as second pilot, Sgt Slánský as W/T operator, Sgt Čtvrtlík as front gunner, and Sgt Janšta as rear gunner. Departure was at 5.45 p.m. and there was perfect visibility up to the coast. We crossed the coast just north of Great Yarmouth, at an altitude of 9,000 feet. Everything seemed perfect as the plane climbed steadily, but the cockpit heating wouldn't work. Over the sea we entered dense clouds, and our troubles began. It was bitterly cold. We later recorded a low of -42 degrees Celsius at 18,000 feet. The aircraft began icing up on the wings and fuselage. We were climbing at a miserable rate, and our airspeed fell gradually until we were going at a mere 80 mph. The Dutch coast became visible by the aid of big beacon at Den Helder (we actually crossed over the middle of the island of Texel).

We left the Zuiderzee behind us and were soon met by some anti-aircraft gunfire from batteries posted somewhere near Leeuwarden. By that time, our starboard engine had begun to fail. Later on, while back on the ground, we learned that all planes sent out that night had the same troubles. The reason might have been that an accumulation of ice built up within the carburettors, which narrowed the channel through which the mixture enters the cylinders. Ice on the propeller shafts might have also had something to do with the failures. The temperature of the starboard engine was rising to a dangerous level, the pressure falling and the Hercules engines' rpms fluctuating. Considering the situation, we decided to attack the secondary target of Emden, which was nearer. We got there around 7.45 p.m. and I am afraid that I bombed rather hastily. The pilot asked me to hurry up because we were at 75 mph with the bomb doors open, and close to stalling speed.[3] The distributor was frozen and didn't work with the firing switch, so I used the push button on the distributor. I pushed the jettison bars to be sure.[4] The pilot jettisoned too, but one of four 500-pounders and one of two containers failed to release as they were frozen solid to the racks.[5] The others didn't fare any better, as everybody came back with some part of their bomb load.

On the way back, our starboard engine was giving us some really serious trouble. It was an uneasy journey. Bufka, who was piloting both ways, was very nervous, asking me every minute, 'Where are we?' and 'How far from the English coast?' Gradually, everything froze. I got a taste of the frigid air when I closed the four oxygen bottles we had used up and opened other four. The cocks were so cold that the fingertips of my left hand froze through the gloves. The first time I tried to get the blood circulating, I was unsuccessful. I put the fingers in my mouth, biting hard on my fingertips, and managed to get the blood flowing again. To make things worse, we had to go through cumulus clouds that put us in a heavy electric storm. Sparks were flying from propellers and wing tips. While the front gunner was turning his turret to prevent it from freezing up, his guns were in a halo of electric discharge. Blue sparks were coming from the radio. With the engines going haywire, the cold, and the storm, it was a ghastly journey home. We got back alright, crossing the English coast precisely at the same spot we had passed over outbound four hours earlier. We landed in East Wretham at 10.10 p.m., thankful to have made it back at all.

Flt Lt Ocelka had turned around near the Dutch coast, Flt Lt Šnajdr and Sgt Šedivý had pushed on to Wilhelmshaven, but the fifth Wellington T2519/KX-Y was missing. It had reported engine trouble—most likely the same situation the rest of us had experienced. Then they suffered an engine failure that forced them to transmit a SOS at 10.18 p.m. They were then fixed by a D/F steer as being at 52° 18'N and 2° 41'E over the North Sea and some 40 miles or so off land. We never heard anything more from them. The next day, four of our planes (under the command of Wg Cdr Toman, Sqn Ldr Pickard, Sgt Uruba and Plt Off. Cigoš respectively) and six planes from No. 9 (B) Squadron, from Honington, searched the sea. There was no trace of the ill-fated crew or plane.[6] Plt Off. Kubizňák, a stout, good-humoured fellow who used to call raids a 'marvellous sport', was the skipper; Sgt Baumruk, one of our best pilots, was the second pilot; Plt Off. Hudec the navigator; Plt Off. Leskauer, a rather melancholic chap, the W/T operator; with Sgt Bolfík and Plt Off. Král as air gunners. I liked little Král very much. He was the driving force behind every social activity in the mess. Král was also chairman of the Wretham Sokol.[7] He was a real idealist and one of our very best men.

Friday 17 January, the day after the raid, was an awkward one. The search planes were in the air, while we on the ground had to endure hours of anxiety, waiting, as hope slowly faded. I volunteered to be in charge of Operations instead of Plt Off. Fantl, who had been up until 4 a.m. and was deadly tired. In the late afternoon, there was nothing left to hope for. To get myself in a better mood, I went with Plt Offs Fantl, Vnouček, and Kirchstein to The Bull Inn in Barton Mills, near Mildenhall. It's a very homey old place. We had quite a number of drinks with a couple of officers from RAF Station Mildenhall. One of them was a very nice and very drunk Squadron Leader with a DFC.

I met a girl, Sheila Close, who is staying with her father in the Old Rectory in Barton Mills. She is an acquaintance of Fantl and seems to be strongly attached to the RAF by her two brothers, who are Squadron Leaders, and otherwise. Sheila seems to be near her thirties, but very attractive. She and I seemed to get affectionate with each other rather quickly, and she was in my arms for a few minutes once we were alone together in the lounge. I promised to come to The Bull again to see her. After midnight, we tried to get a taxi to go home but we couldn't get any, so we spent the night in easy chairs placed in front of the fireplace. I slept quite well for about five hours. We got a taxi the next morning and reached Wretham at about

9.20 a.m. We ran directly into the arms of the CO and the Adjutant, who were on the way to their offices.

I forgot to mention a strange coincidence in connection with the loss of Plt Off. Kubizňák's crew. The sixteenth day of the month plays a prominent part in the fate of the Squadron. On 16 October, we lost three planes and twelve men. On 16 November, there were no losses as the Squadron was then temporarily off operations for training. On 16 December, Křivda crashed his plane near the airport, and on 16 January Kubizňák disappeared in the North Sea. Since October, the Squadron has suffered losses only on the sixteenth day of each month!

On Saturday 18 January, the day we came back from Barton Mills at 9.20 a.m., our squadron was inspected by the King and Queen. We were lined up on an open square. It was bitterly cold, with a freezing wind blowing over the airfield. We stood there for over an hour. Their Majesties finally arrived, accompanied by Air Chief Marshal Sir Richard Peirse, Commander in Chief of Bomber Command, and Air Vice-Marshal John Eustace Arthur Baldwin, Air Officer Commanding of No. 3 (B) Group. The Queen was as charming as ever. Later, in Wretham Hall, I was amongst the officers who were to be presented to Their Majesties. The Queen remembered that I had been for tea at Windsor Castle, and called the King to tell him about it. She then said that she would tell Princess Margaret Rose (beside whom I was sitting on 27 November 1940) that she had seen me. I was very impressed that the Queen should have remembered me after two months. She is really great. The end of the day was less impressive for me; I was Station Duty Officer. One water tank in Wretham Hall broke and I had to get a plumber from Thetford during the night. It was a descent from the blue skies to the realities of common life.

Our squadron has been strengthened by a second flight from Honington—six crews, with Flt Lt Kirby-Green in charge.[8] This was vital, as through losses and illness we are now down to seven complete crews. The new flight will of course remain non-operational for the time being and complete its training on the station.

On Wednesday 22 January, Sqn Ldr Pickard took Wg Cdr Toman and Plt Offs Fantl, Stratton, and myself to The Bull in Barton Mills. Wg Cdr Toman invited us for a good dinner that included chicken and a marvellous old red Chambertin. I phoned Sheila after dinner and asked her to come over. She came and we spent a very nice evening in front of the fireplace. Unfortunately, I couldn't be alone with Sheila except when I accompanied her halfway home. She is very lovely.

Morale in the Squadron is at a low point after Kubizňák and his crew's accident. Firstly, Plt Off. Richter, Flt Lt Ocelka's navigator, reported sick. He is one of the best heads in the Squadron. Richter has been in half a dozen crashes. On that fateful night of 16 October, we lost three planes, with Richter being on one of them. He had to bale out of Flt Lt Šnajdr's aircraft as well. On 16 January, he was in Ocelka's plane, which had engine trouble and had to turn around close to the Dutch coast. It was the old problem of icing again, which was experienced by all our planes and probably Kubizňák's as well. It must have been an uneasy trip back, still over 100 miles out over the North Sea. Richter's morale finally broke after this last episode; I think he has been taken off flying for good. The thirty-year-old Plt Off. Hnátek was then put in Ocelka's crew as navigator. He had been on five of the Squadron's first operations in 1940, but, as far as I know, has not flown since 16 October. Hnátek used his tonsils as an excuse. He promptly asked to be put on a pilot's course, and when this was refused, he asked to be relieved from flying. We are very short of navigators. Now, Plt Off. Nedvěd is Ocelka's navigator—a very intelligent young boy, the same who behaved so gallantly when Křivda's plane crashed on 16 December. There is no danger of him getting windy. Plt Off. Fürbach asked to be transferred to the infantry; he had been in Ocelka's plane on the night of 16 January. However, I hear that he is on the point of changing his mind. Fürbach is one of our commissioned air gunners. It is difficult to ignore or condemn the lack of spirit that is so prevalent in our squadron. The main trouble is the complete lack of confidence in our Czech military leaders. The men hate the Air Ministry and the Czechoslovak Inspectorate General.[9] The main points they are bringing forward against them are as follows:

1. They haven't kept promises they made to our boys in France, and although they themselves had high salaries and sat in Paris, they didn't care about our officers being demoted to privates in the Foreign Legion, making 50 centimes a day. Furthermore, they threatened that if our officers refused to serve with the French Foreign Legion they would be handed over to the Gestapo.

2. They reported our squadron as being fully trained immediately after it had been formed in England, although our men were far from fit for operations.

Then there are our heavy losses. There was plenty of talk about the 'Düsseldorf Murderers' and 'Wretham Butchery', as they were angrily referred to. There are lots of other petty mistakes that eat at the souls of our men. Here are two of them: the RAF has approved promotions for a few of our officers. The promotions would have already gone through if the files weren't being held back by some of our officials. Our men go on operations while officers show no respect for us as they sit in the security of their London armchairs. One Staff Captain, Kulhánek, phoned from London the other day and got connected with Fantl.[10] Fantl is our Operations Officer and the hardest-working man on the station. Staff Captain Kulhánek was shouting down the phone, 'You have had file No. XY with you since December and haven't returned it. You are doing nothing!' He actually used the profane Czech expression '*hovno*' ('crap'). The question remains, who is really doing nothing? An overstaffed Ministry administering just three Czech squadrons (Nos 310 (F) and 312 (F) as well as No. 311 (B)), or an operational bomber squadron that is bombing Germany?

All the discontent has no doubt poisoned this squadron. All the dismissals, cashiering, and reduction of rank in the infantry won't change it. So far, I've seen the Kozák brothers and Úlehla, all three Pilot Officers, along with Sergeants Fák and Novotný, punished in one way or another since late last year. Five officers from our Training Flight in Honington were dismissed and sent to the infantry fourteen days ago.[11] Now Hnátek and Fürbach come along. Richter, who has an acceptable excuse, will probably get away with it. Despite all this, we have some of the best and bravest men I have ever seen. They are keeping high standards and maintaining the reputation of the Squadron.

There has been no flying since 16 January owing to miserable weather. Times are rather dull. On Friday 24 January, I was in the cinema at Thetford watching *Gulliver's Travels*, and then I went to The Anchor. It was quite crowded there. I was standing beside Dr Hora, a Corporal, and his wife. He works in our Orderly Room and is one of those up for a commission from the British; unfortunately, it is being blocked by Czech bureaucracy. Hora had been a solicitor in Prague. A few of our Sergeant Pilots were there, along with two WAAFs from Honington. I enjoyed the company of one of them, Iris Coles. She works in the Accounting Officer's office. Iris has a very attractive, soft, and petite face. The next night, I was with Fantl in The Bull at Barton Mills. I was very tired, and moreover there were too many people around. Practically all the RAF officers from Mildenhall seemed to have decided to surround Sheila. I didn't feel like fighting, so I resigned myself to a spending a dissatisfying evening. Sheila came over later, apologised, and then asked me to see her again on a quieter evening. I was rude and I doubt if I'll go there again. I have a rather bad conscience, and I am homesick and missing Herta. It must be the relative idleness, and it'll be better once we are on operations again. For the moment, I am in a damn-it-all mood. Today is Monday 27 January. I was at Thetford again at the cinema, then in The Anchor for drinks, and, finally, at Hora's home.

The next morning, I was notified by the 1st Czech Brigade Disciplinary Court Martial at Leamington, Yorkshire, that four of the recently cashiered officers, Plt Offs Vaněček, Kovář, Hančil and Matuška, have selected me as their attorney.[12] I have declined, mainly because I don't want to get mixed up in the internal Czech troubles. The reason I gave them was that I wasn't acquainted with Military Law and could not make up for it during criminal proceedings. Incidentally, those officers are in custody because they have refused to serve in the ranks of the infantry and swear an oath. However, I don't know if they have been reduced in rank with the Czechoslovak Army or only cashiered out of the RAF.

Plt Off. Valenta from our squadron has put together statistics that show our performance up to 20 January 1941. It is very interesting, and it demonstrates the heavy losses a frontline bomber squadron has to deal with in a short period of time (four months, of which one and half were non-operational).

Target	Number of raids	Number of aircraft	Number of bombs		
			500 lb	250 lb	4 lb incendiary
Docks, harbours, oil stores in harbours, ships	15 attacks on 11 targets	42	92	159	9,080
Railways	4 attacks on 4 targets	13	28	37	2,280
Plants	2 attacks on 1 target	3	13	1	240
Targets in towns	3 attacks on 3 targets	8	11	36	720
Total	**24 attacks**	**66***	**144**	**233**	**12,320 (111 SBCs)**[13]

* two aircraft did not reach the target for various reasons.

Losses:
Planes: sixty-eight planes dispatched—six lost ... 9 per cent
Personnel: seventy-eight took off, twenty-seven missing ... 35 per cent[14]

This last one is a disturbing number!

I went to Bury St Edmunds on Thursday, 30 January, where I watched Charlie Chaplin's *The Great Dictator* for a second time. Wg Cdr and Mrs Simonds took Wg Cdr Toman and Plt Offs Stratton, Nedvěd and myself in the CO's car. I was supposed to go on leave the following day, but Fantl didn't come back from a dance at AVM Baldwin's place until late Saturday afternoon, and therefore I couldn't leave. On the night of Saturday 1 February, I went out again to The Bull. This time I was with Wg Cdr and Mrs Simonds, Wg Cdr Toman, and Plt Offs Fantl and Kacíř. Sheila was there, being very apologetic and extremely nice too. Kacíř played the harmonica and Fantl got awfully drunk. We arrived back at 2 a.m.

8

Leave in London, 2–6 February 1941

I left for London on Sunday 2 February, on the 9.35 a.m. train from Thetford. Lojza was waiting for me at Liverpool Street station in London. He is living in an enormous complex of apartment houses on Dolphin Square, which is something like London Terrace, where I used to work in New York. Lojza is staying in Mrs Rose's flat at 110 Rodney House. Mrs Rose is a widow, and her son was in the RAF and killed in a flying accident soon after the outbreak of the war.[1] Her daughter Jeanne, whom I have met before, is an officer in the WAAF, and she is stationed at Watton, some 10 miles from our station.

We had tea in Mrs Primrose Osborne's flat on the same gangway. Mrs Osborne was born Primrose Phyllis Salt on 9 April 1915. She was called the loveliest *débutante* of 1933 and 'The Toast of Two Continents' (among other titles). Primrose must have really been a social highlight. She is the daughter of Major-General Harold Francis Salt CB CMG DSO, who served in India from 1936 to 1939. Primrose married Maj. Anthony Hope Osborne in India. Guests invited to the wedding included the Viceroy Lord Willingdon and Lady Willingdon. Her husband, Maj. Osborne—an Australian serving with the 2nd Dragoon Guards (Queen's Bays)—is now with his unit in Chester. She is really very beautiful, not quite twenty-six, with really marvellous light-blue eyes. But she uses a little too much makeup. Primrose has three enormous dogs in her little flat, so one can hardly move. Next door lives one Mrs Sanders. She lived in Italy for some thirty years and has two of her daughters still there. Both are married to high officials of the Fascist Party. Her son, on the other hand, is the well-known Sqn Ldr Arthur Thomas Drake Sanders DFC. He is the Commanding Officer of No. 264 'Madras Presidency' (F) Squadron, a night fighter unit. Mrs Sanders does not like her third daughter's husband, who is also a Squadron Leader in the RAF; it seems he drinks too much. I chatted afterwards with Lojza until midnight.

The next day I was at Lloyds Bank, Canada House, and RCAF Headquarters.[2] We ate lunch in a French restaurant on St Martin's Lane called La Coquille.

Leave in London, 2–6 February 1941

Lojza's girlfriend, Patience, who works in the Foreign Office, joined us. She was accompanied by fellow employee Nancy Bingham, a very petite, dark, and pretty girl. After lunch, I went with Lojza to see his lawyer, Mr Englefield. Dr Hermann, a lawyer from Brno, works in Mr Englefield's office as managing clerk. We then met Dr Palkovský, a Czech politician who seems to be an intermediary to the Russian ambassador Majski, in the Old Vienna coffee shop. We then went out with Karel Česaný for dinner in a Chinese restaurant in Soho, and for a few drinks afterwards at the Carlton bar.

The next morning, I went to see Ivo Ducháček in the Foreign Ministry. I then had lunch with him and Lojza at the Czechoslovak Centre at 3 Clifton Gardens, W9. We had pork, dumplings, and sauerkraut. It was great. I then went to the Czechoslovak Inspectorate General at 19 Woburn Square and met with Air Vice-Marshal RNDr Karel Janoušek KCB. The reason for me visiting him can only be described as ridiculous and pathetic; for the last fourteen months, Dr Pavlásek, the Czechoslovak Consul General in Montreal, has been positive that I am an agent of the Gestapo. The situation started on 11 December 1939, when he sent a letter with his suspicions to Capt. Van Wart in Toronto, Ontario.[3] Since then, he has taken all the pain in the world to persuade different officials that I am a spy. Apparently, he has also sent a warning to the famous Czech '*2eme Bureau*' (Intelligence), and the Chief of Defence Intelligence, Maj. Bartík, has put one Strelinger (an agent from Slovakia) on my trail. Air Vice-Marshal Janoušek heard of the affair and more or less hinted to me (through Dr Palkovský) to come up and see him.

He told me to immediately laugh the silly accusations off as he had already done. Janoušek then questioned me about conditions in Canada and about the chances of us getting volunteers there for the Czech squadrons in the RAF. He asked me to write up a report. I later heard from Strelinger himself that the 2nd Bureau had also dropped the charges. I have been very decent, and up to now I have refrained from any attacks on Dr Pavlásek, but his last step has forced me to retaliate. I told AVM Janoušek (and later Minister Lichner) all I know about our officials in Canada, and that's plenty. In the evening, we were with Patience and Nancy at a dinner dance at the Strand Palace. Ernest Bevin was there.[4] We then went to my guest room in Drake House, located within Dolphin Square. It would be late to bed again.

I forgot to mention that on Monday I went to the Czech Institute at 18 Grosvenor Place, where I met with Plt Off. Janik from the Polish Air Ministry.[5] He is a man with an inscrutable personality. Janik has developed a plan involving a Czecho-Polish symbiosis. It would start during the war, with the amalgamation of Czech and Polish units in the RAF. They would form Slavic squadrons. After the war, a new common state of Czechoslovakia and Poland would emerge. I was able to follow him up to that point, but then he told me about the re-Slavisation of East and West Prussia, Silesia and Pomerania, including which provinces would be incorporated in the future Czecho-Polish state. He went on about a Slavic Union comprising the Czecho-Polish state, the Ukraine, White Russia, Yugoslavia and Bulgaria. That was too much for me to comprehend. After he promised to provide me with heaps of pan-Slav literature, I left the imaginative Plt Off. Janik. It was rather interesting to hear that Professor Hodža, Papírník, and Gen. Prchala were all for the idea.

On Wednesday, I lunched with Lojza, Dr Palkovský, and Strelinger in the Hungarian Csárda on Dean Street. After bringing a letter for Herta to RCAF HQ (an officer going to Canada may take it with him), I went home. I then spent the afternoon with Mrs Osborne in her flat. That evening, I went with Lojza to Minister Lichner's place, where I played bridge with him, Fedor Hodža (the Secretary of Dr Osuský), and Dr Harminc (the Secretary of Minister Lichner). On Thursday, I met Torelli again for lunch at the Old Quebec Café at Marble Arch. I left on the 2.25 p.m. train. Dordie, who was coming back from leave spent with her people in Somerset and Kent, was on the train. I arrived at my station around 6 p.m. on Thursday, 6 February, just in time to see six of our aircraft take off for a raid on Boulogne-sur-Mer, France. The leave had been very nice, although little hectic, Primrose Osborne having been the highlight.

9

Third Stage at East Wretham, 6 February–2 May 1941

I arrived towards dusk on Thursday 6 February 1941, just in time to see our planes disappear southward to Boulogne-sur-Mer. The night was clear, and yet we lost one of our six planes that went out. Its crew was: Fg Off. Cigoš, skipper; Sgt Uruba, second pilot; Fg Off. Bušina, navigator; Plt Off. Valenta, W/T operator; Sgt Kopal, front gunner; and Plt Off. Křížek, rear gunner. The usual navigator of this crew was little Plt Off. Partyk, but since he is sick, Fg Off. Bušina was sent with Cigoš's crew. I think that this was a grave mistake. Firstly, Bušina is much too old. I think he is thirty-nine. He has had some cardiac problems and was very nervous. When Richter and Hnátek became unavailable as navigators, I asked for young replacements from 'B' Flight in Honington, and especially for Plt Off. Kvapil. We got Bušina because he had been a Staff Captain in Czechoslovakia, in addition to having a lot of experience in what was called navigation in our country (but was simply map reading). I gave Bušina one half-day of instruction in astro navigation before I went on leave. I found him to be clever, but nervous and hasty. He was supposed to be Bufka's navigator, which would have given him one month's time for further instruction as both of the pilots of the crew, Sgts Bufka and Kráčmer, are in hospital at present.[1] Instead, Bušina was put in a crew immediately. It may not have been his fault, but it seems strange that the accident occurred on Bušina's first flight. There are other rather appalling circumstances. Cigoš's aircraft took off at 6.06 p.m. and signalled at 7.23 p.m. that they had bombed the target and were returning. At 8.10 p.m., they asked for and received a QDM of 339°.[2] They must then have been comparatively close (perhaps 30 miles) away from Honington. Between 8.10 and 9.10 p.m., they asked for a QDM eleven times. Their calls were heard by our station in Wretham, but unfortunately not by the D/F station in Honington. As a result, no courses were sent to the plane. No signals were heard after 9.10 p.m. Around 11 p.m., a plane was over Scampton aerodrome in Lincolnshire and contacted the field by R/T. Somebody speaking English with a foreign accent—but slowly and clearly—was transmitting. All the aerodrome lights were switched on, but the plane didn't land; it disappeared in a north-easterly direction, towards the North Sea. Mist had fallen by then. That was perhaps the last contact we had with Cigoš's crew.[3]

On Saturday 8 February, I was at Thetford with the new Padre, Sqn Ldr Pouchlý. First we went to the cinema to watch *It's a Date*, starring Deanna Durbin, and then off for drinks at The Anchor. Pouchlý seems to be very nice and also well-educated. He had been at the university in Rome prior to leaving Italy during the spring of 1940. He had only just arrived when Cigoš's accident occurred. His first duty was to break the news to Plt Off. Křížek's Yugoslavian wife.

The next day we had a visit from AVM Janoušek of the Czech Inspectorate. He came over to settle questions ranging from operational training to organisation and establishment. The idea seems to be to withdraw the commissioned W/T operators and gunners (who at this time are an anomaly in the RAF) and retrain them as pilots. The navigators are protesting against the idea as there is a lack of them in the Squadron. There is fear that if the idea is carried out, they will never get a pilot's course. A proposal was put forward that pilot training should be offered only after a certain number of operations, as a sort of reward. I don't know which standpoint will prevail. Fg Off. Fikrle is the main champion of the navigators' plan, and he got into quite a heated argument with Wg Cdr Toman for putting his ideas forward in an overly aggressive manner. I listened to Mr Churchill's speech in the evening and I was very impressed.

On Monday 10 February, we put up five crews—all the Operational Flight had available. Accidents had taken their toll on crews and aircraft. Additionally, one crew was ill and another one on leave. I was supposed to go on Wellington T2972/KX-G for an operation against Hanover, Germany. The crew were: Sgt Korda, skipper; Sgt Rozum, second pilot; myself as navigator; Sgt Slánský, W/T operator; Sgt Čtvrtlík, front gunner; and Plt Off. Zapletal, rear gunner. We were sitting in the plane at 6.45 p.m., ready to start, when Sgt Rozum became ill and began to vomit. It was later rumoured that Rozum had had too much beer after lunch, but this was met with his strong denial. It took more than an hour to find a spare pilot. Fg Off. Breitcetl got ready and headed to the dispersal area. Meanwhile, an air raid was going on, with the Germans dropping pairs of flares somewhere to the south. We could hear explosions and then the characteristic sound of German machines overhead. The flare path was switched off and we waited. After the Germans had passed, we began to roll to the take-off point. We had just left the dispersal and were taxiing along the edge of the aerodrome when a new wave of Germans came in. Flares were dropping 1 or 2 miles from the field, just behind the little wood on the south side. The flare path was shut off again, and as the danger seemed imminent, we exited the plane and waited in a shallow sandpit. The picture of the moonlit night, with the bright flares seemingly dropping from the skies, was very impressive. By the time this second wave passed and the flare path was switched on again, it was 8.15 p.m. It was apparently too late to carry on. I was very disappointed that we did not receive permission to start again.

The next morning, I was awoken at seven o'clock to take over the Operations Room for a search for three dinghies that were supposed to be somewhere in the North Sea.[4] We sent four aircraft, one of which was Wellington T2972/KX-G with Sgt Korda's crew, the other three with crews from Training Flight. During the morning hours, the Group asked for a maximum effort. We had to recall Korda and one of the Training Flight crews for night operations. It was an awful *tohuwabohu* in the Operations Room, with the search going on alongside preparations for the night's sorties.[5] Both Wing Commanders and Sqn Ldr Pickard phoned around continuously, giving orders and then cancelling them one after another.[6] Wg Cdr Simonds, who never flies, declared that he would go as second pilot with Sgt Hrnčíř, himself a flying instructor with Training Flight. When Simonds found out the target was in Germany, he suddenly decided he was not going. We finally managed to put five crews together. Some 90 per cent of the personnel had been out the previous night. I was supposed to go again with Korda's crew on Wellington T2972, Sgt Rozum having been replaced by Sgt Filler. Our target was to be Magdeburg, but it was later changed to Bremen. We started in broad daylight at 6 p.m. All was well until we crossed the English coast south of Great Yarmouth, over a layer of solid white clouds. Then our instruments failed. First the starboard engine's rpm instrument dropped to zero, followed by failure of the vacuum pump, then the rate-of-climb indicator and a seized altimeter. The final snag that caused us to abort our trip was the airspeed indicator; it began to show everything between 80 and 300 miles. We turned for home; we then changed our mind, going eastward again before finally turning back for good. When we came over land again, fog had developed—contrary to all forecasts and with suddenness possible only in England.

We got over Wretham all right by dead reckoning. Later, on the ground, I was told that we had passed overhead precisely at the time when I told our W/T operator, Sgt Slánský, to contact the aerodrome over the R/T. Our R/T had broken down and we weren't able to communicate with the ground to ask for the flare path to be switched on. We therefore went to Honington, but when we got there we decided to try Wretham again. This time, the officer in charge of the flare path lit it up on his own initiative, allowing us see the lights though the fog. Our altimeter didn't work. Despite this, Korda, who is an old commercial airline captain and probably our best pilot, opened a window and stuck his head outside to judge his altitude. He made a perfect landing with almost full petrol tanks, 1 ton of bombs, and a visibility of only 200 yards. It was a masterful piece of flying.

Our other four planes bombed the target, as seen by gun flashes, searchlights and fires reflecting against the clouds. On the return trip, they were diverted to fog-free aerodromes further to the west. Sqn Ldr Pickard and Sgt Anderle thus landed their planes at Newmarket, Fg Off. Breitcetl at Wyton, and Sgt Šedivý crash-landed near Swinderby, Lincolnshire.[7] All the crews are safe, which is a miracle considering the terrible weather conditions.

Our bombing of Germany in 1940 can be judged by the following table.[8]

Month	July	August	September	October	November	December
Number of Sorties	1,814	2,050	3,109	2,219	1,855	1,399
Average per night	59	66	104	71	62	45

The weather in December was so bad that bombing activity was carried out on a very small scale. To the above figures, about 15 to 20 per cent may be added for bombing attacks carried out by Coastal Command. From September, our bombing activity was at least equal (if not more intensive) to that of the Luftwaffe.

On Wednesday 12 February I was invited for dinner at Cavenham Hall, near Bury St Edmunds—the residence of Sir Archibald Home.[9] He is a retired Brigadier General and Honorary Colonel of the 11th Hussars. The regiment, which exchanged horses for armoured cars long ago, is now fighting in Libya. Sir Archibald is also Secretary-Treasurer of the British Empire Services League, and as such he is Field Marshal Lord Douglas Haig's right-hand man.[10] He has assumed a position with the Red Cross. Sir Archibald was recently in the news for forbidding Mrs Fellowes, a member of high society and a nurse at Bury St Edmunds hospital, from wearing lipstick while on duty. Mrs Fellowes decided to stick to wearing lipstick and left her nursing job; this showed where her priorities were in wartime work. His wife is a very friendly old lady, and their daughter, Theresa, is also a nurse at Bury St Edmunds. She is dark, slim, and not very pretty, yet still attractive and clever. Her friend, Lelgarde Philipps, and a friend of the host, Brigadier General Lord Dillon, were there. He looked like the ageing English generals you would see in old photos—tall and slim, with a big, aquiline nose and a white trimmed moustache, his tunic breasts covered by several dozen rows of ribbons. Four of us from 311 Squadron were there—Flt Lt Provazník, and Plt Offs Schneider, Stratton and myself. Everything was very British—the house, the dinner, and the conversation. After dinner, we played darts and ping-pong and danced with the girls. This was followed by a game of 'vingt-et-un'.[11] We left at around 11.30 p.m., after a very enjoyable evening. The next day I went to Honington to take care of a number of official matters. On the return trip, I met our Padre at Thetford and ended up going with him to watch a picture called *Rio*, with Basil Rathbone and Victor McLaglen.

On Friday 14 February, Wellington T2972/KX-G was taken on a morning test flight. It is an awful crate. Firstly, it took the plane thirty-seven minutes to climb to 12,000 feet. After another six minutes, we reached 13,000 feet. That was it—not another inch higher. The radio transmitter burned out when switched off, and the instruments showed everything except the right thing. The plane is definitely unserviceable. In the afternoon, we went to fetch a plane at Llandow, near Cardiff, Wales. We had a reasonably good flight over Cambridge, Oxford, and Swindon until we got over the hills south of Bristol. There we encountered terrible weather, with clouds reaching down to the ground and torrential rain. We turned back when we reached the Bristol Channel. It was 4.15 p.m., and we couldn't see practically anything. It was a pity as we were only some 30 miles or so from Llandow. Upon arriving back home, I found a long-awaited letter dated 9 January and a cable sent on 14 February from Herta, I was overjoyed. Herta seems to be well. She received news from home. My parents are doing fine, but Herta's father died on 20 September from heart failure. My mother-in-law is now back in Brno again.

On Sunday night, we had a party at Wretham Hall. There was the usual drinking and noisy cheerfulness. I enjoyed the evening. I met a remarkably intelligent and attractive lady, Mrs MacDonald, the wife of a Wing Commander from No. 3 (B) Group. I got very tired and went to bed at half past eleven. The next day, we were supposed to raid the Ruhr. As our aerodrome was too soft, we relocated to Honington to operate from there. I was in Šedivý's crew, aboard Wellington T2561/KX-A, but operations were cancelled before the briefing due to bad weather. Weather is pretty terrible throughout. On Tuesday 18 February, I went with Sgt Korda to fetch a new plane from Burtonwood, near Liverpool. We had only been flying for twenty minutes when we hit cloud banks that dropped right to the ground. It was so bad that we couldn't see the ground when flying at 100 feet, and so we returned to Wretham.

The Germans are now attacking Wretham more seriously, or, as Fg Off. Coxwell put it, 'The war's getting personal.' As I wrote already, the Germans have been reconnoitring our area for some time. We recovered an intact flare from a tree on Sunday morning. On Tuesday 18 February, I was still in bed at around 7.50 a.m. when I heard the sound of engines, and then the chatter of machine-gun fire. This was followed by five heavy explosions in close proximity. Bombing must have occurred from a very low altitude—500 feet at the most—and yet there was almost no damage. One plane's port engine was hit by a few bullets, but repairs will not take long. Other bullets went through the roof of a hut on the aerodrome, while a few windows were shattered in the Sergeants' Mess. The raider, a Heinkel 111, was shot down shortly afterwards by Watton Station Defence. After witnessing the embarrassing actions displayed by the Wretham defenders, we described our Army personnel forming the station defence as 'seventy raw recruits commanded by two little boy officers'. Most ran into shelters, with only one machine gun being manned and firing only six rounds. This is despite a warning having been given five minutes beforehand! It is fortunate that Watton seems to be well-organised. I saw the Heinkel lying in a field near Ovington, some 2 miles out of Watton. The plane was riddled with bullets, and moreover had been caught in rocket-cables. It's a beautiful ship, and it seems well-constructed. It looks far lighter than our Wellingtons and gives the impression of great speed. The downed aircraft's armament of five machine guns—mostly in impractical fixed or hand-mounted positions—is rather poor. The crew of five is safe and are now prisoners of war. I am sure that the plane could be relatively easy to repair and put back into service again.

One of the bombs that the Heinkel had dropped the day before remained unexploded in a moor on the boundary of Illington and Great Hockham. I went there on Wednesday with our Senior Armament Instructors, WO Simpson and Sgt Davies. We were led to the spot by the gamekeeper of Illington, Mr Gower, and Constable

Porely of Great Hockham. We had to fetch both of them from the Dog and Partridge pub. The bomb had slid over the ground for a few yards, and it was now sticking nose-up. It was a 550-pounder, with one of its fuses in plain view on one side. We had no tools to unscrew the locking ring and didn't dare to handle the fuse otherwise; we therefore couldn't really do anything other than to advise the civilian authorities to call for a Bomb Disposal Squad.[12] In the afternoon, I went out with the Padre and Plt Off. Bečvář to watch a movie at Thetford. It was a public-school story named *The House Master*. We then had dinner at Sqn Ldr Pickard's home in East Harling. Mrs Pickard and he are living there in a nice little house, and I spent a pleasant evening there. I stayed overnight and once again slept in a real bed instead of a camp cot.

On Friday 21 February, I took part in a raid on Wilhelmshaven. I was in Wellington T2972/KX-G, with Sgt Korda as skipper, the Commanding Officer, Wg Cdr Karel Toman as second pilot, myself as navigator, Sgt Slánský as W/T operator, Sgt Čtvrtlík as front gunner, and famous middleweight boxer Sgt Jakš as rear gunner. The official No. 3 Group report of the action reads as follows:

No. 3 (B) Group Operations—Night of 21–22 February

Owing to weather conditions, the effort was reduced to thirty-seven aircraft, detailed to attack Wilhelmshaven Naval Docks, with an alternative target of Emden Naval Docks, twenty-one aircraft succeeded in reaching the primary target, three aircraft attacked the alternative target, six aircraft attacked last resort target, three returned early and two jettisoned bombs. Two aircraft failed to return to base.[13]

Heavy haze and intense darkness made identification of the target difficult. Fires were seen in the target area and one particularly large fire, visible halfway to Emden, was in the area of gas works, 1,500 yards north-west of the Bauhafen, around the gasworks, causing six green explosions. $5 \times 1,000$-lb, 63×500-lb, 10×250-lb and $2,040 \times 4$-lb bombs were dropped. Three aircraft attacked Emden, dropping 10×500-lb, 2×250-lb, 540×4-lb bombs, but results were not observed. One aircraft attacked Boulogne. Again no results were seen. De Kooy aerodrome was attacked by three aircraft, 5×500-lb, 3×250-lb and 320×4-lb bombs were dropped, two bursts being observed in target area. Leeuwarden aerodrome received attention by three aircraft, 14×500-lb, 1×250-lb and 140×4-lb bombs were dropped, no results were seen.

Stations operating were East Wretham, Feltwell, Honington, Mildenhall, Newmarket and Wyton. Bombs were dropped from heights of 8,000 feet up to 17,000 feet. No successful photographs were taken.

There isn't very much I could add to this report. We got over Wilhelmshaven all right, although we had to fly blind on top of an overcast layer there and back again. Conditions improved right over the target, although there weren't more than a few clear patches in a thick haze. As the new moon had just broken, the night was particularly dark.

Flak was very heavy and there were lots of searchlights. We were picked up by searchlights several times, but we never held long enough to allow the guns to get us. I bombed from a little below 16,000 feet. On the homeward trip we entered thick clouds, and we had to descend through them from 14,000 feet right down to almost 1,500 feet. It was very cold outside. Our thermometer indicated -34 degrees centigrade, but the cockpit heating and de-freezing worked very well, so there was no serious trouble. Before our departure, I had calculated our flight to last four hours and twenty-three minutes. We landed after four hours and twenty-one minutes. Korda piloted the plane both ways.

The main news is that Wg Cdr Toman is finally the only CO of our squadron. Wg Cdr Simonds was posted as 'supernumerary' to Driffield, Yorkshire. That certainly is no promotion, and he doesn't deserve anything else. He is a good chap and a marvellous organiser of social entertainment, but he hasn't succeeded at practically anything and he has never shown himself to be capable of running an operational bomber squadron. Wg Cdr Toman took over on 21 February and began his command by taking part in the Wilhelmshaven raid.

I was out again on Sunday 23 February. We sent out six aircraft, all on Boulogne-sur-Mer, France. I was on Wellington T2971/KX-H. The crew was made up of: Sgt Anderle, skipper; Sgt Filler, second pilot; myself, navigator; Sgt Plzák, W/T operator; Plt Off. Horák, front gunner; and Sgt Valach, rear gunner. We were supposed to bomb the docks, and we cruised above the target area for about fifteen minutes before we were able to locate it by the light of a flare we dropped and two other flares (which, as we would find out later, came from by Flt Lt Šnajdr's plane). I then released the 3,500 lbs of bombs in two sticks. I think that I was lucky this time, as there were at least two very good hits that started enormous fires.

Boulogne must have got an enormous pasting last night. Poor Frenchies. The only noteworthy part of the whole trip was the display of flak the Germans put on. At one time they joined six searchlights and plastered the point they merged with multi-coloured tracers, apparently from pom-poms. There was also a regular barrage of heavy flak, which didn't cause any damage. The aircraft was buffeted about by the turbulence created by the explosions of the guns. With the bursts of our bombs, the huge fires, and the beams of numerous searchlights, it was a big, colourful fireworks display. Upon arriving home, we found that two aircraft from other stations—a Wellington from the New Zealand Squadron, Feltwell, Norfolk, and a Blenheim from Watton, Norfolk—had landed at our aerodrome during their return from operations. The skipper of the Blenheim, Flt Lt Barker (a very nice chap), slept in my room.[14]

I was at two parties in the next two days. On Tuesday, we had a little party of our own in the mess. First we had dinner. I dined with Mrs Simonds, two nice girls from Cavenham Hall, Lelgarde Philipps, Theresa Home, Flt Lt Provazník, and Fg Offs MacNicol, Fantl, and Schneider. We were joined afterwards by Wg Cdr Toman. Our musical trio, Fg Off. Chrást and Plt Offs Kacíř and Hapala, provided the music for a really good little dance. It was much quieter than the usual parties in our mess, and I enjoyed it more than any other party so far.

The next night, I was with Grp Capt. Berounský, Wg Cdr Toman, Sqn Ldrs Pickard and Powell, Flt Lt Provazník, Fg Offs MacNicol and Fantl, and Plt Offs Robinson and Roman at a very official cocktail party. Our host at Ampton Hall was Grp Capt. Gray, the Station Commander of Honington. It is an aristocratic place several miles from Honington, where the aircrew of No. 9 (B) Squadron are lodged. This is in accordance with a new policy that means aircrew don't lodge on permanent stations, which are visible from above and thus often attacked. The valuable aircrew are kept at safer places. Ampton Hall is very beautiful, with a large, wood-panelled dance gallery. The food was excellent. No. 3 Group AOC, AVM Baldwin OBE DSO, appeared for a while. I met Mrs MacDonald once again and was invited to see her at Newmarket.

On Wednesday 26 February, I flew my fifth raid. This one was to Cologne, Germany. Again, I'll refer to the official report of our Group about the raid:

> Forty-three out of forty-nine aircraft detailed reported that they attacked the primary target Cologne, dropping just under 40 tons of HE and 8,000 incendiaries. Seven out of eight from 149 Sqn, eight from 99 Sqn, fourteen out of sixteen from Feltwell, ten out of eleven from 9 Sqn and four out of six 311 Sqn. Darkness and haze obscured definite pin-points, but the last wave reported town well alight on arrival and many fires seen in target area. Three large fires with white sheds of flame and one big red fire at target point. Three big and many small explosions. One A/C reports direct hits on apparent oil storage tanks on west bank of Rhine, resulting in greenish fires and large volumes of smoke. Large yellow fire one mile to north and another 1.5 mile to south. Fires visible for 50 miles. One A/C, which from photograph taken was over Bonn, reports large flak and searchlights concentrations and fires 15-20 miles to north-east. Four out of six freshmen attacked Boulogne Docks, two from 15 Sqn, two out of three from 99 Sqn. Fires with green explosions seen west of docks Nos 3 and 4. A ship in docks appeared to be on fire. Fires were visible for 40 miles. Four A/C attacked SEMO including two from 311 Sqn on Flushing.

It was a very dark night. I flew in Wellington T2561/KX-A, crewed by Sgt Šedivý, skipper, Sgt Čapka, second pilot, myself as navigator, Plt Off. Liška, W/T operator, Sgt Babáček, front gunner, and Sgt Cupák as rear gunner. We got to Cologne all right and located the rough position of the town rather easily. We were aided by the mass of searchlights and flak. Our aircraft was one of the first to get there, arriving at 9.10 p.m. There were only a few small fires. I was sure it was Cologne, and I thought I would see the Rhine even on such a dark night—but I did not. I began to have doubts as to whether the town beneath was really Rheydt, or perhaps Mönchengladbach. We therefore remained on the same course for a further ten minutes. No Rhine appeared. I had a flare dropped and saw wooded, snow-covered hills—obviously the mountains east of the Rhine, known as the Sauerland. We turned back. By this point, there could be no doubt that the town we had passed before was Cologne. Several large fires had been started, and there were a number of planes over the town, all dropping flares. One of these flares illuminated a bend of the Rhine south of the town. We went north and I put my five high-explosives and 120 incendiaries in one stick, dropping it nicely on top of the target. The time over target was 9.35 p.m. The journey back was uneventful; I think I did quite a decent job by guiding my plane straight home, with one slight deviation of 3 degrees over the Dutch coast. I now often use the azimuth of stars to track my location, with the intention of working my bearings on stars for navigation.

Fantl has gone on leave for a week and I am temporarily in charge of the Operations Room.[15] That means that I'll be grounded for a week. We have had some rather funny occurrences too. An Anson from our Training Flight in Honington was flying to Sealand, Flintshire, when the hatch over the pilot's seat was blown open, smashing the aerial. There was quite a cracking sound. The pilot, Flt Lt Earle, apparently became unnerved and let the plane go into a dive. He later tried to explain that he had done so to test his controls. One of the crew members, Plt Off. Engel, thought things to be too dangerous and baled out. This must have been riskier than to stay in the plane—which, incidentally, proceeded without further troubles to Sealand. Engel was apparently mistaken for a parachutist and stopped by a man with a shotgun. Poor English skills resulted in Engel being detained as a supposed German before he was able to identify himself.[16]

A similar thing happened to one of our English W/T operators, Sgt Judson.[17] His aircraft had just crash-landed, but he thought it was breaking up in mid-air. Judson grabbed his parachute and threw himself out, head-first, through a safety hatch—only to fall flat onto the grass from a height of a couple of feet. It happened in the middle of astonished onlookers.

One not-so-funny thing happened at our aerodrome on Wednesday, at around 11.15 p.m., just when they were expecting us to return from Cologne. A plane from No. 9 (B) Squadron had landed. The pilot asked where he was, and then requested permission to start out again for Honington. The Orderly Officer, Plt Off. Bečvář, would not give him permission to start and then ordered him to await further orders. The pilot waited for a few minutes before taxiing across the flare path, almost colliding with Sqn Ldr Ocelka, who had just landed. The pilot then ran into some barbed wire on the west side of the aerodrome, turned right, and ploughed into a Blenheim (which had only recently been repaired after sitting for two and a half months on our airfield). I doubt if they'll repair it again. The pilot of the Wellington from No. 9 Squadron must have been out of his mind.[18]

Lojza and Torelli came on the afternoon of Saturday 1 March. I put them up in The Bell at Thetford, but they went for dinner in the mess. That night, we had seven planes raid Cologne and one freshman crew bomb Boulogne-sur-Mer. This great effort was only made possible by the drive of Sqn Ldr Pickard. Although we only had six serviceable planes in the morning, he shouted, cursed and threatened so much that we had nine available for the evening. Everything worked smoothly. The Cologne raid was a resounding success. I worked in the Operations Room until 4.30 a.m. Our last plane landed at 2.40 a.m., followed by an interrogation of the eight crews, including one cuckoo. They were a Whitley crew from No. 51 (B) Squadron, based at Dishforth, Yorkshire, which landed on our aerodrome.[19] That night, Plt Off. Bečvář, Flt Lt Šnajdr's navigator, had a close shave. While over the target, he left the navigator's desk and went forward to the bombsight. Just then, a heavy shell burst above the plane, spraying it with between thirty and forty splinters, most of which entered the cockpit. The navigator's desk, where Bečvář had been sitting just a few minutes beforehand, took some of the shrapnel. The oxygen tubing was smashed too! Almost everything took a hit, from the rudder to the air screws.

On Sunday, Lojza and Torelli were shown around the aerodrome and went on a short flight with Sqn Ldr Ocelka.[20] Torelli then left on the 5.48 p.m. train, and I went with Lojza, Flt Lt Provazník and Sgt Anderle in the latter's Ford to Sir Archibald's home at Cavenham Hall. I had been there on a previous occasion. We first walked through the huge park, then played billiards. That was followed by a marvellous dinner. Then we played darts and ping-pong, and danced with Theresa and Lelgarde. We stayed overnight, had breakfast with Sir Archibald, and were back at Wretham before 9 a.m.

On Monday 3 March, we sent only one freshman crew to Boulogne-sur-Mer. That night was more exciting than that of 1–2 March, when we were operating with eight crews. Training Flight carried out some night flying, and shortly before 9 p.m., one of the planes overshot the flare path and crashed, with Fg Off. Šejbl at the controls. The port engine caught fire. Šejbl and the W/T operator, Plt Off. Kacíř, were unhurt. The second pilot, Sgt Kalenský—a good man, just about to be transferred to Operational Flight—broke his knee. The fire was put out by the fire tender, but it lasted long enough to damage the machine quite a bit and to attract the attention of the Huns to our aerodrome. They were buzzing overhead merrily and almost got our operational plane when it landed one hour after the crash. Sgt Helma, the skipper, was apparently taxiing with position lights on and almost at his dispersal point when a bomb burst some 10 yards away.[21] Nothing happened except some clumps of earth tearing the fabric of the plane. Six more bombs fell (alongside incendiaries) without hitting anything. One of the incendiaries burned so brightly that all of us in the Operations Room thought that another of our machines was in flames. We were lucky again.

Lojza spent his day by cycling to Watton to lunch there with Mrs Rose, and he spent the evening with the Horas at Thetford. I'm afraid that I haven't been able to spend any appreciable amount of time with him.

Nothing happened for the whole of last week due to miserable weather. There has not been anything noteworthy either. I went to the cinema in Thetford once and watched *Golden Boy*, starring Barbara Stanwyck. I had seen it before in Canada. Afterwards, I visited The Anchor. During another evening, I had dinner at the Pickards' and stayed there overnight. Lojza left on the morning of Wednesday 5 March. I got news from Herta, who is a golden girl. I also got a letter from Božena Hauserová, now Mrs Božena J. Lauwers, Clarenville Hotel, Sea Point, Cape Town, South Africa, who normally stays in Leopoldville, Belgian Congo. Her husband, who, I think, is an American, works there with Baťa. She recognised me from a newsreel about Canadian airmen and sent me a letter addressed to 'Mr Dr John Gellner, Czech pilot, England'. I got it anyway.

On Saturday 8 March, we had a big party in the Officer's Mess—the first to be run by the crews themselves. That day, Sqn Ldr Pickard had received the DSO to go along with his DFC, and I was at his place for a few drinks before dinner.[22] I was at the mess by 7.50 p.m., and there I found my two guests, Theresa Home and Lelgarde Philipps. The party was very lively and I was more cheerful than I ever had been in England. I would later go on to regret inviting the two ladies; the boys had invited some ladies of rather questionable standing from Norwich, and it was quite a brawl. I was glad when my quests left at around 1.30 a.m. Some of the Norwich beauties stayed overnight, and they were seen in the mess the next morning in a dishevelled state. I hope that there won't be any official repercussions.

Yesterday, on 10 March, I travelled to Feltwell, Norfolk, to look up Joe Roberts. He serves there with No. 75 'New Zealand' (B) Squadron. Joe had been just briefed for an operation and I found him in the crew room, brooding over his maps. He likes his job and was thrilled by his first and only operation so far when he went to Boulogne-sur-Mer. The news he gave me about our classmates was not so good. Happy Hill went out in a Beaufort and didn't come back. Craik has been shot down during a mine-laying operation near Wilhelmshaven. Jepson is missing. Pidduck had a nasty crash. He wrote to me about that some time ago. Snell is in hospital with appendicitis. There are rumours that Gilmore has been involved in a crash too. Of the other four boys in our group, Florence is coming to Feltwell next week, Easton is in Stradishall, and Noble and Rose are at Wyton. Noble was sick again with the same stuff he had in Malton. Naughty boy!

There have been promotions in the Czech Army. This goes on independently of rank held in the RAF. Bala, Taiber and Korda were commissioned, but they remain RAF Sergeants for the time being. Sqn Ldr Schejbal was awarded the Czech Military Cross. He went on a few operations last fall and received the Czech Gallantry Medal for them, but since then he has been off operations. He is now in charge of B Training Flight at Honington. Everybody wonders why he got the CMC for administration work. The other two Czech Military Crosses were awarded to Plt Off. Nedvěd (for his bravery in a crash on 16 December) and Sqn Ldr Ocelka, CO of Operational Flight, who has flown more operations than anyone else in the Squadron. The value of the decoration is diminished by being indiscriminately awarded for office work; its real purpose is to honour individual acts of bravery or continuous commendable service in the field.

On Wednesday 12 March, I got two letters from Herta. One was delivered by Plt Off. P. A. Gilbertson, the boyfriend of Herta's friend Margaret Ross.[23] Gilbertson is currently at No. 52 (F) OTU, Debden, Essex. Herta is all right, which is most important thing. The same night I went to Berlin, my longest raid so far. The raid report of our Group reads as follows:

1. Eighty-eight aircraft set out to attack Berlin, Bremen and Boulogne.
2. Berlin: Twenty-seven detailed, nineteen attacked—four out of seven from Feltwell, two out of three from No. 9 Sqn, two from No. 311 Sqn, five out of seven from Marham, three out of four from No. 214 Sqn and three out of four from No. 40 Sqn. Bombs: 4 × 1,000-lb, 38 × 500-lb, 11 × 250-lb and 2,820 × 4-lb incendiaries. Many bursts were seen within half a mile circle of aiming point, causing many fires there and on railway yards. All A/C arriving after 00.01 a.m. reported good fires burning on arrival. One A/C came down to 50 feet, shot out searchlight and machine-gunned military barracks at Kreuzbach. Fires at Berlin were seen by returning A/C from 50 to 100 miles. Of the other eight A/C, three attacked Hamburg docks and Schiphol and Oostvoorne aerodromes, four made no attack and one is missing.[24]
3. Boulogne: Seven detailed, six—each from Nos 75, 9, 311 and 7 Sqns and two from No. 40 Sqn attacked target and one of No. 40 Sqn was shot down over target [see Appendix V—Sgt Rose]. Bombs: 45 × 500-lb, 2 × 250-lb and 600 × 4-lb incendiaries. Bursts round No. 4 dock and on quay between Nos 4 and 5 docks causing fires seen 25 miles away.
4. Bremen: Focke-Wulf Works. Fifty-four detailed, thirty-three attacked—four out of five from No. 149 Sqn, two out of five from No. 99 Sqn, eight out of eleven from Marham, three out of six from No. 9 Sqn, one out of five from No. 311 Sqn, six out of seven from No. 214 Sqn, six out of seven from No. 40 Sqn and three out of eight from Feltwell. Bombs: 6 × 1,000-lb, 162 × 500-lb, 16 × 250-lb, and 840 × 4-lb incendiaries. Many direct hits, including one 1,000-lb bomb on buildings in factory area causing fires, followed by explosions. Fires were still visible 80 miles away. Seven A/C one each Nos 149, 311, 214 Sqns, Marham and Feltwell and two from 99 Sqn attacked Bremen industrial area. Bombs: 1 × 1,000-lb, 41 × 500-lb and 3 × 250-lb. Good fires started between aiming point and rail station. Railway 1 mile to east straddled one stick including one 1,000-lb. Bombs across south end of docks produced particularly good results. All bombs seen to burst and two big fires started. One A/C of No. 40 Sqn attacked Leeuwarden aerodrome. Two A/C of Nos 9 and 311 Sqns attacked Hamburg starting fires in the dock area and three A/C from Feltwell attacked Schiphol and Vechta (believed) aerodromes. Six A/C failed to attacks any target (one each from Marham, Feltwell, Nos 99 and 9 Sqns, and two from No. 311 Sqn) and two—one from Marham and one of No. 9 Sqn are missing.[25]

I was on Wellington T2972/KX-G, with Sgt Korda as skipper, Sgt Kráčmer as second pilot, myself as navigator, Sgt Slánský as W/T operator, Sgt Čtvrtlík as the front gunner, and Sgt Kovařík at the back in the rear gunner's position. The other Squadron aircraft going to Berlin was R1410/KX-M, which was flown by Flt Lt Šnajdr. It was a marvellous moonlit night. The flight over the North Sea was a sheer pleasure, with the moonlight reflecting on the water. We crossed the Dutch coast at Wijk aan

Zee, over the mouth of the channel connecting the Zuiderzee with the North Sea. Amsterdam is on the same channel, and it remained close to our right. We then flew over Osnabrück, Minden, Hanover, and Braunschweig, and approached Berlin south of a line of lakes between Brandenburg and Potsdam. There were lots of searchlights west of Berlin, most of them beaming their lights straight out in an attempt to indicate our direction of travel to night fighters. While I lay at the bomb-aimer's window, I saw two unidentified enemy aircraft in line astern, coming at us from about 1,000 feet below. Flak was very fierce over Berlin. We were soon enveloped by shell bursts. I first took their smoke for loose balloons. Another aircraft, above ours, was coned by thirty searchlights. They got peppered by very accurate flak. Large fires raged below in the town. Our gunners reported that we started another large one, and it was visible for 60 miles. We carried out our attack from 13,000 feet, which is rather low considering the intense anti-aircraft defences built up in the Berlin area. Owing to a strong headwind, we took five hours to get to Berlin, but the return trip took just two and half. Our total airborne time that night was seven hours and forty minutes. On the outbound leg, we saw fires and flak over Bremen and from the residential areas of Hanover, some 50 miles away. We went straight back to our base. It was also my best flight, navigationally wise. My ETAs were dead-on as we crossed every point exactly as planned. I am glad that I have been over Berlin.

The next day, I took a long walk with Bečvář and Nedvěd. In the evening, I consumed a large number of drinks—first in the mess and then in The Bell at Thetford. While there, I had dinner with Sqn Ldr and Mrs Pickard, who were accompanied by Mr Bertrand John Henry Daventry, an official photographer for the Royal Air Force. I then slept soundly for nine hours and awoke fresh once again.

Fg Off. Hnátek, the last one to refuse to go on operations, left us on Saturday 15 March. He has been posted to Czech RAF Depot Wilmslow, near Manchester. Everyone except him knows that he'll go from there to the infantry. We took him by plane to the nearest aerodrome, Woodford, on the outskirts of Manchester. Anderle was supposed to fly Wellington R1466/KX-D, but Flt Lt Kirby-Green persuaded me to take one of his pupils, Fg Off. Vildomec, from Training Flight as the Second Dickie. It was quite an eventful trip—certainly more exciting than a raid on Berlin. Anderle took off and then gave the controls to Vildomec. His flying was a little erratic, but not so bad until we reached Burton-upon-Trent. There had previously been some haze in the area, and there was a wall of mist and smoke that severely restricted our visibility to a few hundred yards. Vildomec panicked and did a 180-degree turn for home. The radio wasn't working, so we couldn't do anything else other than map read. We were flanked by two balloon-barrages, with a third in front of us. I got angry and asked Anderle to take over and to proceed to Woodford. After a while, I got my relative bearings just in time to find Macclesfield and Woodford aerodrome. Hnátek, the hero, rushed forward, running over half of the crew, and cried, desperately, 'Balloons, balloons!' Woodford, which is close to Manchester, seems to be a big testing station. We saw numbers of Avro Manchesters and Douglas

Bostons. The former looks ugly, but its size and super engines are impressive. We left Hnátek in the care of a Home Guard officer and then flew home. Again, Vildomec took over once Anderle got it airborne. He was decidedly better this time around, except when landing at Wretham. That was a rather hair-raising affair as we were side slipping with the right wing and almost touching the ground. Anderle had him level out at the last moment, so we only bounced a bit upon landing.

We remembered the second anniversary of the occupation of our country after dinner with some 1934 Château Lagrange (St Julien), a fine-tasting red Bordeaux we found in the dingy cellar of the mess.

During the next day, Sqn Ldr Pickard took myself and Plt Off. Bečvář to Wittering, a fighter station 10 miles west-northwest of Peterborough, Nottinghamshire. We were to pick up Plt Off. Carlin. We only left at 4.20 p.m. and got to Wittering shortly before 5 p.m. Carlin had been a fighter pilot in the last war, with the final rank of Major. He shot down eighteen planes and fifteen balloons. Carlin was awarded the MC and DFC. On top of that, he lost a leg as a result of battle. Carlin is now fifty-two, but he has volunteered again. Although he is physically unsuitable for being a pilot, he nevertheless now serves as a Pilot Officer air gunner in a Boulton Paul Defiant-equipped squadron. Wittering is a very large station, home to three very active squadrons. One squadron flies Supermarine Spitfires in the day fighter role, while the other two are night fighters operating the Bristol Beaufighter and a mix of Defiants and Hawker Hurricanes.[26] The station was bombed severely last Friday, 14 March. One bomb landed right in front of the Officers' Mess, smashing all windows and part of the front of the building. A hangar took a direct hit, resulting in the destruction of two Beaufighters that were under repair. Some men had been killed and wounded.[27] We had tea and met the Station Commander, Grp Capt. Basil Edward Embry DSO and Two Bars. Embry, who was shot down on 26 May 1940 over Saint-Omer, was captured by the Germans. He escaped during a march to a prisoner of war camp. After three months full of adventure, Embry made it back to England. We met also Wg Cdr Richard Llewellyn Roger Atcherley, of Schneider Cup fame. He is now the CO of the Bristol Beaufighter-equipped No. 54 OTU. We looked around the aerodrome and duly admired the Beaufighters as real examples of power and usefulness. We began to head back home at around 7 p.m., with half an hour of light left. We had just passed Peterborough when we entered fog. Sqn Ldr Pickard realised that we had only a short spell of light ahead. Here we were, on a pleasure flight in an operational aircraft, with no W/T operator or harnesses on the parachutes—so we landed at Peterborough. Later, we looked in vain for hotel accommodation. We ended up spending our night rather comfortably in the mess of the No. 13 Elementary Flying Training School at RAF Station Peterborough. The next day was St Patrick's Day, and the fog lifted around noon. We got back in the aircraft and returned to Wretham at around 1.30 p.m.

On arrival, we put together a crew for the night's raid. Sqn Ldr Pickard was to go as skipper, Sgt Filler as second pilot, myself as navigator, Sgt Slánský as W/T operator, Sgt Čtvrtlík as front gunner, and our guest, Plt Off. Carlin, as rear gunner.

Our Wellington for this operation was R1371/KX-F.[28] We started up at 12.52 a.m. on 18 March. Our target was Bremen, Germany. There was a 10/10 overcast layer of low-lying cloud over England. It cleared completely once we were over the North Sea. Over the continent, it was completely lovely, with excellent visibility. I went a little bit too far to the north and we thus crossed the Dutch coast over the southern tip of Terschelling. We changed course a little later by eleven degrees to starboard, which took us right to the target. Suddenly, searchlights beamed upwards. We began to get heavy flak from a small peninsula to our right. It was surprising how accurate the gunners' height and direction was during their first shots. It was an awkward moment to see all the flashes around us. Sqn Ldr Pickard dodged and finally dived to get out of it. We didn't have any other exciting experiences like that prior to reaching Bremen. It was a raid on docks with high-explosive bombs. There were not very many fires at the target. Opposition wasn't as heavy as one would have expected. What the flak lacked in quantity was made up with quality; we were soon again enveloped by shell bursts, and explosions rocked the plane several times. The docks were plainly visible and I think we worked them over well. We made for home at 4 a.m. sharp and landed at 6.02 a.m. after an uneventful return flight. Shortly before we landed, I had seen the day breaking gloriously in the east from the astrodome. It was almost light when we landed—the last machine to come home.

Anderle's plane had caught fire in the air, but it made a successful wheels-up landing on the extreme south-east edge of the aerodrome to save the plane and crew.[29] It really was a great performance. The fire (caused by excessive friction in the reduction gear of the starboard engine) was extinguished. It was only after landing that I heard from the other crewmembers that we had encountered an enemy fighter and almost bumped into enemy balloons over Bremen docks.

Our complete station command was practically put out of action during the night of 18–19 March. Wg Cdr Toman, Grp Capt. Berounský, Sqn Ldr Pickard, Mrs Pickard, Fg Off. Fantl and Plt Off. Carlin had been in The Bull at Barton Mills. On the way back, Wg Cdr Toman, who was driving, collided with an Army lorry.[30] The first reports are that Grp Capt. Berounský will be out for one week, Wg Cdr Toman for six weeks, and Fg Off. Fantl for two months. I was supposed to go on leave starting Friday 21 March, but I am the Operations Officer now, which means no leave and grounded on top of that.

I had had the most disagreeable twenty-four hours that I have had since landing in this country. I had been on a raid on Bremen, returning at 6 a.m. on 18 March, and I was in charge of operations on the night of 19–20 March, when we had five planes over Cologne. I had expected to get a good sleep the next night, and I went to bed early. I was awoken by the Station Duty Officer at 2.30 a.m. on 21 March. There had been a report of some big ships approaching the shores of England, and we were ordered to stand by for action.[31]

The alert was called off by about 4.30 a.m. Sqn Ldr Pickard (who had been picked up from East Harling), Sqn Ldr Schejbal (temporary commander of the Squadron while Wg Cdr Toman was hospitalised at Ely), Fg Off. Roman (the Armament Officer), Plt Off. Le Grand (the Intelligence Officer), and myself stumbled back to the mess for a very early breakfast. The next morning, I sent out two operational crews—Fg Off. Breitcetl's and Sgt Čapka's—with two aircraft to collect two new planes that have been allocated to us from Ternhill, Shropshire. I told them to return straight away because both crews and planes would be needed for operations. They had barely left when Group asked for seven planes to attack targets at Lorient, France, and one for Ostend, Belgium. Our ferry crews didn't return, forcing me to report by 3 p.m. that we wouldn't be able to send out any more than six planes to Lorient. We became concerned about the ferry crews and started to search for them by phoning Ternhill. We were told that they hadn't arrived there at all! We mobilised Regional Control, only to hear at around 4.30 p.m. that our two dispatched aircraft and one of the new ones had safely landed at Honington. They had been to Ternhill and started back together in line-astern, but somehow they lost one of the new planes (piloted by Sgt Bernát). A frantic search all over the area commenced again. At around 7 p.m., Regional Control reported that they were detecting an unidentified plane; it turned out to be Bernát. He landed not long afterwards. During the afternoon prior to the raid, a pilot from Training Flight taxied a Wellington into a hole and damaged it.[32] When the six operational planes were lined up for the start, one of them—Helma's R1015/KX-L—broke down with engine trouble. It turned out to be the fault of bad servicing by the mechanics. The leader of the plane's ground crew, Cpl Harrison, was placed under arrest. We had to keep R1015 on the ground, which effectively cut our effort from eight to five aircraft. To make things worse, Wellington T2553/KX-B, flown by Šejbl, had its starboard landing gear collapse after a ferry flight from Honington to Wretham. The aircraft also suffered damage to a wing and propeller. After the operation, Sgt Fencl taxied T2972/KX-G into some bushes, bringing the score for the day to three planes damaged, one broken down with engine trouble, and three failing to start for operations. I got to bed at 2.30 a.m. on 22 March, twenty-four hours after having been forced out of bed by a false alert. What a disgraceful twenty-four hours these were!

Flt Lt Provazník brought me the following message from Wg Cdr Toman, who is in hospital in Ely with Grp Capt. Berounský and Fg Off. Fantl: 'You should only walk between the mess and Operations Room, never go by car, never go anywhere near an aeroplane, and don't even think of going on operations.' Now that Fantl is out for quite a time, Wg Cdr Toman is afraid of losing the only Czech and English-speaking officer capable of running operations. Fantl and I have insisted for quite some time that we need to have somebody else trained for duties in the Operations Room. We proposed it be Plt Off. Zafouk, who speaks English fairly well. It was postponed again and again, so now they haven't got anybody except me to call upon—hence all their current troubles. There have been repeated attempts to give me some sort of compensation for my grounding, including the promise of a Czech medal and promotion to Flight Lieutenant. I am not so sure that all these promises will be kept. I flew again anyway, to Berlin on the night of 23–24 March. Our plane was T2990/KX-T, crewed by Sgt Anderle, skipper, Sgt Bernát, second pilot, myself as navigator, Sgt Plzák, W/T operator, Plt Off. Horák, front gunner, and Sgt Janšta, rear gunner. The trip wasn't as nice as my first to Berlin, mainly due to the heating system packing up altogether. Even in the cockpit, the cold was bone-chilling. We also had to deal with empty oxygen tanks after only five hours of flight, as they had not been properly filled. The flak over Berlin was terrific. We were hit in the tail, resulting in two splinters penetrating the fuselage and another one severing the wire leading to the tail of the plane. It was very cloudy over Berlin, but the gaps were big enough to make out the target. I think they received a good plastering again that night. On the journey back, our oxygen supply was exhausted by 12.30 a.m. The cold was unbearable, and our aerial was covered with ice. At a height of 20,000 feet we experienced a minimum temperature of -30 degrees Celsius. We couldn't receive on our W/T set until we crossed the English coast. Anyhow, we managed to find our way back home, landing after some seven hours and forty-five minutes in the air.

After the raid a whole succession of officials—including Sqn Ldr Schejbal, acting CO, Sqn Ldr Pickard, and Wg Cdr McKee, Officer in charge of training in our Group—tore a strip off me for going on the operation. I was told not to go on any more without written permission from Group. There was further bad news; Tommy Rose hasn't returned from his first operational flight. After Hill, Craik, and Jepson, he was the fourth of our class of thirty-seven to be killed in action. The good news is that according to intelligence reports, our bombing of Germany is getting very effective. In one raid on Cologne, 4,000 houses were destroyed and 100 fires started, one of which burned for three days. I think that the Germans are getting it now.

On Friday 28 March, Theresa and Lelgarde came over and had dinner in the mess with Flt Lt Provazník, Plt Offs Schneider and Podstránecký, and myself. I had been in the Operations Room continuously for twenty-four hours straight from 9 a.m. yesterday until 9 a.m. this morning. I was tired to death.

I haven't made any entries in this book for one week now. The reason is that there wasn't anything to report. I am now going through the whole ordeal of being in the Operations Room with very little sleep, always on stand-by, with no air. Fantl is supposed to come back on 8 April, next Tuesday. I'll be only too glad to be rid of the Operations Room. On 31 March, Mavor came to Wretham and stayed in the Operations Room throughout the entire Bremen operation that night. We had a rather exciting time during operations on 4 April. Our boys went to Brest to bomb the *Scharnhorst* and *Gneisenau*, which were supposed to be in dock there. A single German aircraft had been flying above our aerodrome and dropped three bombs that fell on the south-east edge. At around 2 a.m., Sqn Ldr Schejbal and I had just left the Operations Room and were walking toward the Hall when we again heard the distinctive sound of German aero engines and then a sharp whistle. Sqn Ldr Schejbal shouted, 'Bombs! Down!' He ducked behind a rail along the path. I followed in the same direction, right into some muddy water. Of course, I didn't care to end up in such a mess. I stood there, waiting. There were two strong explosions. We later found out that four bombs were dropped, two pairs on the same place somewhere on the aerodrome. We went back, took a car, and tried to find the craters. The flare path had been switched off just a few minutes ago, so we didn't find anything. The next morning, we learned that the bombs had fallen in a stick about 50 yards away along the flare path. That's pretty good bombing when considering that the German was flying low.

A lady in Cambridge got a postcard from Germany sent by Bušina. He is now a prisoner of war in the same camp as Cigoš and Valenta. They are part of the crew we lost on 6 February over Boulogne-sur-Mer.

Our squadron was out on two consecutive nights. They were on 6–7 April (against Brest, where the German battleships *Scharnhorst* and *Gneisenau* are laying) and on 7–8 April (against Kiel, greeting the Japanese naval delegation, which was there inspecting dockyards and so on). Our Group's Intelligence narrative of this operation is worth noting:

113 A/C detailed
104 A/C attacked primary target
4 A/C attacked last resort target
2 A/C jettisoned
2 A/C missing

Primary target Kiel: nine out of ten from Waterbeach, twenty-one out of twenty-two from Marham, five out of eight from Stradishall and eighteen out of nineteen from Wyton dropped 15 × 1,000-lb, 191 × 500-lb, 29 × 250-lb and 10,020 × 4-lb incendiaries on aiming point A.

Twelve from Mildenhall, eighteen from Feltwell, seven out of nine from Honington, eight from East Wretham, one of two Stirlings from Stradishall and one from 3 PRU dropped 16 × 1,000-lb, 158 × 500-lb, 22 × 250-lb and 7,996 × 4-lb incendiaries on aiming point B.[33]

A total of 31 × 1,000-lb, 349 × 500-lb, 51 × 250-lb, or about 93 tons, and 18,016 × 4-lb incendiaries.

It would appear that this was the most successful large attack yet made by the Group, being more concentrated than before. Area B was reported as having more large fires than area A. By 1.30 a.m. there were fires all round area B within a radius of a mile and clouds of smoke made it difficult for later A/C to see where their bombs had fallen. A good breeze should have helped to make the fires more difficult to extinguish.

It is thought that the Japanese delegation, which was reported to be in Kiel inspecting shipyards etc., will now have left, if able to do so.

Freshmen out of three detailed from Feltwell, Stradishall and Wyton, attacked

Emden dropping 16 × 500-lb, 2 × 250-lb and 720 × 4-lb incendiaries, but did not see much results.

Four A/C bombed last resort targets.

The attacking force over Kiel consisted of ten Wellingtons from No. 1 Group, forty-five Whitleys from No. 4 Group, and fifty-four Hampdens from No. 5 Group. It must have been a real slaughter, supposedly surpassing in intensity everything the Germans have up to now delivered against a single target of this size.

The next day, on 8 April, our Medical Officer, MUDr Krůta, and I took in quite a good picture at Thetford called *Contraband*, starring Conrad Veidt. It was a moonlit night and we decided to walk home. The whole time we saw two aircraft from our A Training Flight practising night flying. Their navigation lights were plainly visible and so were the planes themselves against the bright sky. We had only just reached Wretham Hall when we heard that one of our training planes (with instructor Plt Off. Hrnčíř and student pilot Sgt Nýč) was shot down by a German night fighter marauding around our flare path.[34] Hrnčíř was probably struck by canon shell on the back of his head. He is unconscious, but gradually awakening in the Newmarket hospital. The shell must have first struck the frame of the fuselage and lost most of its force, as it did not penetrate Hrnčíř's skull. It just pushed the bone and lodged beneath the skin. A trepanation has been carried out successfully and he will probably recover. Other canon shells practically shot the plane's tail off. Nýč wasn't hurt and succeeded in crash-landing the plane at West Tofts, near Mundford, Thetford, in Norfolk. It was a fine performance by a pupil—he saved Hrnčíř's life.

Fantl returned during the afternoon of 11 April, which also happened to be Good Friday. I am finally returning to flying duties. That same night, I was supposed to fly again on T2972/KX-G, with Sqn Ldr Pickard as skipper, Plt Off. Korda as second pilot, Sgt Slánský as W/T operator, Sgt Čtvrtlík as front gunner, and Flt Lt Stevens, our Group's Gunnery Officer, as rear gunner. We would have gone to bomb the *Scharnhorst* and *Gneisenau* at Brest and then shoot up some German aerodrome in Brittany, perhaps Vannes or St Brieuc. We were already in the plane and ready to taxi out when the order cancelling the raid came through. We were very disappointed.

In the evening of the next day, Sgt Langer took Plt Off. Korda, Sgt Čtvrtlík and me by car to Bury St Edmunds. We had a really good dinner and saw two good pictures—one with Gloria Jean, a kind of younger Deanna Durbin, and the other, *Queen of the Yukon*, which was a really good Wild West story. We stopped on the way back for a beer in The Anchor.

Today, 13 April, is Easter Sunday. Sqn Ldr Pickard took me by air to Bassingbourn, Cambridgeshire, home to No. 11 Operational Training Unit. I met up with Williams and three chaps from the second class of observers. Williams had somehow managed to remain at the OTU. I heard lots of news, both good and bad. The fifth and sixth students from our class are gone—Easton, who was with No. 214

'Federated Malay States' (B) Squadron at Stradishall, Suffolk, and Waldron, who was at Newmarket, Suffolk, I think with No. 99 'Madras Presidency' (B) Squadron. So Oily Joe, the great lady-killer, has crossed the line forever. The second class also had its first loss—Davidson, killed in a flying accident, as far as one knows in one of the new Liberators.[35] Brander has left Bassingbourn only three days ago. Dimi got his commission and is now at Stranraer, Wigtownshire, on Sunderland flying boats.[36] Training is now being stepped up tremendously. We are now sending lots of crews out east. No. 3 Group is alone, having lost 148 Wellington's crews, who are now in Egypt. We therefore have lots of newly minted crews around here, which explains the heavy losses our Group is having lately.

On Easter Monday, 14 April, Plt Off. Korda flew me to Debden. It is home to No. 85 (NF) Squadron, an operational unit using Douglas Bostons known as 'Havocs' when operated in the night-fighter role. The station also supports the big, Hurricane-equipped No. 52 OTU. I got hold of Paul Gilbertson, the boyfriend of Marguerite Ross, Herta's best friend. He has been in England some six weeks now and is ready for a posting to go to an operational squadron. There are several Czech pilot instructors at Debden, one of them being Sgt Kaucký, Korda's brother-in-law.[37] In the evening, we had a really decent meal compared to the terrible food we are occasionally getting. Plt Off. Korda and Nedvěd (who share a room), old Roth (a former factory-owner at Uherský Brod), their batman and I, had a duck with Czech sauerkraut and excellent beer.[38] Afterwards, we had duck fat and liver on bread. I am becoming very much a materialist. After dinner, Plt Off. Schneider took me by car to Thetford. We saw *Road to Singapore*, starring Dorothy Lamour, Bing Crosby, and Bob Hope. I had a very enjoyable day.

On 15 April, we took Plt Off. Carlin, who has finally been released from hospital after the accident on 18 March, by air to his station at Wittering. In the evening, I was on my first raid after more than three weeks of ground duties. It was Kiel, and we started shortly before 10.30 p.m. We were back on Wellington T2972/KX-G with the regulars; Korda, Slánský, Čtvrtlík, Jakš and myself. Sgt Schoř flew with us as Second Dickie. His regular skipper, Sgt Helma, is in hospital recovering from frostbitten fingers.[39] We had to go through some thick clouds while we were still over England, and we experienced some icing while having the uncomfortable sensation of our own searchlights combing the skies for us. We then flew over a more or less solid overcast from the English coast to the target. We remained at least 5 miles off the Frisian Islands in the North Sea, well aware of the intense flak from these islands. The worst of the enemy fire was from Borkum and the German mainland. Kiel was also covered by clouds. The Wellington circled awhile, but as the gaps in the cloud cover didn't widen any further, we attacked at around 1.10 a.m. from somewhere over 11,000 feet. Flak was multi-coloured and erratic. We couldn't make out the dockyards we were after, and therefore we bombed the town west of the deep harbour. For the homeward-bound journey, we chose a route much more to the north, all of it out in the North Sea. We had a quiet trip. Slánský was working particularly well that night, and he got me a succession of loop bearings from two German radio beacons. One was at Texel, and the other off the coast of Schleswig, around Amrum Island. We landed shortly before 4 a.m. We got a transport from the dispersal point to the crew room, and then to the Operations Room for the mandatory interrogation. It was around 5.30 a.m. and time to have breakfast. I had intended to leave for London at 7 a.m. by staff car. I therefore laid down, still dressed, for half an hour or so on my bed, before washing and departing at the designated time with next to no sleep.

It was a glorious morning, and the drive to London was really beautiful. Plt Off. Schneider was going too. We parked at Golders Green tube station and I went straight to Fursecroft to see Česaný.[40] On the corner of Edgware Road, I met Lojza. I then saw Česaný and Wichta at the Czech Ministry of Finance, and afterwards I went to the office of the magazine *Čechoslovák*. While there, I had a long conversation with the editor, Bohuš Beneš, who is the nephew of the President.[41] I had two articles in the paper and have sent three more for a book on the Czech Air Force in England. Later, I met with Lojza and Dr Hermann, a former Brno solicitor who now works in the offices of an English solicitor, Mr Englefield. I then had lunch with Věra Uhlířová, Česaný, Wichta and Lojza in a Czech restaurant called The Seaport on Edgware Road. In the afternoon I met Dr Procházka, a former professor at Brno Law School and husband of my former classmate Helen Koželuhová. At 5 p.m. I met our car again at Golders Green. We stopped on the way back at Duxford, where I saw Sqn Ldr Weber, CO of our No. 310 (F) Squadron.[42] We were back in Wretham by 8.30 p.m. By then I had been awake for more than thirty-six hours and I was totally exhausted. During this time, I had been to Kiel, over Heligoland, and in London. I slept for ten hours that night—something I wouldn't have been able to do in London. It was the night of 16–17 April, the worst attack of the *Blitz* so far, with lots of destruction and much loss of life.[43]

We had quite a busy morning and afternoon on 17 April. Our own Wellington, T2972/KX-G, was undergoing a routine eighty-hour inspection, so we were to use R1021, the Squadron's veteran. It had sat idle for weeks and was in a non-airworthy condition.[44] After a test flight, loops and compass swinging, adding and replacing all kinds of odd equipment, the machine was more or less fit for operations. We then started for Berlin at 8.49 p.m., in a clear but pitch-dark night. I'd like to include the Intelligence summary of our Group concerning this operation, and thus I will only convey my own impressions of this trip. German anti-aircraft defences are getting extremely good and are far better now than when I started operating, around the middle of January. To go to Berlin, we chose a route taking us north of Great Yarmouth, to the southern tip of Texel, to Celle, and then south of Berlin. On paper, it seemed pretty safe compared to the north of Osnabrück, Hanover, Braunschweig, and other well-known centres of resistance. We were mistaken. First, we crossed an obvious fighter area just past the Dutch coast, forming a belt on the line from Lathen to Meppen and Lingen. It is a ghastly site. Well over 100 searchlights are dispersed around the countryside, where they comb the skies hoping to light up British planes.

It took us a few minutes to cross this belt, but it seemed like an eternity. We had just passed the belt when we spotted a German aircraft crossing our bows at high speed, in a north-westerly direction about 100 yards from us and at the same height. He didn't see us, though. We then flew on according to our plan, and we thought we were comfortably safe. We saw the flak working furiously at Hanover, far away to our right, when we suddenly came into a terrible barrage of heavy flak. We experienced the same thing as on 18 March, south of Emden. Without the aid of searchlights, the guns suddenly zeroed in on us. They had acquired our height and direction with great accuracy. Explosions rocked our aircraft, and despite the roar of the engines, we heard the shells shriek by and burst all around us. We got away, but were mighty lucky. It was Celle, and, by God, I shall never forget it. Berlin was comparatively quiet. For the homeward-bound leg, we took a much more northerly route and fared much better. We first flew for 75 miles west-northwest, then turned to leave the mainland slightly north of Texel, and from there we went straight to base. Going home, there was no opposition to speak of. It was a relatively quick trip of seven hours by the time we landed. I was rather exhausted as we nearly ran out of petrol on the homeward journey.

I slept from 6 a.m. to 11.30 a.m. Last night we had seven crews out: Sqn Ldr Ocelka, Fg Off. Breitcetl, Plt Off. Korda, Sgt Anderle, and Sgt Šedivý went to Berlin, while Sgt Doktor and Sgt Kráčmer attacked Cologne. This would turn out to be a deadly trip for the Squadron. Fg Off. Breitcetl had to return just off the English coast with engine trouble. Sgt Kráčmer's plane was crewed by him as skipper, Fg Off. Sixta as second pilot, Plt Off. Kubíček as navigator, Plt Off. Košulič as W/T operator, Sgt Štětka as front gunner, and Sgt Lifczicz as rear gunner. They were shot down by a fighter around Erkelenz, just inside Germany. There's a fighter box around there somewhere. The entire tragic event was witnessed by Sgt Doktor's crew. They saw one crew member bale out and later watched the plane burning on the ground. The rest of the crew may have succeeded in leaving the aircraft too.[45] Honington lost two planes on the same night as well. One was probably shot up over the same area where we had lost Kráčmer; someone sent out a radio transmission stating 'Abandoning plane' somewhere on the Dutch-Belgian border. My former classmate Mavor was in this plane. He is the seventh of us to go. I hope that he got away all right. The other plane from Honington crashed into the sea. Our squadron sent three planes out to look for the dinghy. One crew found an empty inflated dinghy and a parachute floating nearby.[46]

I can now add the Group Intelligence Narrative for the Berlin raid:

Twenty-eight A/C out of thirty-four which started for point B in Berlin, reached the target-area. Four out of five from Mildenhall, seven out of eight from Feltwell, five out of seven from Honington, four out of five from No. 311 Sqn, seven out of eight from Wyton and one Stirling from No. 7 Sqn, dropping 1 × 4,000-lb, 13 × 1,000-lb, 71 × 500-lb, 17 × 250-lb and 4,225 × 4-lb incendiaries. There was little cloud over the target, but a thick ground mist made pin-pointing of the target extremely difficult. In consequence bombing was distributed over a wide area. Fires were reported at the aiming point, up to 3 miles west of it and 1,000 yards to the south. The last A/C reported many scattered fires.

The first 4,000-lb bomb to reach Berlin was carried by a Mildenhall A/C. It was reported as making a very large yellow flash which developed into a large area of yellow fires.

Ten A/C were detailed to attack aiming point B at Cologne and four reached this objective, one out of two from Honington, two out of three from Wyton, one out of two from No. 311 Sqn, none of three from Mildenhall, dropping 1 × 1,000-lb, 13 × 500-lb, 4 × 250-lb, 1,080 × 4-lb incendiaries. Bursts were seen half mile east and south of aiming point and along the river-bank. One explosion gave off a vivid greenish blue flash.

The late A/C reported fires visible for 20 miles.

Emden, Bremen, Aachen/Weiden aerodromes, Euskirchen and what was believed to be Troisdorf aerodrome were attacked as last resort targets.

No photos of value were got.

A force of eighty-two aircraft was dispatched to attack Berlin that night. The force was comprised of fourteen Wellingtons from No. 1 Group, twenty-seven Wellingtons and one Stirling from No. 3 Group, seventeen Whitleys and twenty-three Hampdens.[47]

The following evening, six of us—Plt Offs Schneider, Podstránecký, Kacíř, Hapala, Doubrava and I—went to La Hogue Hall, Chippenham, the home of Capt. Lewis. He threw a smashing cocktail party. Several dozen people were stuffed into a not-so-very-big drawing room. I met lots of people whose names I have long forgotten. There were two or three quite attractive girls. One of them, nicknamed 'Baffy', is a secretary at our Bomber Group's HQ. We headed to The Bull afterwards.

On Saturday 19 April, operations were cancelled after briefing. Sqn Ldr Schejbal took Plt Offs Motyčka, Smrček and myself to Bury St Edmunds. I saw quite a good picture called *The Mark of Zorro*, with Tyrone Power and Linda Darnell.

On Sunday 20 April, we were out on a raid over Cologne. Once again we were flying T2972/KX-G with the same crew as the two previous times. To avoid the fighter box located west-northwest of Cologne, where Sgt Kráčmer and his crew were shot down on 17 April, we decided to go on a round-about route over Orford Ness, a point halfway between Dunkirk, Ostend, and Lille. It was an extremely uncomfortable night, with thunderstorms and severe icing. Just south of Brussels, our course took us right through a massive formation of cumulus clouds, where we experienced a wild electrical storm. At the same time, we were violently rocked by intense updrafts. The plane climbed vertically for almost 4,000 feet, despite the nose pointing downwards. There was solid overcast over the target, so the best we could do was to bomb existing fires and concentrations of flak. It was Cologne all right, but I could not tell what part of town it was. Hurricane-like winds blew, and it was no easy task to navigate in a pitch-dark night above the clouds. I succeeded in re-crossing the

Belgian coast precisely over the same spot where we had come in more than three hours before. There were lots of searchlights to our right, over Ostend, but they were no concern to us. We landed safely after five and half hours of flying.

Yesterday, on 21 April, I borrowed Plt Off. Bimbo Bečvář's tiny Morris car and went to Cavenham Park. I spent a quiet day walking with Theresa Home, followed by tea. I wrote a long letter to Herta and later read some Woodhouse.[48] Dinner was excellent. I played some bridge and went to bed early. I left Cavenham at 9 a.m. today after a very relaxing break from the war.

On 23 April, five navigators from our squadron, Plt Offs Dvorský, Nedvěd, Bečvář, Motyčka and myself, were sent to No. 3 Group HQ at Exning, Suffolk, to be shown a new type of target map with fluorescing lines. Personally, I couldn't see any advantage to it. On the way home in the staff-car, we stopped in The Bull at Barton Mills for a drink before lunch. Sheila was there, apparently very glad to meet me after such a long time. She is a nice girl, but I am now so homesick that I haven't any interest in girls, even if they are as pretty as movie stars.

In the evening, we took off from Honington to bomb the *Scharnhorst* and *Gneisenau* at Brest. Our Wellingtons carried one 2,000-lb bomb each. We were unable to load them at our home aerodrome because we did not have a crane to lift them. We therefore flew to Honington to get bombed-up. While at the mess in Honington, I met Plt Off. Smith, who was in Dimi's class in Canada. I also met an Australian Plt Off. who was at Uplands with Jim Thompson. Jim bunked beside me at Eglinton.[49] The raid itself was quite interesting. We had to cross the coast near Bridport in Dorset, so we had a bit of a cross-country lasting an hour and a half. This took us over the Southern Midlands and to the south. We climbed to operational height over the Channel and reached the westernmost tip of Brittany. There was quite a sea-haze, which resulted in us missing Brest the first time around. The pilot turned us back when we were about 20 miles south-west of the city. We went a little to the east and soon found the target by the glare of searchlights piercing the haze. We bombed the dock area, but we couldn't make out any results. Both ships have been hit though. According to the agent's last report, the *Scharnhorst* is resting stern-down, with water up to her hawser-holes. The damage was light to the *Gneisenau*, which now has a twisted stern turret. In any case, the ships haven't been able to leave port. Both have been deadly menaces as commerce-raiders in the Atlantic. For this reason alone, it makes the continuous bombing of Brest justifiable. You have to keep in mind that one cannot sink a ship in dry dock, only damage it, and that has been done successfully. The flak wasn't very bad over Brest, and our return home was uneventful. From the middle of the Channel, we could see gun flashes, searchlights and fires in Plymouth. They took a terrible beating that night.[50] I forgot to mention that we were again on Wellington T2972/KX-G with our usual crew, the exception being that the second pilot, Schoř, was replaced by Sgt Bufka (who was the skipper on my first raid on 16 January).

On 25 April, Plt Off. Korda, Fg Off. Fantl and I walked to the cinema in Thetford. While there, we watched *Dodge City*, a picture in Technicolor. I had watched it at Plainfield, New Jersey, a few days before the outbreak of the war in August 1939. On 24 April, I had been in a cinema at Bury St Edmunds with Plt Off. Korda and Sgt Jakš. I was buying our tickets when a lady of thirty-five or so approached me and started a kind of incoherent conversation. As she was obviously a little intoxicated, I cut the conversation short. I waited until she had entered the dimly lit theatre and then chose seats on the opposite side. We had just only settled down when she came again. 'Won't you come over and sit with us?' she said. 'I am awaiting for two girls who are quite alone, and if you like…' I refused politely. 'Do you know Vera?' she continued. I emphatically denied I did, and, after a few further attempts, the lady withdrew. It was the only time I had seen open prostitution in England.

On Saturday 26 April, I went on my thirteenth raid. It was again on good old T2972/KX-G, with the same crew as last time, and to Brest. Here is our Group's Intelligence Report:

Owing to a late adverse Met report, the effort was reduced and twenty-two A/C were detailed to attack aiming-point B at Hamburg. Six out of eight from Mildenhall, one outstanding, six out of eight from Honington and six from East Wretham attacked their primary target, dropping 1 × 4,000-lb, 5 × 1,000-lb, 71 × 500-lb, 6 × 250-lb and 2,520 × 4-lb incendiaries.

It was very dark haze and later low cloud made it difficult to pinpoint accurately. However the river and docks were found to be visible in spite of the weather conditions. Fires were seen to be north and north-east of the aiming point and a large red fire with much smoke to the north. There were also fires to the west of the aiming-point. 1 × 4,000-lb was dropped probably south-west of the Binnenalster. There was a very large red explosion a half-mile in diameter.

One freshmen crew out of four detailed and one Honington A/C, which had been detailed for Hamburg, but had technical trouble, bombed Emden, dropping 13 × 500-lb, 1 × 250-lb and 120 × 4-lb incendiaries. Bursts were seen in the dock area, but no other results.

One A/C unable to bomb Hamburg owing to low cloud, dropped 1 × 4,000-lb near Bremerhaven. There was a huge burst and two or three houses in a row were seen to disintegrate. One A/C having been hit by flak at Hamburg, bombed Cuxhaven and one A/C, failing to find Hamburg, bombed Wilhelmshaven.

The weather wasn't all that bad, but the wind was changing constantly. It was varying between a northern and east-south-eastern direction. I was initially puzzled, causing me to go off-track several times before finally reaching the Wash north-northeast of Wretham. Flak was extremely strong all along the Frisian Islands and down the Elbe River. Cloud cover offered us protection from the enemy guns.

One of our aircraft—flown by Sgt Doktor, with Fg Off. Machálek navigating—was also drifting northward. Machálek is a good chap from the Haná. He's a little too noisy, but by God he is also no master navigator. Their transmitter packed up and thus they couldn't get any QDMs. For some reason, Sgt Procházka, the W/T operator, wasn't familiar with taking loop-bearings, nor Machálek with taking astro shots. They got themselves lost while crossing the English coast somewhere around Scarborough, and ended up flying around over northern Yorkshire. Finally, when they had only 30 gallons of petrol left, Doktor made a perfect wheels-down landing. They came to a stop on a very small field near Wetherby, situated between a wood and a steep road cutting.[51] It was a masterful display of airmanship. The plane sustained minimal damage and could have been easily flown off if it were not for the small field. The crew is okay except for the second pilot, Sgt Styblík, who suffered slight injuries to his knee.

The CO, Wg Cdr Schejbal, woke me up on the Sunday morning after the Hamburg raid and told me that I should fly with Plt Off. Korda and Sgt Slánský to RAF Station Church Fenton, Yorkshire, to pick up Sgt Doktor's crew. We took off after 1.30 p.m. and flew over Spalding and Lincoln to Selby, in the neighbourhood where Church Fenton was supposed to be. We saw an aerodrome and landed. We learned from some officers that we were on Church Fenton's satellite field, Sherburn-in-Elmet. No. 46 'Uganda' (F) Squadron is based there with Hurricanes.[52] Church Fenton is 3 miles away to the north, so it was off again. Getting airborne from the small, uneven, and very soft field was a tricky job. We scoured the countryside looking for Church Fenton while in low clouds and a rainstorm. It took a while, but we found it. No. 54 OTU is based there. This large unit is where night-fighter training is conducted. The CO, a Group Captain, is from British Columbia.[53] One of the Sqn Ldrs on the station is James Brindley Nicolson VC. He shot down a Messerschmitt despite his own Hurricane being engulfed in flames. We left Styblík in hospital and then rounded up our crew and their kit after some delay. On landing at Wretham, we shot off a Very pistol flare just for fun. This started a fire that rapidly spread into some brush. Fire extinguishers had to be used to put it out—not so funny after all.

I was back on operations on Monday 28 April. There are two changes in our crew. Sgt Bufka has taken over Sgt Anderle's crew (Anderle is now a flying instructor in Training Flight), and Plt Off. Vildomec is now our second pilot. He flew Potez 63 fighter-bombers in France and received the *Croix de Guerre* for a daylight attack against a German armoured column.[54] Vildomec hasn't been on operations in England yet. Our rear gunner, Sgt Jakš, is not physically fit, which is rather strange for a middleweight boxer of European fame. He can't tolerate sitting in an icy tail turret for very long, and therefore Sgt Janšta has taken his place. As usual, our plane was T2972/KX-G. The two German battleships at Brest were once again the object of our attention. The night was very bad—pitch-dark, with a solid layer of low cloud—meaning we could only bomb the dock area of Brest. Our route took us over the whole south of England again. We had to fly below the clouds, at a height of approximately 2,000 feet, for more than an hour and a half. There are lots of training stations all over, with aircraft flying above and below us, making it dangerous to fly in such darkness. Despite this, the night was a big success for our squadron, which was the only Wellington unit to have all its aircraft at least reach the target. Here is the official report:

> A dark night with an extremely heavy ground haze made the attack on the *Gneisenau* and *Scharnhorst* at Brest extremely difficult. Three Stirlings of No. 7 Sqn dropped 12 × 2,000-lb bombs in the target-area without seeing any result. Four Wellingtons from East Wretham reached the objectives, dropping 4 × 2,000-lb, 8 × 500-lb, 4 × 250-lb bombs from 14,500–16,000 feet. One A/C claims to have straddled No. 1 Dock, but here again thick ground haze prevented accurate observation. Of the seven detailed from Honington, two A/C jettisoned bombs and five attacked dropping 3 × 2,000-lb, 18 × 500-lb, 3 × 250-lb in the target-area from 11,000–13,000 feet. One very brilliant white flash was seen at or near No. 10 dock. Of the eleven A/C setting out from Stradishall, one returned early, two brought bombs back, the remaining eight jettisoned their bombs into the sea. No photographs were taken and all A/C returned to their bases.

The next morning I slept until about 10 a.m. I then had a bath and played a good game of football in the afternoon, before Fg Off. Fantl, Plt Offs Korda and Vildomec, and I went to Norwich, which is a very interesting old town.

Our crew is due for leave from midnight on 3 May. On Thursday 1 May, we got a visit from AVMs Janoušek and Baldwin, who came to see the Squadron in operation. We were supposed to go to Hamburg, but operations were cancelled late in the afternoon—probably due to bad weather over Germany. I went with Korda and Bečvář to Thetford to see a good Wild West picture called *Oklahoma Kid*, starring with James Cagney. We returned early and found a party going on with both the Air Vice-Marshals present. The next morning, the two usual Czech decorations—the Czech Gallantry Medal and the Czech Military Cross—were dished out. I have been recommended for both, but as I am in the RCAF, the recommendation has to go to the Air Ministry and Foreign Office and God-knows-where. It'll take time before I actually get them [see Appendix II].

Before going on leave, I had the rather unenviable duty of defending Sgt Anderle at the Police Court in Ixworth, Suffolk. Anderle had accidentally killed a cyclist with his car. The police found out that he had no road-fare licence, no insurance, and no blinds on his headlamps at the time of the accident. It looked like it could be rather serious, especially if the victim had anybody to support. Anderle's pay would hardly have been sufficient to pay the damages. I did my best, pointing to Anderle's twenty-four operations and his two decorations.[55] He got off with a fine of £11 and the loss of his driver's licence.[56] My leave—which, as I am on the British establishment, has to be approved by the Station Commander at Honington—didn't come through yet, but with Wg Cdr Schejbal's approval I proceeded on leave anyway and left from Thetford on Friday May 2, on the 3.35 p.m. train.

10
Nottingham and London, 2–9 May 1941

I arrived in Nottingham at 8.51 p.m. An interpreter from our Orderly Room, Cpl Bloch, lived in Nottingham for several years, and he had undertaken to find the best train connection for me and telegraph my cousin Ernest. He messed things up completely, of course. I arrived at 8.51 p.m. at Victoria station (LNER), while Ernest waited at LMS station for a train arriving from Kettering at 9.24 p.m. After looking in vain for a taxi, I got a bus and eventually arrived at 2 Hazel Grove, Mapperley. This is where Ernest lives with Mrs Hearson. Emmy was there with Mrs Leroin, the lady she is staying with (also in Nottingham—Mapperley, on Ward Avenue). After a while, Ernest returned from the station. Both look very well. It seems that Emmy will be very pretty. Ernest is a grown-up lad of eighteen, and he looks very much like his mother—including the glasses. He is a little too bright and has made his mind up on everything already.

I spent three days in Nottingham, from Saturday 3 to Monday 5 May. One afternoon I took Ernest and Emmy to a show. It was called *No Taxi on Laughing*, and it was a little naughty and not altogether appropriate at my cousin's age. We went for a walk to the little village of Lambley. We stopped in at The Nag's Head, a very picturesque old inn. I also watched Ernest performing as the High Priest in the Passion Play. The whole show was terrific, and I had a hard time trying not to laugh. Ernest was talking into the ground throughout, with his head bent to one side and one hand playing nervously with his phoney beard.

Aunt Hella is probably already in Mexico by now, and the two children are supposed to join her. They both have Mexican visas, but they cannot get over the Atlantic for lack of accommodation. I was at the Refugee Committee in Nottingham and later at the one in London. I heard lots of proposals there—that the refugees could go via the United States, Uruguay, or Jamaica—but nothing really definite. The children are well-off though, and Nottingham hasn't been seriously bombed yet. Ernest should join up, as another cousin of ours did.[1] Our Uncle Felix's son, John, is now at the Czech RAF Depot in Wilmslow.[2]

I left Nottingham at 10.12 a.m. on Tuesday 6 May. Lojza was waiting for me when I pulled into London's St Pancras railway station at 1.09 p.m. I'll describe the main events of my three-day *séjour* in London in the form of a short diary.

6 May

We went for lunch at a canteen in the Arts Gallery on Trafalgar Square, which is run by some society ladies. Mrs Primrose Osborne is also working there. The food was terrible. I got settled in at Dolphin Square and went to Mrs Osborne's flat at around 4 p.m. for a drink. Unfortunately, Maj. Osborne is on leave, and he arrived home shortly after me. We then went to see Česaný and Wichta at the Ministry of Finance. From there, it was off to an old inn on Edgware Road called The Dickens. I had more drinks with them and Wichta's charming wife, the former Miss Přecechtělová of Brno. We were invited for dinner to the town house of the Honourable Mrs S. Tollemache, an owner of a big brewery.[3] She is short, fat, and rather odd-looking with so much jewellery on her large evening gown. She is very nice though, and invited me to look her up at her country house, Bentley Manor, near Ipswich. Her telephone number is Bentley, Copdock 54. There was also another middle-aged lady at the house with her. After an excellent dinner—a far cry from mess-hall food—we had a good game of bridge. Both Lojza and I lost.

7 May

In the morning, I made all kinds of official visits. I first went to RCAF HQ to inquire about the chances of me going home to Canada on leave. It would seem this is highly unlikely. The situation on the Atlantic is still a very dangerous one. HQ won't risk trained men unless they absolutely have to, as they are so much more valuable after half a year of operational flying over Germany. I also saw the editor of the *Čechoslovák*, Mr Bohuš Beneš. He paid me £4 for the two stories I submitted. This was rather fortunate timing, as I had spent lots of money while on leave. Mr Bohuš Beneš went on to inform me that my first contribution—about Kubizňák's death on 16 January—was to appear in *The Observer*, and that negotiations were ongoing to have my stories published in both Americas through the International News Service, which is run by Walter Tschuppik.[4] We had lunch with Česaný at the Czech Restaurant on Edgware Road. Then we visited Dr Lefort, who is now working as a mechanic at a service station. He met us in oily overalls and a greasy cap that covered his few remaining hairs. Nevertheless, he looks fit and is much slimmer than he was back home. The doctor has the satisfaction of being able to support his wife by working with his own hands. We had tea with Dr and Mrs Palkovský. During the evening, at the Montparnasse, we met Lojza's new girlfriend, a Pole by name of Bella.

She is quite attractive—but not beautiful—and works in the Cumberland. With her, we went to the Hungaria, on Lower Regent Street, to have dinner. The Hungarian Badacsony wine and dancing to a good band made for a delightful night. The Hungaria is frequented by Allied officers—mostly Poles, Dutch, and Norwegians.

8 May

I went out for lunch with Mrs Boissier. She is the wife of a naval officer, who appears to be on shore duty at Milford Haven. She is very beautiful, tall, slim, and blonde, but perhaps a little too cultured and down-to-earth. She certainly is a *Grande Dame*—something I soon discovered after lunch, during a short talk in her flat. God knows that I have had almost no interest in other women since I've been married. This time I had a purely psychological interest, seeking to determine whether this great lady's character was a façade that hid her true personality. She avoided any close physical contact, just touching me casually, lightly, and amiably. I wasn't sorry. I forgot to mention that our lunch at La Coquille, on St Martin's Lane, went extremely well.

At 5 p.m., I grabbed Lojza at the Czechoslovak Institute at 18 Grosvenor Place. He had been at a gathering of the Czech Society for International Law. Also in attendance were Professor Procházka, Helen Koželuhová's husband, Dr Táborský, the President's secretary, Dr Palkovský, Dr Hermann, and some fifteen or so other very professional-looking gentlemen. They talked the same professional poppycock that I used to hear at home. I then had tea with Lojza, Dr Palkovský and Dr Hermann. After 7 p.m. I went with Lojza to dine with some acquaintances of his who live in an old house off The Strand, at 10 Buckingham Street, London, WC2. There were seven of us. The two hostesses were Yvonne, who just got a job as a driver with American Ambulance, and Joan Duff, an employee of the Ministry for Aircraft Production. Besides Lojza and myself, the others included Hazel (a girl who works at the Foreign Office) and Sqn Ldr Malý, a tall young lad in civvies from the Czech Inspectorate. The dinner, served in the kitchen, was very delicious. The girls told us about the two big raids on 16 and 19 April, which destroyed houses all around while shaking and damaging their own homes. They behaved as all civilians behave here; they fought disaster valiantly, without fear, leaving the rest to destiny. Joan is very tall, almost 6 feet in height. She is not particularly pretty, but very nice and happy. We left the party soon after dinner and went to the Hungaria, alone, to dance. Both of us had a great time. A very drunk American was there too and we had our fun with him. We went home after the other guests had already left. I stayed with Joan a little longer. I left at around 2.30 a.m. It was a marvellous, moonlit night. A small raid was in progress. Streaks of exhaust smoke criss-crossed the sky, which was highlighted by occasional bursts of flak. I walked around the Houses of Parliament and Westminster Abbey, then along the river to Dolphin Square. It had been an enjoyable evening.

9 May

I went to the Czech Inspectorate and saw AVM Janoušek and our former Adjutant, Flt Lt Provazník. I then had lunch with Česaný and Wichta in a Chinese restaurant. After a last-minute talk with Lojza in his flat, I left London from Liverpool Street station at 5.47 p.m. I arrived at Wretham just as six of our crews were strolling to the aerodrome to take off for Mannheim. I watched them take off and felt a little bit of annoyance. Leave is okay, but flying is better.

I have to mention a strange thing; I have never been in a real air raid. We arrived at Liverpool on 24 November. The city had been raided night after night for two months straight. The first raid-less night was on 24–25 November, which, coincidentally, was the only one I spent in Liverpool. On 29 April I was in Norwich. We left at 10 p.m., and it was bombed an hour later. I was in London on 16 April and left in the late afternoon. That same night, London suffered its worst bombing of the *Blitz*. Close to 1,500 people were killed, and considerable damage was done. This last time, there was practically no bombing for the entire length of time I was in London. On the night of 10 May, just after I had left, the city took a terrific beating at the hands of the Luftwaffe. The House of Commons and Westminster Abbey also sustained damage.[5]

11

Back with No. 311 (B) Squadron, 9 May–3 June 1941

I started flying again on 11 May, two weeks after I had last set a foot in an aircraft. That morning, we flew eastward for a while to view the sea. From above Saxmundham, Suffolk, the North Sea looked gentle in the sunshine. We left for Hamburg the same night. We flew on Wellington T2972/KX-G, with Plt Off. Korda as skipper, Wg Cdr Toman as second pilot, myself as navigator, Sgt Slánský as W/T operator, Plt Off. Šimon as front gunner, and Sgt Čtvrtlík as rear gunner. The target was the docks in Hamburg-Altona, located on the left bank of the Elbe River. Our squadron was sending seven planes to that target and an eighth to the docks at Dieppe. It was a glorious night, with a full moon and marvellous visibility. We flew along our usual, well-known route, along the Frisian Islands some 10 miles out to sea, from Texel to the Elbe River Estuary. It was a very easy job. The Wing Commander asked for the map and was able to pinpoint positions almost the whole way. I often left my desk to look out beside the pilots or from the astrodome. There was such a marvellous view of the silver sea and the black shape of islands bathed in moonlight. The danger of night fighters was of course a constant threat under such conditions, but we didn't worry. After some three hours of flying, we saw the bend of the Elbe north of Hamburg and followed the river down toward our target. It was like on a bombing range. We made a perfect level approach, crossing the entire town from north-northeast to south-southwest and getting a very good shot at our objective. We were mostly carrying incendiaries, and we started a big new fire to add to several others that were already burning in the target area. That was our main task. Our plane was among the fire-starters sent with the first wave of bombers, whose job it was to light up the target for the following oncoming waves. Two hundred and eight bombers had been detailed to attack Hamburg that night, and, according to all reports, the town and the harbour must have got a terrific pasting. We flew away, crossing the whole town again; just past it, an incoming Wellington flew by us at no more than 50 yards away. On the way back, I spent as much time as possible in the astrodome, admiring the splendid night around us. We landed without any problems after 5.35 hours of flying.

The other planes in our squadron weren't as lucky. On the outward-bound leg over the North Sea, Sgt Bernát got in a scrap with a German night fighter—presumed to be a Junkers 88. The German attacked twice and our gunners replied. In the course of the action, Sgt Bernát had to jettison his bombs into the sea to get more manoeuvrability. The German eventually broke off the fight without having scored a single hit in two attacks—not a very good effort for a night fighter. Having nothing left to drop, Sgt Bernát returned to base.[1]

Sgt Blatný, with the troublesome Plt Off. Bečvář as navigator, was over Hamburg at 13,000 feet when he was caught in searchlights and instantly bracketed by flak. Blatný broke away from the gunfire but not before being hit by a splinter in the head, just behind the ear. He remained at the controls. The bombing was carried out after all the excitement. Blatný brought the plane out into the relative quietness of the North Sea. Only then did he turn the controls over to the second pilot, Sgt Musálek, who was on his first operation. After Blatný's wound was bandaged, he laid down on the field bed. Musálek flew Wellington T2971/KX-H the rest of the way back. He found he could not lower the landing gear; he was unaware that a hydraulic pipe had been smashed by a splinter. Blatný made a perfect belly landing on an aerodrome. The plane had ninety-three holes. The luck of the crew that night was incredible. One splinter went through the wing, just between the two fuel tanks, while another went clear through the cowling of the airscrew. A third splinter went through the cabin, entering and leaving without hitting anybody or anything.[2] Flt Lt Šnajdr's plane also came back with several holes.

We received the good news that Czech pilots from No. 310 (F) Squadron at Duxford have accounted for six out of thirty-one planes shot down by night fighters. This took place on the night of 10–11 May, during the big *Blitz* against on London. Sgt Dygrýn has shot down three enemy aircraft, including two Heinkel 111s and one Dornier 17Z. Plt Off. Běhal shot down one, but he was later killed in action.[3]

Sqn Ldr Pickard DSO DFC has left us and will be Squadron Leader (Flying) with No. 9 (B) Squadron at Honington, effective 15 May. He was very nice but a little too vain, and in the end he lost most of his popularity. His last exploit occurred in the early morning of 18 April. Fg Off. Breitcetl, who is now a Flight Lieutenant, had to return early from a raid on Berlin due to engine trouble. Sqn Ldr Pickard took on his usual air; he muttered something about cold feet and turning about for no reason. When a request came through for three planes to search for a dinghy, he said that he would fly Breitcetl's plane himself, proving that it could be flown all right. When the engines were started, it became obvious that one of them really was unserviceable. Sqn Ldr Pickard took another plane, neglecting to apologise to Breitcetl, who has been on something like twenty-five operations and has always done more than his fair share.[4] Such things occurred every once in a while, and I am afraid that nobody here is sorry to see him leave. Pickard was always nice to me. I was guest of his at East Harling on a number of occasions. We flew an operation together to Bremen on 18 March. For a brief period of time, we had the fifty-year-old Plt Off. 'Timbertoes' Carlin with us. He's a marvellous, adventurous chap. Carlin had been with us since he shot down two Germans and damaged a third while serving as a gunner on a Defiant night-fighter. Sadly, he was killed a few days ago. He died as he had lived, an ageing warrior [see Appendix VI].

Here is a summary of our Bombing Group's effort for the month of April 1941.

Squadron	Number of sorties	Hours flown	Weight of bombs dropped (lbs)
115	102	569.22	266,880
149	101	581.44	311,620
99	99	543.14	297,870
75	95	592.16	208,670
218	92	491.37	210,886
9	87	496.18	216,590
214	84	457.13	200,940
40	83	521.42	240,460
311	63	349.17	176,074
57	37	197.34	80,130
15	32	182.49	103,540
7	31	167.50	194,500
3 PRU	6	35.53	5,500
Total	**912**	**5,186.49**	**2,513,660**

Our average bomb load is thus 2,795 lbs per plane; that of our neighbouring No. 9 (B) Squadron is a total of 2,490 lbs.

My next operation was on Thursday 15 May. Our own plane, T2972/KX-G, is undergoing an overhaul, and so we were assigned R1451/KX-P. There is no comparison between it and good old 'seventy-two'. Our crew was Plt Off. Korda, skipper, Sgt Horáček, second pilot (on his first trip), myself as navigator, Sgt Slánský, W/T operator, Grp Capt. Berounský, front gunner, and Sgt Janšta as rear gunner.[5]

Our Group's official account of this operation reads as follows:

Hanover was attacked by twenty-six Wellingtons and three Stirlings (six out of eight from East Wretham, six out of seven from Honington, nine out of eleven from Mildenhall, five out of eight Wellingtons and two Stirlings from Wyton and one Stirling from Oakington). Dropped 23 × 1,000-lb, 132 × 500-lb, 12 × 250-lb and 4,920 × 4-lb incendiary bombs. Observation was difficult owing to haze and slight dazzle, the latter in some cases preventing A/C finding target. Bursts seen near aiming point and within half mile of target. A few good fires started visible for 20 miles. A Stirling returning from Berlin ten minutes after main attack concluded dropped 5 × 1,000-lb and 9 × 500-lb bombs in middle of large fire in centre of city. Two A/C from East Wretham, one from Honington and three from Wyton, attacked Münster, Vahrenwalder, an unidentified aerodrome and concentrations of searchlights and flak at Hanover and Schiphol aerodrome, some bursts and fires seen. Two A/C from Mildenhall made no attack. Two A/C from East Wretham crash-landed, crew safe, and one A/C Wyton is missing.[6] Those three all sent NGZ and are included above.[7]

Of seven Stirlings, three from Wyton and four from Oakington, detailed to attack Berlin, only two Oakington aircraft succeeded in reaching their destination, dropping 10 × 1,000-lb and 10 × 500-lb through 7/10 clouds.[8] One fire seen. The other two from Oakington turning back from Berlin owing to excessive petrol consumption attacked Hanover and Waalhaven. Of the three A/C from Wyton, one did not start. One was diverted to Hanover owing to late start, and one A/C was unable to penetrate the searchlight barrages owing to glare and eventually attacked flak and searchlight concentrations at Cologne.

On this night, the total RAF Bomber Command effort amounted to a medium-sized raid. It was divided as follows:

Hanover
101 detailed, seventy-seven attacked, two Wellingtons and one Hampden lost (No. 1 Group—six Wellingtons, No. 3 Group—twenty-six Wellingtons and three Stirlings, No. 4 Group—thirteen Whitleys and eight Wellingtons, No. 5 Group—twenty Hampdens and one Manchester).

Berlin
Fifteen detailed, one Manchester lost (No. 3 Group—seven Stirlings, No. 5 Group—seven Manchesters with one Stirling cancelling before the raid). Two Stirlings and three Manchesters carried out the attack by dropping 28 × 1,000-lb and 10 × 500-lb.

Boulogne
No. 4 Group—nine Whitleys, no losses.

Dieppe
No. 4 Group—eight Whitleys, no losses.[9]

Secondary Targets
Aircraft failing to reach primary targets above, four aircraft lost.

I am noting this merely to show bombing activity over Germany on the odd night when the RAF activity is not called '*Blitz*'.

We had a good and interesting flight, and I think we bombed successfully. Near Hague, we witnessed a Wellington coned by searchlights get plastered by flak. A German fighter was not far from there as well. We crossed a very nasty fighter box north of the Ruhr, and that was about it. Our only concern was the plane, which was not up to standard at all. There was no heating, and the cold—with

-32 degrees Celsius outside—was brutal. Oxygen was escaping through a cock that couldn't be shut off. The intercom system to the front gunner was dead, while all the other positions were experiencing communication problems. The oil pumps froze up and ceased functioning. The oil temperature of the starboard engine rose to 100°, which is 25° above the allowed maximum of 75°. The pressure fell to 60 lbs, which is under the allowed minimum of 70 lbs. We didn't want to turn back, but the starboard engine could have stopped for good at any minute.

Two planes from our squadron crash-landed. Wellington R1410/KX-M, flown by Flt Lt Šnajdr, experienced an engine fire in the vicinity of Münster while at 14,000 feet. He flew some 300 miles on one engine and landed near Wattisham after fuel starvation caused the second engine to quit.[10] Wellington R1466/KX-D, flown by Sgt Fencl, was coned by searchlights above Hanover and hit by flak. To avoid more searchlights, Fencl dived to 200 feet. He crossed Germany at this height and escaped damage. This was despite him having to fly through machine-gun fire on three separate occasions. Out of petrol, Fencl landed south-east of Norwich.[11] It was a very good show by both crews as they managed to make it home unscathed.

Again, I haven't made any entries in this book for ten days. The weather has been terrible, so there haven't been any operations. There have been a few incidents of common interest (or, rather, three) that are worth mentioning:

1. There was a deadly accident on 25 May involving one of our training planes, Wellington N3010/KX-L. The crew was: Plt Off. Zeinert, skipper, Plt Off. Švic, second pilot, Plt Off. Čermák, navigator, Plt Off. Vild, W/T operator, Sgt Dušek, front gunner, and Sgt Stoček, rear gunner. Along for the flight were two passengers—Plt Off. Van der Bijl, our new Education Officer, and one Corporal from Marham. The crew were taking off from the auxiliary field at Langham to carry out some air gunnery work over the Weybourne Range. A reconstruction of the accident with the known facts gave the following picture. Plt Off. Zeinert made a standard take-off run into the wind for some 200 yards. It is probable that the throttle lock was loose, which made the starboard throttle slide back, causing the aircraft to make a 90-degree turn to starboard. Zeinert pushed the throttle forward again. Upon noticing that the plane had gathered speed and was running straight, he probably decided that he would not abort his roll and continued with a crosswind take-off. After a further 700 yards, the plane became airborne, hanging to one side on account of the crosswind. Zeinert fully applied the opposite rudder, after which the plane turned abruptly to port and ran into a row of trees around 15 feet in height. The shock of impact must have been enormous. The plane broke in two and burst into flames. Both gunners must have been killed instantly or soon after the crash. Plt Off. Zeinert died the next day in hospital. Švic and the Corporal are seriously wounded, while the other three got off rather lightly. The funeral of the three killed will be tomorrow, 30 May, at Wretham cemetery.[12] Stoček was a well-known boxer.

2. A plan has been drawn up for the rest cure of the crews who have completed their tour of operational flying. English crews usually undertake six months of non-operational duties like courses, ground work, and instructing at OTUs. Six weeks are spent on leave. As non-operational occupations are scarce for Czechs, there seems to be a plan to give the Czech crew nine weeks' leave after thirty-five missions and then put them back on operations. However, a few non-operational jobs will be available—Plt Offs Nedvěd, Doubrava, Horák, and Študent and Sgts Valach and Košek are going to a pilot's school. That makes Plt Off. Vnouček the new administrative officer and navigation instructor. Fg Off. Machálek, a boisterous chap and one of the few I do not like here, will be in charge of propaganda at the Czech Inspectorate. Others will be attending Bombing Leaders, Gunnery Leaders, and parachute courses. Plt Off. Kirchstein has already been attached to the Operations Room as an assistant. The bulk of the crews will get nine weeks' rest and then go back to flying; so shall I, if I can help it. It may mean seven weeks in Canada for me by approximately 15 July. Hurrah!

3. Personnel: Wg Cdr Toman has been posted to the Czech Ministry of Defence. This is his first office job after more than 3,200 hours in the air. It will be like a glorified retirement for him. Sqn Ldr Pickard has relinquished his position as Liaison Officer to Sqn Ldr Batchelor. Fg Off. Richter, the man who had a nervous breakdown, has been posted to No. 313 'Czechoslovak' (F) Squadron at Catterick, Yorkshire, as an Intelligence Officer. He will not be alone as MUDr Krůta is now serving as a Medical Officer there. Plt Off. Nedvěd was awarded the MBE for his gallantry after his plane crashed on 16 December 1940.

On 27 May, after doing nothing for twelve days, I was going back out on operations. The target was Cologne. I would be flying in Wellington T2972/KX-G with Korda, Horáček, Slánský, Čtvrtlík and Janšta. We elected to fly the southern route, although we wouldn't go as south as the last time. Our track took us by Zeebrugge, Brussels, Aachen, and Bonn. The Germans seem to be increasingly reliant on night fighters. Avoiding flak has become easier from one concentration of searchlights to the next. The night was quite cloudy, with some scattered opaline clouds up to 18,000 feet—not good weather for the night fighters. I wouldn't like to fly on a moonlit night through all these light barrages around Ostend, Ghent, Brussels, and the Belgian-German border, nor anywhere along the entire Rhine. We had a rather quiet flight despite being very heavily loaded; it took us three hours to cover the distance from base to target. There were lots of searchlights in the target area, but relatively little flak. Homeward bound, we met one of our Whitleys over Brussels. Altogether it was an uneventful trip, despite the cold discomfort after the heating system became unserviceable again.

That night, our squadron had been the only one from our Group to operate. The rest of the Group had been out during the day, taking part in the big hunt for the *Bismarck*. They arrived too late, as the German ship had already been sunk by torpedoes from

HMS *Dorsetshire* at 11.01 a.m. Naval officers had flown on our bombers to provide instant ship recognition and to prevent novice and overzealous crews from bombing our own vessels. That's the reason why our squadron wasn't sent as well. There was the real danger of our crews misunderstanding the naval advisers.

I slept deeply until 1 p.m., and after a very hurried lunch there was a parade for Sqn Ldr Pickard to bid the operational crews farewell. Sqn Ldr Batchelor, the new Liaison Officer, then look over. We went to Bury St Edmunds in the afternoon and watched a terrible picture starring Basil Rathbone. We then rushed back as our crew was ordered to test Wretham's D/F station. It's a miserable contraption with a range of only 20 miles or so. We'd like to see it replaced with something decent. Korda was flying the plane, with Sgt Mareš as W/T operator and myself as navigator. Between 11 p.m. and midnight, we were flying on a transit line through Honington and Wretham south and then northwards. We found out what we already knew—that our D/F station was no good.

I should also mention something about my social activities during this spell of idleness. I went to the cinema several times. I drank in a horrible pub at Woolpit that is frequented by some of our officers, two of whom are Richter and Dvorský. They somehow now consider it to be their home. On 26 May, I went back to Cavenham. On 31 May, I entertained Theresa Home, Lelgarde Philipps and a friend of theirs, Yvonne Davies, at Wretham, during a garden party held in conjunction with War Charities Week. Afterwards, Flt Lt Šnajdr and Plt Offs Schneider, Kacíř, and I went to La Hogue Hall for a cocktail party. That's all.

Here are the statistics highlighting the dangers of night bombing and the operational tempo by RAF Bomber Command for the month of April 1941. The command operated on twenty-three out of thirty nights, dispatching a total of 2,276 sorties. Losses were 2.4 per cent—i.e. fifty-four to fifty-five aircraft, an average of just over two per operational night. The following groups participated:

No. 1 Group—Wellingtons—228 sorties
No. 2 Group—Blenheims—99 sorties
No. 3 Group—Wellingtons—890 sorties
No. 4 Group—Whitleys—445 sorties
No. 5 Group—Hampdens—548 sorties (this Group does mine-laying as well)

The following new types were introduced:

No. 3 Group—Short Stirling
No. 4 Group—Handley Page Halifax
No. 5 Group—Avro Manchester

Altogether, they flew total of sixty-six sorties.

The slower Wellingtons were intercepted by Luftwaffe fighters more often than the faster types. The new Stirlings, Halifaxes, and Manchesters fared much better, with only one Manchester attacked. This would seem to validate the thought that it pays to build bigger and more powerful machines.

On 30 May, a funeral service presided over by our Padre, Sqn Ldr Pouchlý, was held in the little graveyard at East Wretham for Zeinert, Dušek, and Stoček. All the flying crews were present for this solemn occasion, which included the honour guard firing three salvoes.

It was 2 June, Whit Monday, and I was once again on operations. The target was Düsseldorf. I flew in T2972/KX-G with our regular crew (with the exception of Sgt Horáček, who was replaced as Second Dickie by the CO, Wg Cdr Schejbal). It was a ghastly night. We finished the usual circuit to gain altitude after take-off. By the time we approached our aerodrome to set course, we were already in cloud. We later found that there were three main layers of cloud—one at about 1,000 feet, another extremely dense formation from 9,000 to 15,000 feet, and a third one at about 18,000 feet. Visibility was nil, with the upper layer mostly obscuring the sky. This allowed for only intermittent astro fixes. To make navigation even more difficult, the German radio beacons (which we are using to great advantage) were not operating that night. It is most likely that they did not have any aircraft operating on the other side of the Channel in such weather. However, we didn't do too badly; after failing to get a good H/F fix east of Cologne, we reached the target area. The Ruhr is a large, expansive area. Everywhere we looked, there was the glow of searchlights under the cloud cover, accompanied by erratic flak. We flew around in desperation. Wg Cdr Schejbal later told me that he thought that I had done it on purpose, to 'take him around' through the flak for quite a while.

There wasn't any chance of pinpointing anything on the ground, so we finally released our bombs on a large concentration of searchlights and flak. It could have been Düsseldorf, but it might also have been a little more to the east— perhaps Solingen or Wuppertal. Our rear gunner, Janšta, saw burning houses after our bombing, so our efforts do not appear to have been wasted after all. On our flight back, I think I did some rather good navigating in bringing us straight over Wretham (after half a dozen changes of course) on such a night.

By then, the clouds were already as low as 700 feet and it was raining below. All our crews—we had eight out that night—returned safely, although only four had actually been over the Ruhr. A crew from a Polish bomber squadron (No. 304, I think) landed on our field on the return trip from Germany. Their squadron have only been operating since 25 April, but they have already lost five crews.[13] This gives quite a poor outlook on their efficiency and training.

In the late afternoon of the next day, I was told that I would be attached to the Air Ministry for special duty for a few days. I was to leave for London the next morning at 7.35 a.m., and I was to report to the Czech Inspectorate immediately after my arrival. No-one, even including the CO and Grp Capt. Berounský, was aware of what this order was all about.

12

London and Kemble, 4–11 June 1941

I left Thetford at 7.35 a.m. on Wednesday 4 June. Fantl had phoned ahead for me, and I thus found Lojza waiting for me at Liverpool Street station. I then went straight to the Czech Inspectorate. AVM Janoušek informed me of what my special duty was all about. Compared to what Wg Cdr Toman would tell me later (and the actual inside story), his official explanation was interesting.

He told me that there is a scheme for the use of tour-expired Czech crews to ferry aircraft across the Atlantic. First of all, it is essential to know the requirements for such a service and to be able to pick the right men, or to give those suitable further training. Wg Cdr Toman has been chosen to try his hand in transatlantic flying first. Later, he will be in charge of the Czech ferrying group. My job was finding everything required for the organisation, and to send a report to the Inspectorate. I was to be Wg Cdr Toman's navigator on his test flight over the Atlantic. After that, I would be his ADC in the organisation of future large-scale ferrying operations.

On the other hand, Wg Cdr Toman told me that there is a fight on for the future top position in Czechoslovakia. Gen. Janoušek is currently the leading candidate. He is the head of the Czech Inspectorate and Commander in Chief of the Czech Air Force in Britain. Gen. Slezák (whose real last name is Vicherek) is head of the Aeronautical Department of the Czech Ministry of National Defence. That means absolutely nothing here, although it would make him the boss back home if the organisation of the Czech Air Force, as part of the Army, remains as it was before Munich. Gen. Janoušek is therefore out to create a position for himself that would leave him in charge of the Czech Air Force in Czechoslovakia, too.

The scheme is to create an independent Air Ministry based on the one already here in England, where Gen. Janoušek's leadership cannot be contested. It means that Gen. Janoušek would come home as a Minister and therefore be Gen. Slezák's superior. It is a cunning scheme, but hard to execute. The Janoušek-Slezák fight seems to have reached fever pitch now. Gen. Janoušek considers Wg Cdr Toman not only to be a supporter of Gen. Slezák, but also a very dangerous person of considerable influence. Wg Cdr Toman had gained widespread notoriety for his outstanding flying exploits and also for having been selected to command the first Czech bomber squadron in the Royal Air Force.

Gen. Janoušek thus used his influence at the Air Ministry to have Wg Cdr Toman removed from London as quickly as possible. The General's connections came through, and Wg Cdr Toman's swift departure was arranged after the he had been in London for a mere three days. Wg Cdr Toman was then sent to Kemble, Gloucestershire. He went through a series of examinations to see if he would be suitable as an Atlantic ferry pilot—a Czech Colonel, a British Wg Cdr as a ferry pilot! Wg Cdr Toman stated that he would go, but only if I would be his ADC. I would help him through the initial stages due to his lack of English-language skills. Gen. Janoušek didn't like that one bit. His desire to get Wg Cdr Toman removed from London was so overwhelming that he consented to having me attached for four or five days—but no more than a week, maximum—to RAF Station Kemble. According to Wg Cdr Toman, the explanation he later gave for this move was 'sheer poppycock'.

I had lunch with Wg Cdr Toman, Torelli and Lojza at the Czech Restaurant on Edgware Road, before going to see the editor of the *Čechoslovák*, Bohuš Beneš. They are about to publish a book about the Czech flyers in England called *Wings in Exile*, to which I have contributed several stories. The printing of this book has been delayed as a result of it sitting on Gen. Janoušek's desk for the past three weeks. Mr Beneš thinks that Gen. Janoušek is trying to force him to print it as an official publication; this would allow him to get his picture on the front cover.[1]

Wg Cdr Toman and I left Paddington station at 4.15 p.m. After changing at Swindon, we reached Kemble at around 6.45 p.m. The aerodrome is close to the railway station, but the officers are billeted all over the countryside. We were put into Croft House, Somerford Keynes—about 5 miles from the aerodrome. Wg Cdr Dawkins, the CO of the Service Ferry Squadron, is living there with about fifteen officers (several of them Poles), a dog, a black cat, a badger by the name of Rasters, and Georgie, a parrot. We share a room with a bath and Plt Off. Ritchie. There are three different units on the station:

1. No. 41 (Maintenance) Group's HQ Service Ferry Pools, based at Kemble, is responsible for training pilots to ferry a large variety of aircraft around the United Kingdom and overseas. Its Chief Instructor is Flt Lt Cox, and it is him who we have to deal with for the time being.

2. No. 5 Maintenance Unit, which is equipping American aircraft (mostly Martin Marylands) for operations and fitting other aircraft with overload tanks for flights to the Middle East.[2] Apart from Wellingtons with two overload-tanks in both outside bomb-bay compartments, we saw Hurricanes with auxiliary tanks under the wings.[3] This is supposed to give them an endurance of seven hours,

which should be enough to reach Gibraltar, refuel there, and then to fly to Egypt. The Marylands look very impressive.

3. Overseas Air Deliveries Flight, run by Air Transport Auxiliary (ATA), a civilian organisation, which is responsible for providing transatlantic crews.[4]

On 5 June, we reported to HQ SFP and were told that Wg Cdr Toman would be examined the following day on Vickers Wellington, Bristol Blenheim, and Douglas Havoc aircraft. In the afternoon, Wg Cdr Toman and I walked about 5 miles to the nearest town, Cirencester. We visited the parish church there, parts of which were built in the eleventh century. It is worth seeing. We wandered through the picturesque streets of the old town, saw a movie, and then walked back to Somerford Keynes. The following morning was spent inspecting a Blenheim and a Havoc on the ground as the weather was too bad for flying. In the afternoon, we walked from the aerodrome to Cirencester, did some shopping, and saw a picture called *The Thief of Baghdad*, starring Conrad Veidt, Sabu, and June Duprez. This was the second time I watched it, the first being at Bury St Edmunds. We were driven back in a taxi by a lovely young girl. I forgot to say that in the afternoon we had watched the famous Scottish aviator Jim Mollison taking off in a Cunliffe-Owen OA Mk I Flying Wing.[5] This odd-looking aircraft is a modified version of Vincent Burnelli's UB-14 Flying Wing. It is an odd-looking thing with no nose, the cabin in the immense wing as middle-nacelle, twin tails, and a strangely curved body.[6]

There are three Czech Sergeants on the station—Mašek, Šeda, and Březovský. Mašek had served with No. 311 (B) Squadron, but he has tuberculosis and is afraid that he will be discharged. He insists that he is fit and longing to fly. The other two are former fighter pilots with No. 310 (F) Squadron and have been posted out. Šeda was considered to be too old at thirty-three, while Březovský, who is a pale, timid little chap, was considered as not being suited for an operational assignment. Březovský should have been a grocery clerk, not a pilot, as he isn't doing too well at Kemble either. Šeda is an excellent pilot, obviously overjoyed to be where he is. When Wg Cdr Toman asked him if he would like to go back to operating as a bomber pilot, he very decidedly said, 'No.'

It took me some energy to persuade Flt Lt Cox to begin with Wg Cdr Toman's flying programme in the afternoon of 7 June. The weather was terrible in the morning and still very uncertain by the afternoon. Altogether, we flew three circuits in a dual-control Bristol Blenheim Mk IV. The instructor, FS Sanders, and Wg Cdr Toman were up front, while was I uncomfortably stuffed in the turret. A thunderstorm moved through the area, forcing all flying activities to be washed out. The weather is appalling around here. Since we've arrived, we have not seen anything else except fog, drizzle, and torrential rain.

There was a cocktail party at Croft House the same evening. It was the usual affair, with innumerable people stuffed into a few rooms. The food was exceptionally good though, especially some asparagus rolls, of which I must have had a dozen at least. A bald Squadron Leader from No. 41 Group (which is doing ferrying), joined us and professed his desire to talk over the problem of Czech crews doing transatlantic ferrying.[7] He told us that previously they had required complete knowledge of English for this job, but that he would consider our proposal of using Czech crews of three, one of whom could speak English. Of course, the man in charge was Sqn Ldr Stannard from the Air Ministry at 424 Adastral House, who was supposed to attend the party. The Sqn Ldr from Group promised that he would call on us later that evening for a more thorough talk. Well, the man from the Air Ministry didn't arrive and the Sqn Ldr from Group got drunk and thus altogether incapable of conducting any conversation whatsoever. I wasn't too sorry, as I had spotted a rather lovely girl—Joy Power, from Cirencester—with whom I danced quite a lot. As usual, my bad luck got in the way.

Mrs Duffy, the wife of Flt Lt Duffy, Chief Test Pilot at No. 8 MU Little Rissington, had cast an eye on me and didn't leave me alone for the whole evening. She is very black and rather solidly built and as she went so far as to bite me during a dance, a thing I hate more than anything else, I had to retreat and go to bed, although the party was still going strong and I would have loved to look in Joy's clear eyes a little longer.

On Sunday afternoon, Wg Cdr Toman and I walked to Cirencester again to see a picture. At noon on Monday, after spending the whole morning shivering in the hangar, with torrential rain pouring down outside, I left Kemble rather gladly. I had sent Lojza a telegram, but it didn't reach him as he had just reached Leamington. I went straight to the Czech Inspectorate to report, but I could not find AVM Janoušek nor his deputy, Grp Capt. Kubita. I thus went to the Overseas League, Park Place, St James's Street, and got a nice room with a bath in a part of the building not destroyed by bombs, which have so badly damaged the main building. From there I went to see Joan. She was at home, and we spent a nice evening together with dinner in the Strand Palace, dancing and drinks in a private club—the Liaison—and then at her home.

The next day, Tuesday 10 June, I was again at the Inspectorate and saw both AVM Janoušek and Grp Capt. Kubita. First, I was presented with an honorary Czechoslovak Air Force badge, and then I gave a report about Kemble and the business of transatlantic ferrying.[8] I had lunch with Česaný and Wichta, met Lojza, and went at 7 p.m. to meet Joan again. This time we had dinner at La Coquille, and after that I spent a quiet evening in her home. She is a very nice girl.

When I arrived home, I found a slip of paper stuck to the door of my room; it was from Flaherty, who is staying at the club too. We met the next morning. He looks well; he has become an Fg Off., and he remains the old, self-conscious, and slightly boastful old shamus he always was. He has been on Beauforts and seems to have done exceptionally well on operations. He is now going to a Long N course held at Prince Albert, Ontario.[9] That course is just about the highest instruction in air-navigation one can get, and afterwards one usually becomes something big (e.g. a Group Navigation Officer or something like that). He gave me quite a lot of gossip, of which the most interesting were stories of Bill Scott's heroic end and Jepson. Here they are.

In Brest harbour, the *Scharnhorst* and *Gneisenau* had been bombed several times without conclusive results. Thus Coastal Command decided to come to close quarters and to make a dawn attack, with a first wave dropping landmines from a low altitude and a second making a torpedo-attack through the Rade Abri.[10] Flaherty was in the first wave, Scott in the second. His plane was last seen low over the water, heading right into the terrific barrage from the ships and shore batteries. Flaherty is positive that Scott scored a hit on one of the battleships before being shot to pieces. Scott had been living a charmed life at his squadron. He was in every scrap, in every spectacular operation, and he found his death precisely as we expected from the colourful head of our 'Camel Corps'.

He was very much afraid. He didn't return from one of his very first operations, and after that a voluminous booklet was found amongst his things. It was a sort of diary, but it was much more fantastic than true. According the diary, he had been on innumerable raids, bombed Berlin, baled out from his severely damaged plane by parachute, and so on. He must have spent all his evenings writing this stuff; for him, it must have been a compensation for all the fear he had to go through in this war.

I left Liverpool Street station at 11.55 p.m. and arrived in Thetford at 2.45 p.m., in time to prepare myself for the night's raid. I forgot to say that in London I met one of the Los Angeles boys who had come over on the *Duchess of Richmond* last November to enlist in the RAF. He is an LAC now, and training at an SFTS to be a fighter pilot. His nice wife joined him two months ago from the United States.

13
Back in Wretham, 11–23 June 1941

I will start my account of the occurrences during what might be my last *séjour* in Wretham with the two operations of 11 June and 12 June. They were both spoiled by the weather, which had been unforeseen by our bright meteorologists.

11 June

Target: Düsseldorf.
Aeroplane: Wellington W5682/KX-Y, Sqn Ldr Ocelka's, while our T2972/KX-G was over Boulogne-sur-Mer with a freshman crew.
Crew: the old one—Korda, Horáček, myself, Slánský, Čtvrtlík and Janšta. Little Slánský is on his thirtieth trip and he has promised the mechanics £1 if he gets back from this one.
Over Germany there was almost complete overcast, only broken by occasional gaps. We passed over Cologne to find Düsseldorf under thick clouds. We pushed on a little further to find a reasonably big gap over Duisburg. We were afraid that even this gap would close if we were to go back to Düsseldorf and persist in finding the primary target, and we therefore unloaded our bombs—which were mostly incendiaries—on Duisburg. We started quite a big fire in the middle of the town; it was visible from more than 40 miles away by the time we reached south of Cologne. This use of occasional gaps for bombing was going on everywhere, and we saw scattered fires all over the Ruhr area. When we passed Cologne, it was just almost clear over the town, which was further lit by an immense fire. It was burning on the east bank of the Rhine and must have been burning petrol, because I have never before seen a single fire produce such a glare. The Germans also used the gap in the clouds to give us a taste of their flak. There wasn't anything as spectacular on the homeward journey.

12 June

Target: Hamm.
Aircraft: T2972/KX-G.
Crew: The same as the night before.

It was fairly clear over the North Sea. The sky was so clear that we could easily see a Ju 88 some 500 feet above us, heading westward. The weather deteriorated over the continent, and when we arrived over the target-area the ground was completely covered by a thick haze. There were a number of planes around dropping flares, and we did as well, but the flares were swallowed by the mist and we couldn't see anything. After some cruising about, we decided to look for a target in the Ruhr. Hamm is a comparatively small place situated in open country, and there was a 100:1 chance of our bombs falling into fields if we were looking to only bomb the searchlights. On the other hand, it is practically impossible to not hit something if one bombs the area between Dortmund, in the east, and Duisburg, in the west, which is practically one big town. We thus turned on course 245° magnetic for ten minutes, and got thus over the Ruhr. To aid orientation by stirring up enemy opposition, we released one bomb and were rewarded by switched-on searchlights and both heavy and light flak. We cruised around again until we became satisfied by various indications (including an H/F-fix obtained by British plane about 1 mile away) that we were over Essen. We then released our remaining seven bombs, which fell close to a good fire started by another plane. It was a great pity that the weather was so bad, as Bomber Command had made a big effort to smash up the four main railway yards in Western Germany—Osnabrück, Hamm, Soest, and Schwerte. It had put four whole Groups (1, 3, 4 and 5) on the job, each on one of the four centres. On the way home, we dropped leaflets over the Netherlands. It was fair there, and it was also fair over England when we reached Wretham at around 3.40 a.m. It took us further thirty-five minutes to land because all our twelve aircraft that had set out that night—plus one English plane—were over the aerodrome at the same time, and we preferred to stay away from the rodeo that was going on.

Our parent station, Honington, paid dearly for a useless escapade a few days ago. The fame of the Blenheims of 2 Group, which since March 12 have sunk close to ninety German ships in broad daylight, aroused the envy of the professional heroes of No. 9 Squadron. They somehow got permission to try their hand in a daylight attack. They took off in four planes with practically the whole staff aboard, including the CO, Wg Cdr Arnold, Sqn Ldr Pickard, Bruce, the Bombing Leader, and so on. The Wellington is perhaps the most unsuitable plane for day operations—a cumbersome, slow, and indifferent climber. The result was according to the merit of the idea—no damage done to the Germans, and two planes lost.[1] Of the staff, only Sqn Ldr Pickard came back. The Blenheims, well-suited for such a job, sunk two ships the same day. Wg Cdr Arnold was an excellent man, and his death is a severe blow to Honington.

I may have related in this book that Sgt Filler, a pilot, is a drunkard. He was supposed to be in my crew on 23 March (my second raid on Berlin), but as he was drunk, Sgt Bernát, who was then a Duty Pilot, had to get dressed in a hurry and fly instead of Filler. Sgt Filler did precisely the same thing on 11 June, when he was to be second pilot to Sgt Fencl. Fg Off. Stránský, who is still in training, had to take over for him. At least it broke Filler's neck; he shall be demoted, dishonourably discharged, and sent to Leamington and the Czech Brigade. He is a good chap, but a drunk pilot is a menace to all, and I am glad that he will be removed.[2]

I read an official report about the effect of the new 4,000-lb bombs. The report concentrates on those dropped on Hamburg, and it reads as follows:

> East of Steinwerder Kanal, an area which consisted entirely of industrial building, 450 × 380 feet, has been completely demolished and only parts of a few walls remain. The further effect of blast which caused this destruction can be seen within an area which measures 900 × 750 feet. The blast is clearly seen on the coal dump along the Reiherstieg and buildings alongside the railway line, the distance between the two points being 1,107 feet.

Imagine—one bomb!

We have been doing lots of work lately, and I think it would be best for me to describe my last three raids while ignoring the order of other events.

June 16

A spell of very hot weather has broken. This is the fate of the bomber crew; when it is cold, one struggles against icing, and when it is hot, one struggles against overheating. My last three operations (16, 17, and 19 June) have all been affected by the heat, the temperature only usually dropping under 0 degrees Celsius above 13,000 or even 14,000 feet.

On 16 June, we flew in Wellington R1598/KX-C (Sgt Čapka's) with our normal crew (Korda, Horáček, Slánský, Čtvrtlík, Janšta, myself), and the target was Düsseldorf. Soon after take-off, we saw that the plane was rapidly getting overheated and would not climb. We usually reach 9,000 feet by the time we reach the English coast, but this time we could only get to 4,800 feet. By the time we reached the enemy coast, crossing a little north of Ostend, we were at 8,500 feet instead of the usual 13,000–14,000 feet. To south of our position, an aircraft was lit up by close to fifty searchlights and plastered by accurate flak. The aircraft refused to climb any further than 9,000 feet, and our speed was limited to 90 mph in level flight. Meanwhile, the oil temperature had reached 96° and still mounting, and the pressure had fallen to 58 psi. The cylinder temperature of one engine was 250°, the other 230°, even with the gills wide open. Under these circumstances, it was obvious that an attack on the Ruhr would have been suicide, or—most likely—that we would never reach the Ruhr at all. Very much *à contre coeur*, we were thus forced to abandon our task south of Ghent.[3]

Seeking to at least bomb something, we chose the big aerodrome of Aalter, west of Ghent.[4] We were mostly carrying incendiaries of course, and, moreover, the flare path was switched off immediately after the first bomb came whistling down. We had quite a trying experience in re-crossing the coast, with heaps of searchlights pointed at us and our aircraft still losing height. Nevertheless, we came back unharmed.

June 17

There was a misunderstanding the next morning. Plt Off. Kirchstein was on duty in the Operations Room and Grp Capt. Gray asked politely, as always, if No. 311 Squadron would operate that night. Kirchstein took that conventional phrase as if our squadron would have the choice of going out or not, and notified the CO accordingly. Those wanting to go on missions had to volunteer while on parade, and, as the Squadron had been over enemy lines already on the 15th (with freshman crews) and the 16th, only five crews were put together for the night's raids. In our crew, Sgt Horáček reported ill and the CO, Wg Cdr Schejbal, thus went with our old crew as second pilot. We had our plane, T2972/KX-G, and the target was Düsseldorf. It was a rather uneventful trip, and our old good 'seventy-two', which was on her thirtieth raid, was almost running normally (notwithstanding the heat). The flak and searchlights were hampered by the huge number of attacking machines and some ground-haze, and we bombed almost at leisure. On this occasion, when both departing and returning we crossed the enemy coast close to the Schelde estuary, north of Knokke, and encountered almost no opposition.

June 19

Slánský and Janšta were commissioned and went off to London. Čtvrtlík, who has been promoted to Flight Sergeant, has gone to Leamington to have his teeth fixed. Horáček is still ill. Our T2972/KX-G was thus carrying a very mixed crew: Korda as skipper; Sgt Blatný as second pilot; myself as navigator; Plt Off. Parolek (on his first trip) as W/T operator; Plt Off. Študent as front gunner; and Sgt Košek as rear gunner. The target was Cologne.

We had bad luck from the very beginning. Parolek is a very nervy fellow; I saw him pathetically kiss a picture of his girl before take-off. He messed up the R/T soon afterwards, so we had no inter-communication for the whole of the five and a half hours of the raid. We found ourselves in a terrific barrage over Cologne, which we had to cross and re-cross several times as it was very difficult to pick up the actual target. Some shells were bursting so close to us that the plane rocked.

The real trouble started later on, when we had just crossed the Belgian coast and were over the North Sea. Suddenly, the pressure of the starboard engine fell to zero.

Korda instantly throttled back completely so that the starboard airscrew was just only turning, and carried on with the port engine alone. We were slowly losing height, but the English coast was close and we crossed it by 4 a.m. We went over Wretham and found it covered by thick fog, which we had been warned about beforehand. The fog ended some 20 miles west of Wretham, where we found the fog-free aerodrome at Waterbeach (No. 99 Sqn). We decided to land there. It is very difficult to land on one engine, and so Korda gave the ill starboard engine a few short bursts—just enough to keep level. We had barely touched down when the starboard engine caught fire. We extinguished it ourselves with the fire extinguisher; we were lucky that the fire had only broken out after we had landed. We received a marvellous reception from Grp Capt. Bell and his staff, and we were brought to Wretham by car. We arrived there at 7.30 a.m. I bathed and dressed and just skipped sleep. Our old good T2972 remained in Waterbeach. She has done thirty-one raids faithfully, and we like her.[5]

June 22

I should have been on leave since midnight on the 22nd, but my crew was detailed for operations and so I went anyhow. We four genuine crew members (Korda, Horáček, Slánský and myself) had two new gunners, Sgts Mikulík and Chmura. We flew on R1598/KX-C and our target was Bremen, where I haven't been since 18 March.

We initially experienced the well-known troubles connected with the heat (30 degrees Celsius on the ground at 11 p.m.). The plane would not climb, and we actually crossed the coast of England at only slightly more than 3,000 feet. By then, the temperature of the oil and under the cylinder heads was again dangerously high, and we doubted that we would be able to carry on. However, the performance of the engines later improved, we crossed the Dutch coast just over the big aerodrome of De Kooy, close to Den Helder, at 12,000 feet, and we were able to reach the usual 15,000 feet over the target. It was rather good that we did, as over Bremen we reached by far the worse flak I have ever experienced. It was a terrific sight. We were soon enveloped by shell-bursts and hit by six in total. One splinter pierced the fabric on my left, just missing my shoulder, below, by a few inches; I was laying at the bomb-sight. The splinter passed under Korda's feet and fell on the floor. We found another nasty hole between the fuselage and the port engine. Flak was exceptionally heavy everywhere over the target area, but also over Vegesack and Oldenburg. I had never before seen such a gorgeous display of multi-coloured tracers. We bombed, went around 'Hell's kitchen' in a big circle from east to north and west, and returned on the same route by which we came.

An aircraft from our squadron, T2990/KX-T, didn't return that night. The crew was: FS Bufka, skipper; FS Rozum, second pilot; Plt Off. Konštacký, navigator; Plt Off. Smrček, W/T operator; and Sgts Valach and Hejna, gunners.[6] It was bad luck—especially for Konštacký and Valach, who were in their last trip before proceeding to EFTS for a pilot's course. I went on my first raid with Bufka, over Emden on that terrible night on 16 January. I liked Konštacký very much; he was a rough but frank and sociable fellow. Valach was married to an English girl from Bury St Edmunds, whose father is running a garage there. The next afternoon, 23 June, the Padre and I went to Bury to break the bad news to Mrs Valach's parents and to ask them to carefully inform Mrs Valach herself, who is expecting a child. It was a very disagreeable job. Afterwards, we went to have tea with Sqn Ldr Pickard, who is now staying in Bury St Edmunds (6 Hatter Street).

I will now go back to what happened on our station over the same period. On Friday 20 June, Dr Beneš visited the station with a very large suite, including the Generals Ingr, Nižborský and Janoušek, Dr Smutný, and several reporters and cameramen (Lamač, Heller). The whole show was rather interesting in so far as the sentiments of our boys toward the President could be seen very clearly. The President himself is well-liked, but there is a marked hatred against his counsellors, who are around him all the time and make it impossible to speak freely with the President. They are also responsible for all the petty mistakes that are creating a wall of distrust between the President and the nation. In our case, they were responsible for an arrangement that offended us as hosts of the President and was ridiculous on top of that. There was a dinner for seventy-two, but only twelve crew-members (six officers and six NCOs) were invited. At parades, Sqn Ldr Ocelka called for volunteers for these twelve places at the President's table. Only one officer (Fg Off. Svátek) volunteered. The Sqn Ldr had to order five other officers and six NCOs to attend at the dinner, and there were still several who managed to avoid that pleasure by using petty excuses.

There was another instance of the counsellors' difficulty. The President slept in the room just across from the one that I share with Fantl and Plt Off. Engel. In front of his door was not only his airman-servant, but also an officer, pistol in hand. It was completely ridiculous. After dinner, the President sat down on the terrace and gave a speech. About half (or slightly less) of the crews were present, the other half preferring to go to Norwich or elsewhere for their amusement. The speech was political and well-framed, but over-optimistic, with too many references to the President's own merits and his foresight. It was rather odd that Russia's entry into the war two days later proved that he had failed to foresee this most important event. I was rather annoyed—not only by the speech, but most of all by the official photographers, who wouldn't stop taking pictures, making it difficult at times to hear the President's words. I went to bed dissatisfied.

The next day I went to Grp Capt. Berounský's place with Korda. He is staying in a castle, Merton Hall, which is now a kind of super-boarding-house. He is staying there with his wife and little daughter—his son is at school somewhere—and one Mrs Kumpošt, whose husband, Colonel Kumpošt, seems to be CO of the Czech detachment in the Middle East. I had a long talk with Grp Capt. Berounský about the President's visit. Berounský is by far the most capable of the Czech military leaders I have seen so far. He seems to have very much the same views as me, and he isn't very enthusiastic about the President either. It was very hot, and I think that I drunk a little too much whisky—I didn't feel well that night.

14

Third Leave, 24–30 June 1941

June 24

I left Thetford on the 9.35 a.m. train and arrived in London before 1 p.m. Korda, Slánský and Mareš were already at the station, waiting for me. I took my things to the Overseas Club and then we all went to have lunch at the Chinese restaurant off Piccadilly. Surprisingly, some of the waiters there are Czech. Korda and I then went to see a picture called *The Letter*, starring Bette Davis. At 6 p.m., we went to the Baders, where Korda stays when he is in London. Mr Baders had been the manager of the Anglo-Czechoslovak Bank in Brno. I was once his guest at a garden party at his home. The Bellak brothers, two textile manufacturers from Krnov, are sharing the same flat at 54 Northway, Swiss Cottage, NW3.[1] After we had finished dinner, Paul Kohn, another industrialist from Brno, showed up. Mr Kohn's wife—the well-known pilot Margaretha Leopoldine Kohn-Ferraris—and their children are still in unoccupied France. For some reason, they are having great difficulty leaving the country. I have no love lost for the refugees, and this was a typical refugee gathering. Mr Bader himself is very nice though.

June 25

I met Lojza and went with him to see Dr Hermann. His offices are almost completely burned out, but he continues to work in the few remaining rooms. I then had dinner with Lojza and Torelli at the same Chinese restaurant as the previous day. Later, I went to watch another picture. After that, I took part in a South American reception at the Overseas League. Lord Willingdon, whom I think is a former Viceroy of India, was chairman. The Ambassadors of Argentina and Chile and Rear Admiral Sir Henry Harwood, the victor of the Battle of the River Plate, were guest speakers. Of the four speeches made, his was the most entertaining, with moments of sheer wit. I kept very close to a pretty girl I had noticed. She was slim, with dark hair and big, light eyes. A member of the committee worked his way over and offered to make an introduction. I found her to be a quite lovely, well-educated girl. Her name is Nancy Douglas. She lives at Latymer Court, Hammersmith, London W6, and works in the Hammersmith post office. Nancy doesn't look as if she had ever worked a day before the war. Now every girl works to help free up a man for military service. I invited her for dinner at Grosvenor House. We both had a wonderful time. We met Dr Hermann there, as well as Lojza, who was accompanied by a very beautiful girl named Heda Ippen. Heda is the daughter of the well-known Viennese merchant Wilhelm Ippen. Her mother was divorced but later married Lt. Alfred Kitchin, who is serving with the British Intelligence Service.[2] She is an Austrian by birth, but she speaks fluent English and is trying to get a job in the film business. We danced and were as merry as possible.

June 26

In the morning, I went up to the Czech Inspectorate and saw Gen. Janoušek and Grp Capt. Kubita. The plan to use Czech crews for transatlantic ferrying seems to have more or less fallen apart.[3] I then met Lojza and wandered around with him. We saw Dr Lefort at his gas station and then dined at the Czechoslovak Centre. The both of us then went to visit Ing. Malík. He seems to be the most disgruntled of all and constantly curses everyone and everything. Malík openly refers to the President as 'this dwarf'. I know that everything isn't the best it could be in the Czech movement right now, but Ing. Malík's manners are rather disgusting.

I accompanied Lojza to the Czech Ministry of Public Welfare. When we arrived, the antechamber was crowded with young men getting seeking support. I suppose they were looking for help with their education, or something along those lines. They would do better to join the services. In the evening, we met Heda Ippen and Nancy Douglas at the Regent Palace. They would be our guests at the Piccadilly Hotel for dinner and dancing.

June 27

The room next to mine in the Overseas League is occupied by Mrs Long, who lived in Kenya for several years. She must be well over thirty—looking a little tired already—but she is very intelligent, and she knows Prague and a greater part of the world. I had a very interesting chat with her in the morning. I then went to Swiss Cottage and had lunch with Korda, the Baders and the Bellaks. Mr Bader and Korda took me to King's Cross, from where I left for Bradford, Yorkshire, on the 4 p.m. train. In the same compartment with me was a very interesting fellow, a merchant who lost a leg in the last war. He is employed with the Ministry of Aircraft

Production and is a playwright on top of that. His company ensured that the five-hour journey would be very interesting indeed. Kurt and Vally were at the station when I arrived.

June 28

Kurt's marriage is a very unfortunate one. Vally left him for Paul Hecht, but then returned. Kurt took her back, but they are not living like husband and wife. Now it would appear that Vally wants move back with Paul again. If only this 'gentleman' would care for her. Things are made worse by the bunch of really awful refugees residing in Bradford. They take a real delight in the scandal, and they are doing everything to pit one side against the other. The worst of the bunch appears seems to be Fritz Veith. He is the brother of a solicitor from Brno who is now living in Brazil. With a few exceptions, all of these refugees are people of low character; they are disloyal cowards through and through.

Here is one example. When the war broke out, Mr Hecht was afraid that he would be put in an internment camp. He thus volunteered for service with the Czech Army. Hecht knew that the Czech authorities were only calling up men for service in France, and that he need not worry. He was gambling that his offer of service would be well-looked-upon by the British authorities. Then France collapsed, and the remnants of the Czech Army that managed to escape and regrouped in Britain. Mr Hecht received a letter—with a rail ticket included—ordering him to report to the Army camp at Leamington, Yorkshire. He ignored the letter and stayed put. Hecht was afraid that the Czechs could call on the British authorities to make him honour his voluntary engagement. He decided to see the MP for Bradford, to whom he told unflattering stories about the Czechs; Hecht described them as fascists and anti-Semites. He asked for protection from the Czech authorities, unaware that they had no interest in pursuing the matter. All the local Czech refugees did more or less the same, but perhaps not to the same degree. I was told that Mr Veith went to Leamington and got six months' deferred service for a bribe of £50. *Relata referro*.[4]

In the morning, I visited Vally's millinery shop and then went by bus with Tommy to Dewsbury. Later we met with Kurt, who is the manager of a factory. By the afternoon we were on our way to Leeds with Mr Veith. During our time together, I became thoroughly convinced that he was indeed the perfect pest. Then I was off to dinner at the Victoria Hotel in Bradford.

June 29

Before lunch on Sunday, I visited the Czech Consul of Bradford, Mr Lester, accompanied by Kurt. The Consul came to England more than fifty years ago and still speaks excellent Czech and English with a decidedly noticeable Czech accent. After dinner, we went to Bolton Abbey in Kurt's car. There, we walked to the summit of a small hill, where we were treated to a nice view of the moors around Bradford. Afterwards, we went to the Fishers', admittedly the most decent couple of the refugee gang. I know them from the *Ruderverein* at Brno.[5] There were several other refugees around. I called up Wretham and arranged to be picked up from Yeadon aerodrome, a few miles north of Bradford.

June 30

In the morning, I went by taxi to Yeadon, where I waited for a little more than an hour before the plane arrived. In the meantime, I had a good chat with some of the instructors from No. 20 EFTS, which operates from there. Sqn Ldr Ocelka finally arrived in Wellington R1598/KX-C. It was quite hot, and I didn't feel very comfortable during the 1.5-hour journey back to Wretham via York. We arrived home just in time for lunch. In the afternoon, I had a swim in one of our lakes. I then went with Korda and Parolek to Bury St Edmunds to see two rather dull pictures, *Rumba* and *Ghost of St Michaels*. That is how I ended my third leave.

15

No. 311 (B) Squadron, 1 July–11 August 1941

On Tuesday 1 July, I took part in a raid in Brest that will always remain memorable to me. This is the story.

Our old T2972/KX-G was still undergoing repairs at Waterbeach, so we flew on Wellington R1015/KX-L. The crew consisted of Korda, Horáček, myself, Plt Off. Parolek, and Sgts Valeš and Kovařík. The night was clear, with a full moon lighting our way. As usual, the route took us from our station over Northampton, Northamptonshire, to Bridport, Dorset. We crossed the Channel, and as we were flying directly into the moon, we had perfect visibility over Brittany. We must have been the first to reach the target, as Brest was perfectly quiet when we approached. It was only when we came over the city that the searchlights were switched on and the flak batteries began to fire.

Our target was the heavy cruiser *Prinz Eugen*, moored on the east side of the jetty of Dock No. 8. One of the defences at Brest is a smokescreen, but the southerly wind would work against the Germans; it blew the smoke from the generators inland, leaving the harbour clear. We were very careful, orbiting the target area to get an accurate position on Dock No. 8. The approach was flown from west to east, along the waterfront. The cruiser itself was invisible against the dark water, but we scored a direct hit with our 1,000-pounder on Dock No. 8. We should have hit the ship, based on our heading and the spacing of the released stick of 500-pounders. This was even more probable as we saw that all the bombs following the 1,000-pounder burst on solid ground. When we returned, we couldn't claim to have hit the ship, but we reported direct hits on the jetty and other areas, which made us think that we may have hit it after all. Two days later, the Station Commander, Grp Capt. Gray, rang up and conveyed the AOC's congratulations on us having hit the *Prinz Eugen*. The ship was about to leave the harbour the next morning. It was hit at the precise time of our bombing in the stern and the rudder, with one screw damaged. A later report tells of two hits, which killed fifty people aboard the ship [see Appendix III]. Brest has proved to be a veritable mouse trap for German warships. Although it is only probable and not absolutely certain that we hit the ship, I am glad that the trap has closed on the *Prinz Eugen* too. The *Scharnhorst* and *Gneisenau* have been in Brest for many months, undergoing some kind of Tantalus' work—i.e. to repair damage sustained during raid after raid.[1]

Sqn Ldr Ocelka received the DFC and then assumed command of the Squadron from Wg Cdr Schejbal, who is going to the Czech Inspectorate, London. Sqn Ldr Ocelka is the first CO to have been selected from within the ranks of the Squadron's crews. He has been a keen skipper, flying thirty-four sorties, and an efficient Flight Commander despite his rough and undiplomatic exterior.

I will present our Group's Operational Narrative for the raid on Münster in full:

Night of 5/6 July

Primary target Münster. The attack was a complete surprise and the town was unprepared and almost undefended. A sudden and effective *Blitz*. Weather: No cloud, slight haze with excellent visibility until smoke from rapidly increasing fires covered the aiming point. One Wellington Mk II out of two from Waterbeach and sixty Wellington Mk ICs out of sixty-three (9/10 from Mildenhall, 26/27 from Feltwell, 11/11 from Honington, 10/10 from East Wretham, 4/5 from Waterbeach) dropped $1 \times 4{,}000$-lb, $26 \times 1{,}000$-lb, 296×500-lb, 53×250-lb and $5{,}400 \times 4$-lb incendiaries. A/C attacked from 17,000 down to 15,000 feet. First A/C to arrive saw no fires, but many large fires with explosions were soon started. One A/C saw one very large central fire with twenty-two others and another A/C, which dived from 3,500 to 1,500 feet for his second run, saw many explosions and much smoke around the aiming point. A third scored a direct hit on the railway sheds from 2,000 feet. The 4,000-lb bomb dropped in the middle of fires at or close to aiming point. Later A/C could not locate the aiming point owing to smoke, which rose to 8,000 feet, flames lit up the interior of A/C and other attacking Wellingtons were clearly visible. The last A/C reported the whole town to be ablaze, with fires visible from the Zuiderzee. Some balloons were reported, of which at least two were shot down.

Of three Stirlings from Oakington detailed to attack Magdeburg, one dropped $5 \times 1{,}000$-lb, 1×500-lb and 480×4-lb incendiary. Bomb-bursts and whitish explosions from the sources of the fires were seen. Weather was very hazy.

Rotterdam. Three freshman crews, Wellington Mk ICs from Waterbeach. One attacked and in addition one Wellington Mk IC from main target. The latter scored a direct hit on a large gasometer or oil tank, setting it well alight. The other A/C saw very large fires north of the river in the area Z3C.[2] Fires were visible for at least 50 miles.

Four A/C of the Czech Squadron were intercepted by fighters off the Dutch coast. In one, the tail gunner was wounded. In the other, the fuselage caught fire, the crew putting the fire out with extinguisher. The undercarriage was unserviceable, but the Captain brought the A/C back to base and landed it safely on its belly.

The main operation was an outstanding success and has been compared to the attack on Kiel in April.

Münster was also attacked by twenty-eight Whitleys from No. 4 (B) Group. All eighty-nine aircraft bombed between 1.08 and 2.13 a.m., which gives an average attack of almost 1.5 aircraft per minute. We flew on W5682/KX-Y, with our crew of Korda, Horáček, myself, Parolek, Čtvrtlík and Kovařík. I have nothing to add to the official account.

The two aircraft attacked were R1451/KX-P, flown by FS Schoř, and R1532/KX-R, flown by FS Bernát. At first, the rear gunner, Sgt Kadlec, a very nice young chap, returned fire against the fighter. It was hit and broke off the engagement. The rear turret of our aircraft was hit by three bullets or cannon shells. Two rounds travelled to the right and left around the gunner's head, while the third smashed his leg. Kadlec had his leg amputated below the knee during an emergency surgery at Ely Hospital. The wound is now comparatively better. In R1532, the fuselage was set ablaze by incendiary bullets. According to the skipper's report, the navigator, Plt Off. Kula, was the only one to panic and rush to the escape hatch to bale out. Bernát prevented that and had him help extinguish the fires instead. The second pilot, Sgt Linka, flew the plane while Bernát (with the aid of W/T operator FS Haering) was instrumental in putting out the fire. Plt Off. Kula received bad burns to his face and both hands as he rushed right through the flames to reach the hatch. He had previously jumped from a burning Anson over Peterborough with his skipper, Fg Off. Němec. The remaining five airmen were killed. FS Bernát proclaimed that he would never fly with Plt Off. Kula again.[3]

I forgot to mention that on 1 July we lost Sgt Helma and his freshman crew in R1516/KX-U. The crew comprised Sgt Helma, Sgt Plocek, Plt Off. Hapala, Sgt Dolejš, Sgt Petrucha and Sgt Lančík. Helma had done over twenty sorties, while the rest of the crew was on its first trip.[4] While on their way back from Cherbourg, France, at 12,000 feet, near the aerodrome at Old Sarum, Wiltshire, they appear to have been shot down by one of our own fighters. The Wing Commander who was flying the Beaufighter that possibly shot Helma down came to Honington. He was very depressed about his tragic error. The Wing Commander has already shot down seventeen enemy aircraft.[5] It was the fault of both sides; Helma ignored all rules of flying over England. He was way too high and without resin lights. The fighter pilot wasn't careful enough either when it came to identifying his target. This should not have been too difficult in such a clear night. Hapala was one of our crack musicians. On the same night, Wellington T2561/KX-A, piloted by Fg Off. Pohlodek, with Plt Off. Macenauer as navigator, hit a balloon cable over Coventry, Warwickshire, but got away with it.[6] The navigation must have been pretty awful in that case.[7]

My next raid was on 7 July, against Cologne, Germany. We were reunited with an old friend, T2972/KX-G. Our crew that night was Korda, Horáček, myself, Parolek, Čtvrtlík and Janšta. Bomber Command sent out 301 aircraft. Here is Bomber Command's Intelligence Report in its entirety:

Cologne
Forty-seven Wellingtons of No. 1 Group and forty-three of No. 3 Group attacked in perfect weather. Slight ground haze, subdued searchlight glare and many satisfactory results were seen. 1 × 4,000-lb bomb fell 2 miles north-east of aiming-point of eastern side of river, another half way between aiming points A and C and the last one between aiming point C and the river. All three caused colossal explosions, which illuminated a vast area, and yet another tremendous explosion took place in the centre of the town. No. 3 Group report the majority of their bombs well within target area, including one on a large gas holder on the west bank of river, which caused black smoke to raise to a great height, followed by flames, having the appearance of some gigantic torch. Direct hits were also observed on the marshalling yards of Cologne-Kalk and Cologne-Gereon. A/C from No. 1 Group also noted the pall of smoke covering the town and gave up the idea of counting the smaller fires burning throughout the city.

Münster
Forty-one Wellingtons of No. 3 Group in excellent weather added to the havoc wrought on previous nights. Map reading was possible from the Dutch coast to the target area and it was possible to note the devastation around the aiming point. On this account one A/C deliberately bombed the railway junction, registering a direct hit, the fires from which were confirmed by other A/C. It was difficult to record individual bursts in the town itself, owing to the fires raging, but a warehouse was seen in the act of collapsing and aerodrome buildings were set on fire. One terrific flame visible for 60 miles is thought to have been the gas works.

Rheydt
Eleven Hampdens identified and attacked the goods siding at Rheydt and a further seven attacked targets in the town. Large fires and several smaller ones were started. One Hampden was forced to jettison owing to an attack by a Bf 110, which was last seen spinning earthwards.

Osnabrück
Forty-four A/C from No. 4 Group attacked the marshalling yard and immediate vicinity. Many fires were started, the glow from which could be clearly seen up to 60–80 miles. Many bursts were seen in the marshalling yard and also in the town itself, and reports generally indicate a highly successful attack.

Frankfurt
Twelve Halifaxes of No. 4 Group and three Stirlings of No. 3 Group attacked their target. A direct hit was registered on the marshalling yard, starting a very large fire, and other bombs straddled the railway station. Fires had obtained a good hold when later arrivals appeared over the area.

Boulogne
Five Wellingtons of No. 1 Group attacked the docks and harbour installations with good results.

Other targets attacked
No. 1 Group—Dunkirk and Aachen by two A/C unable to climb sufficiently to attack their primary. Good results seen in dock area at the former place and fires increasing in size at Aachen.

No. 3 Group—Tidal basin at Dunkirk by one A/C, Ostend—outer harbour by two A/C, Burgsteinfurt to the north-west of Münster by two A/C, starting fires visible for 60 miles, Rheine by one A/C, results not seen.

No. 4 Group—Lengerich, Texel aerodrome, Terschelling, Den Helder dock and the Münster-conflagrations were attacked by A/C unable to bomb their primary targets for various reasons.

No. 5 Group—Düsseldorf by five A/C, Duisburg by two A/C, Rheydt by two A/C, Ehrenfeld by two A/C, one very large fire in building near railway Wesel, the marshalling yard at Neuss, Krupps' works Essen and the railway between Möchengladbach and Cologne by one A/C apiece.

In the early morning of 8 July, we had only just returned when we were informed that we would be required for another raid that same evening. One largely underestimates the strain of operating on two consecutive nights. It's 4.30 a.m., and you've just returned from a raid. You sit through an intelligence debriefing and then have breakfast. From 6 a.m. until noon, you sleep—or at least try to. Very often you are woken up by the noise in the overcrowded house, which is compounded by the stifling daytime. After a late lunch it is off to parade from 2.15 to 3 p.m. The pre-flight inspection of aircraft and subsequent test flight goes from 3 p.m. to 4.30 p.m. After that, from 6.00 to 7.00 p.m., is an operational briefing on flight details. After dinner, we head out to the aircraft at 10 p.m. and are soon airborne. I think that the 'Manitou' realises that it doesn't pay to have the same crews operate on consecutive nights. Two raids in a row is an exception.

The night of 8–9 July was a moonlit one; things have a tendency of happening on nights like this. We had the same crew and Wellington as we did the previous night.

Our aircraft was part of a force of forty-nine Wellingtons detailed to bomb Münster again. It must be in a sorry state by now, after all the attacks. Visibility was exceptional due to the aforementioned moonlight, as long as we were not too far inland. While over the Netherlands, we had a marvellous view of the big streams in the southern part of the country. We looked down upon the Waal, Rhine, and the Meuse, the strange bends of the river Ijssel, and finally the Rhine itself, turning southwards towards the Ruhr basin and Cologne.

Ground haze in Germany made it difficult to identify the comparatively small target that night. Quite a number of crews had the same trouble. Flares were seen everywhere in the area. We cruised around over Münster for around half an hour. There was little danger because the city's defences were almost non-existent. We finally were able to pick up the characteristic Dortmund-Ems-Kanal on the eastern boundaries of the town and make a satisfactory bombing run. The air was full of our aircraft—maybe too full, as I saw another Wellington through my bottom window, passing underneath us only a few scant yards away. We returned without any incident. The only drawback was the sub-standard performance of Plt Off. Parolek. He is a really a nice boy, but perhaps he is still too much of a little boy for such a serious job. He cut one of his fingers over the target. According to Parolek, this injury rendered him unable to throw flares or photo flashes. On the way back he had some trouble with his W/T set, and instead of trying to repair it, he sat back and did nothing.

The big news in the Squadron is that Sgt Blatný received the DFM for his act of bravery while over Hamburg on 11 May. He was struck in the head by a splinter, but persevered at the controls, bombed the target, and only turned the controls over to the second pilot when he had brought his aircraft safely out over the North Sea.

We are finally a complete crew once again, with Korda, Horáček, Slánský, Čtvrtlík, Janšta and me on our 'old' T2972/KX-G. Our old team went on a raid on Cologne on 10 July. It had been an unusually long spell of clear weather, with great visibility. On 7 July, we had been able to see the smallest of details in the town below us, including being able to count the number of bridges crossing the Rhine. Things were to be very different this time. We had to deal with solid clouds that prevented us from seeing a single thing. Accordingly, the bombing was very haphazard. Many of the crews mistakenly bombed towns ranging from Koblenz, in the south, and Duisburg, in the north, mistaking them for Cologne. The Germans didn't waste too much ammunition on us. If it had not been for the groups of searchlights trying in vain to pierce the clouds, we wouldn't even have been able to determine the approximate position of the town. Altogether, it was a very unsatisfactory raid.

On Saturday 12 July, I attended a conference of Navigation Officers from No. 3 (B) Group at Mildenhall. Before noon, we were shown a new invention known as the 'Synthetic Astro Trainer'. Its purpose is to teach astro navigation on the ground. The trainer was built by Sqn Ldr Cruickshanks, and it allows the navigator to take a ground sight in times of complete overcast by projecting a lighted dot on a lens instead of the actual star. We then had lunch, which was very good indeed compared to what we are getting on our station. The adulate conference started at 2 p.m., with Flt Lt Cousins, Group Navigation Officer, presiding. After the conference, I went to the aerodrome, where I should have been picked up by plane. Sqn Ldr Ocelka (in R1371/KX-F) did not arrive until almost 5.30 p.m. I just about managed to get to Wretham in time for briefing. That night, we went to Bremen with the same plane and the same crew as the two nights beforehand. The No. 3 (B) Group Operational Narrative for this raid is as follows:

> Owing to probable adverse weather conditions, the effort was cut down to twenty-nine Wellingtons, including two Mark IIs.
>
> Waterbeach ran into a series of thunderstorms stretching from Ijmuiden to the south of the Zuiderzee, and of the ten A/C detailed, five turned back, one being due to engine trouble. One A/C reached Bremen, but could not identify anything and brought bombs back. Three A/C, including one Mk II, bombed around Bremen. The Mk II thought the 4,000-lb dropped in Wildeshausen. The other 4,000-lb-bomb is believed to have dropped in Bremen between the large marshalling yard and the Deschimag Werke after making several runs over the target and sustaining flak hits.[8]
>
> East Wretham had better luck, seven out of eight A/C reaching Bremen, where one fire south of the town was seen on arrival. Bombs were dropped near the river south-west of the town, near the railway station, and 1 mile south-east of the railway several small fires started. The eighth A/C ran in the tail end of a storm around Emden and heavy icing accumulation caused the A/C to lose height rapidly, so bombs were jettisoned and the A/C returned to base.
>
> Honington got A/C on to the target area and through they report nil to 2/10 cloud over the target area, visibility was rotten. One A/C going north to avoid thunderstorms reached Wilhelmshaven and bombed this, another bombed Leer, and a third Dreye, south-east of Bremen. The total number of the bombs dropped on Bremen was 1 × 4,000-lb, 3 × 1,000-lb, 55 × 500-lb, 3 × 250-lb and 2,040 × 4-lb incendiary bombs.

We ran into our first thunderstorm just as we reached the Dutch coast. Huge thunderclouds were towering several thousand feet above our heads. The view of the fantastic cloud formations was marvellous as we flew through a narrow gap between the cells. We encountered another thunderstorm over the east bank of the Zuiderzee, but it was less powerful than the first. We must have reached the target during a spell of clear weather, and we were able to make a perfect run downriver from south-east to north-west. Flak was extremely heavy, and our plane was rocked by explosions. We brought back a photo of the target area that showed the fire from bursting shrapnel. The bursts must have been uncomfortably close. We decided to leave the area travelling northwards, so as to cross the German coast between

Emden and Wilhelmshaven. It would then be a quiet homeward-bound trip over the sea. However, I doubt if it was worthwhile. All along the comparatively short run overland, we had to make many erratic manoeuvres to avoid exceptionally strong flak. It wasn't until we flew out to sea, over the island of Spiekeroog, that we were out of what amounted to one of the worst 'Hell's kitchens' I have ever experienced. The rest of the trip was uneventful except for a miserable area of rain we had to pass through just off the coast of England.

There are a few famous personalities around. Mr Boothby MP is infamous for his connection to the scandal involving Mr Weisenger and financial claims against Czech banks.[9] He is now a Plt Off. at the Administration Branch in Honington. As he has no apparent special skills, he performs various duties, and as such he is also Court Martial Officer. He must be pretty good at that, judging by his own record.

On the 14 July we were off to Bremen again with T2972/KX-G. Sgts Kubalík and Kocman are filling in temporarily, while our regular air gunners, Plt Off. Janšta and FS Čtvrtlík, are on a refresher course at Newmarket.[10] We were faced with thunderstorms again. We went through one just over the English coast and experienced a very bumpy fifteen minutes. By the time we reached the Netherlands, the aircraft had gained enough altitude to be above the thunderclouds. There was no further trouble until we reached Bremen itself. We were lucky, but Germans not. The skies were cloudy everywhere except for over the town. We had an unrestricted view of the terrible mess below. There were countless fires burning, several of which were huge, with lots of smoke hanging over the town. It seemed to be an exceedingly successful raid. The flak wasn't as bad as last time; the gunners were probably blinded by flames and smoke. For the route home, we had decided to go around Oldenburg from the south, and then to turn straight north. We would then cross the German coast halfway between Emden and Wilhelmshaven. However, our plans were spoiled by the extraordinarily heavy barrage all along the German coast. We kept on a westerly heading to avoid it, and after we had passed Emden, we considered it unnecessary to go any further north, remaining on track. We crossed the Dutch coast slightly south of Texel.

Our squadron is operating with trying regularity every other day. On 16 July, the destination was Hamburg, Germany, in T2972/KX-G. We flew with the normal bulk of the crew, including Plt Off. Šimon and Sgt Kovařík as air gunners. Šimon has the notorious reputation of being the Squadron's biggest drunk. It was an extremely unpleasant raid. We went in overland and ran right into the flak barrage at Bremen. Hamburg and its whole surrounding area was covered by 10/10 cloud (with the exception of a few occasional gaps). Despite this, the Germans were shooting with surprising accuracy. After stooging around for some time, we couldn't do any better than to release our bombs on the apparent centre of flak and searchlights. I gave a course of 326° magnetic, which would have brought us out to sea along the east bank of the Elbe River. Here, the flak was so fierce that Vašek considered it necessary to divert to the north and north-northeast.[11] It wasn't any more pleasant there, either. We got into some extremely nasty flak over Neumünster and in the area of Kiel. I was in the astrodome—what an exciting view of the gun flashes that lit up the clouds from below and of the shells bursting all around us. The German sound locators must be pretty good. We saw a row of shells bursting behind our tail. The next salvo was much closer. Vašek would react by sharply turning left or right. The German flak gunners would be baffled for a few moments, but they usually had us again after half a minute or so. To me, it seemed like a miracle that we got out of there without a scratch. We eventually succeeded in getting out over the sea, above the group of islands of Sylt and Amrum, along the outer fringes of the old Danish-German frontier. We intentionally went fairly far out to sea to avoid the German fighter patrols. Now north of the Frisian Islands, the pilot turned the Wellington to a south-south-westerly heading, eventually crossing the Norfolk coast around Cromer. We finally touched down in daylight, after six hours and fifteen minutes in the air.

We lost another crew that night. They were Sgt Nýč, Sgt Šťastný, Plt Off. Zafouk, Plt Off. Černý, Sgt Mareš, and Sgt Knap, who were flying R1718/KX-N. Černý was twenty-one and married to a Danish girl. She was also twenty-one. I seldom saw a nicer couple. Both were very young, very blonde, and very much in love. He reminded me of young Purser, who, alas, has gone over the line too, during a raid against Hamburg. Nýč was very nice and keen, but got into trouble for a spectacular low-flying display over Bury St Edmunds. He was about to appear before a Court Martial.[12] Šťastný was a funny little guy whom they called 'Coyote', or '*Ušák*' in Czech. I think he was only twenty. Zafouk was one of our smartest officers and one of the few to speak good English. We certainly lost an excellent crew. Incidentally, we received news that of the crew we lost on 22 June, Bufka is safe and a prisoner of war, but the five others seem to have been killed.

Yesterday, on 17 July, I cycled to Thetford during the afternoon with Plt Offs Zimmer, Mareš, and Slánský. We watched *The Bluebird*, starring Shirley Temple. I enjoyed the 15-mile ride and the picture as well.

The Germans have paid us visits over the past few nights. Our main concerns lay with the Czech Training Flight, which is now at Wretham. When the OTF is carrying out night flying, the flare path is fully lit for several hours. The 'Chance Light' is switched on at intervals of some ten minutes or so.[13] Moreover, one or two planes continuously circle the aerodrome with their navigation lights switched on. A German machine came in regularly between midnight and 1 a.m. from 17–19 July. On the first night, there was no real attack. On 18 July, the Germans released a stick of ten bombs close to the flare path on the east side of the aerodrome. The following night, the Germans initially shot at one of our training planes, then releasing a stick of bombs on the south-west edge of our field. Two did not explode.[14] There was no damage at all, which again proves how senseless it is to bomb an auxiliary field with dispersed aircraft. On 18–19 July, the bombing kept me awake for a short time. Our roommate, Plt Off. Engel, ran out of the room, stating he wanted a better view of things.

From the window, I saw him with a group of four or five others in pyjamas; one was our Gunnery Leader, Fg Off. Fürbach, who was standing in front of the Wretham Hall close to the shelter entrance.

On 19 July, at around 11.30 a.m., Fg Off. Stránský took off for an air test in Wellington R1804/KX-D. For some unexplained reason, during take-off he veered from his track and ran straight into a steamroller working on the aerodrome. The plane caught fire and the civilian driver of the steamroller was killed. It is possible that a wheel may have been punctured. I arrived at the aerodrome after the plane was already half burnt-out. The steamroller's civilian driver lay unrecognisable, a smouldering mass, just a few short paces from the wreckage. The crew escaped, with Stránský receiving slight injuries to his left hand.[15]

In the evening, we went on a raid to Hanover aboard T2972/KX-G. Our gunners on this occasion were Sgts Svoboda and Kovařík. Svoboda was studying law in Brno, and during his seventh semester, in the autumn of 1939, he had been arrested by the Germans. The weather was again rather unsettled, but over the target it was clearer than anywhere else. Visibility was hampered by the dark night and layers of cloud. We circled around over the target for more than half an hour, running into all kinds of flak barrages. Hanover is in the centre of the Steinhuder Meer–Hildesheim–Celle triangle. Countless guns were laying a terrific barrage there. In the midst of shells bursting all around us, we finally released our bombs. Slánský had a typical experience; he had just opened the flare chute and dropped a reconnaissance flare when a shell burst just underneath. The force of the blast came up through the chute opening, causing him to stumble backwards. On the trip home, searchlights and flak bothered us quite a bit. Over England, in some places the cloud stretched all the way to the ground. I got as far as the beacon at Waterbeach before I successfully corrected myself and set a course for home.

That night we lost another crew—the fourth in four weeks. The crew of R1371/KX-F was Sgt Netík, Sgt Jindra, Plt Off. Partyk, Sgt J. Čtvrtlík, Sgt Valeš and Sgt Babáček. An aircraft was seen by the crew of another aircraft in combat with a fighter over the searchlight belt close to Osnabrück. Both the bomber and the fighter went down in flames. It may have been Netík. Čtvrtlík is the brother of our crew's front gunner, FS M. Čtvrtlík. Valeš has been our front gunner since 1 July. Babáček had been Šedivý's gunner. FS Šedivý finished his 200 hours on 16 July, and Babáček, who was short by thirty hours on account of illness, was with another crew for the first time. So was Šedivý's old plane, R1371. That's fate for you. Šedivý's old gunners, Cupák and Babáček, were called the 'Israelites' because they are very dark. They were inseparable friends. Our last losses are Bufka (22. 6.), Helma (1. 7.), and Netík (19. 7.).[16]

The Group's activity during June 41 is shown in this table:

Squadron	Day/Night-sorties	Hours flown	Bombs dropped in pounds
75	0/128	655.08	412,330
57	0/118	637.50	375,640
214	0/116	579.40	355,790
218	0/112	586.21	338,248
115	0/95	470.20	262,460
40	0/86	419.22	260,820
311	0/82	385.58	256,180
9	10/81	413.04	237,620
149	0/78	409.38	227,820
99	0/78	339.54	212,240
7	7/58	321.11	447,800
15	7/48	262.18	419,980
Total	24/1,080	5,480.44	3,806,928

By now, Stirlings are mostly relegated to daylight operations. Daylight activity consisted of fourteen sorties by Stirlings from Nos 7 and 15 (B) Squadrons. No. 9 (B) Squadron flew ten sorties, the most notable one involving the tragic loss of Wg Cdr Arnold, who lost his life while part of a flight of four over Calais. The six other North Sea sweeps were not considered to be air raids.

Our squadron is not doing badly as far as the weight of bombs per sortie is concerned. Here is the list (pounds of bombs per sortie):

1. No. 75 (New Zealand) Sqn   3,221
2. No. 57 Sqn   3,183
3. No. 311 (Czech) Sqn   3,124
4. No. 40 Sqn   3,033
5. No. 218 Sqn   3,020
6. No. 214 Sqn   3,015
7. No. 149 Sqn   2,921
8. No. 9 Sqn   2,795
9. No. 115 Sqn   2,768
10. No. 99 Sqn   2,721

I have not included Nos 7 and 15 (B) Squadrons, who are operating Stirlings.

We have had an easier spell, not going on another raid until July 23. However, we were on continuous standby, with preparations being made for daylight raids. We practised formation flying and there were rumours that beam guns would be mounted. I, for one, have not seen them yet.

On 23 July our target was Mannheim, Germany. We flew Wellington T2972/KX-G, with our usual crew except for the inclusion of Sgt Šebela, from Flt Lt Šejbl's crew, instead of Sgt Horáček, who is ill again. The flight wasn't very exciting, although Mannheim is well-defended by flak and searchlight belts running in a semicircle around the town. It was very hazy, and we were fortunate to at least see the Rhine in the glow of a flare. The only interesting thing we saw was a big 'V' formed by white lights in the Ghent area. The point of the 'V' was pointing inland, while the two sides opened towards the coast. The whole show was switched off when we passed.

On 25 July, we went to Hamburg in Wellington T2972/KX-G. We had the same old crew with the exception of Plt Off. Nejezchleba, who was flying instead of Horáček. The weather was not great on the way to the target, but it was just lovely in the target area. Although there was no moon, the visibility was exceptional. We had crossed the Schleswig coast somewhat to the north of the Elbe Estuary before simply flying down the river, which was plainly visible from a distance of 5–10 miles. It so happened that we were the first aircraft to reach the target. The German defences were caught off-guard and only started to fire when we were right over them. We dropped two flares, the second during our bombing run. The town below was clearly visible. There was virtually no response from flak, although less lucky aircraft were hotly engaged by ground defences all over the area, especially over Cuxhaven. We started a good fire practically in the centre of town. German clothing-ration cards were dropped instead of leaflets.[17] These should prove to be hard nuts to crack for the Germans. On the way back, we passed a very powerful searchlight on the Schleswig coast. It beamed dots of light up—presumably some type of code for the marauding night fighters. This was an uncomfortable sight, but nothing happened. On the way back, the oil temperature gauge for the starboard engine dropped to zero and for a short while we were worried. However, we soon saw that it was only that the counter had become unserviceable.

We've had a number of visitors to the station lately. Wg Cdr Toman came over during the weekend. There were two military judges—Lt Dupel and 2nd Lt Maláč from Leamington—and one 2nd Lt Pavlík. Maláč pretended to know me from Brno. Pavlík made a name for himself as a successful climber in the Tatra Mountains. He and I rejoiced in memories of climbs in better times. It is interesting to hear that at Leamington, where they have 2,800 officers and other ranks all together, there are 265 court martial procedures running—mostly for cases of absence without leave, desertion, and insubordination. It's an appalling state of affairs.

Here is another interesting set of statistics about Bomber Command's night-bombing activities during June 1941:

Operations carried out over a twenty-four-night period with more than 100 aircraft being dispatched. Altogether, 3,239 night sorties were made.
  Sorties and losses:

No. 311 (B) Squadron, 1 July–11 August 1941

Group	A/C type	Sorties	Losses
1	Wellington I	432	10 (2.3%)
2	Wellington I	46	–
3	Wellington I	975	15 (1.5%)
3	Wellington II	32	3 (9.4%)
3	Stirling	112	5 (4.5%)
4	Whitley	630	25 (4%)
4	Wellington II	82	1 (1.2%)
4	Halifax	67	1 (1.5%)
5	Hampden	802	12 (1.5%)
5	Manchester	61	2 (3.3%)
Total		**3,239**	**74 (2.3%)**

Only 'missing' aircraft are tabulated—not those which crashed in England or close to the shore. Day activities, mainly by Blenheims of No. 2 (B) Group and Stirlings of No. 3 (B) Group, are taken into account.

Details are now also available of the big daylight operation on 24 July 1941, concentrated on ports in north-western France. The following Squadrons participated: Nos 90, 44, 144, 106, 18, 139, 226, 114, 107, 35, 76, 40, 218, 115, 75, 57, 99, 101, 405, 104, 150, 103, 12, and 142. Altogether, 150 aircraft were dispatched.

Target	A/C type	Group	A/C Dispatched	A/C Attacked	Bombs in pounds	Bomb height in feet
BREST *Gneisenau*	Fortress	2	3	3	12 × 1,000	30,000–32,000
	Hampden	5	18	18	67 × 500 2 × 250	13,000–14,500
CHERBOURG Docks	Blenheim	2	35	34	135 × 250 68 × 40	12,000–13,000
LA PALLICE *Scharnhorst*	Halifax	4	15	8	15 × 2,000 53 × 500	13,500–14,500
BREST *Gneisenau*	Wellington	3	36	30	162 × 500	12,800–15,200
	Wellington	4	18	14	8 × 2,000 80 × 500	12,000–14,000
	Wellington	1	24	19	6 × 1,000 96 × 500	14,800–16,000
BREST *Prinz Eugen*	Wellington	1	1	1	6× 500	

Table of losses:

Group	A/C type	A/C lost (one A/C per squadron unless stated)	German A/C destroyed	German A/C probably destroyed	German A/C damaged
1	Wellington	12 Sqn, 103 Sqn	6	1	2
3	Wellington	75 Sqn, 101 Sqn, 218 Sqn, 40 Sqn	7	–	4
4	Halifax	35 Sqn (2 A/C), 76 Sqn (3 A/C)	4	1	4
	Wellington	405 Sqn (2 A/C), 104 Sqn	1	2	–
5	Hampden	44 Sqn, 144 Sqn	5	1	–
Total		**16**	**23**	**5**	**10**

Accompanying fighters from twenty-nine squadrons destroyed twelve enemy aircraft, probably destroying a further four, and damaged five, while losing seven aircraft themselves. The enemy aircraft destroyed were Bf 109 Es, Bf 109 Fs, and one He 113.[18] The number of enemy fighters destroyed by our bombers is rather surprising. It was our biggest daylight attack, with 300 fighters and 150 bombers taking part.

I was awarded the Czech Military Cross and Czech Gallantry Medal.[19] We received the news that of the crew we lost on 16 July, at least four members—Plt Off. Zafouk, Sgt Nýč (the skipper), Sgt Šťastný, and Sgt Knap—are safe and being held as prisoners of war. There is no news yet about Plt Off. Černý and Sgt Mareš, who were with them.

After a rather long lull, we were out again to Hamburg, Germany, on 2 August, aboard Wellington T2972/KX-G. We had our usual crew, with Sgt Filler as second pilot. He somehow managed to wangle his way out his Court Martial ceremony. It was a rather good effort. A total of 206 aircraft were dispatched, with 106 sent to Hamburg, fifty-two to Kiel, twenty-nine to Berlin, fourteen to Cherbourg, and five on mining. Bomber Command's official report on the night's operations reads as follows:

Berlin
Three Wellingtons of No. 1 Group, four Wellingtons and three Stirlings of No. 3 Group and eight Halifaxes and fourteen Wellingtons of No. 4 Group reached the Berlin area. There was little cloud, but some ground haze resulted in poor visibility. There were no signs of a smokescreen. Four Wellingtons of No. 3 Group delivered their 4 × 4,000-lb bombs, with one of them diving from 16,500 feet to 6,000 feet to make the bombing more accurate. In all cases, terrific explosions and flashes were seen which started many fires. All other aircraft dropped their bombs

in the area and saw bomb blasts start a number of fires and explosions. One report mentions about ten of our aircraft over Berlin at the same time.

Hamburg
Seven Wellingtons of No. 1 Group, twenty-eight Wellingtons and one Stirling of No. 3 Group, and twenty-one Whitleys and one Wellington of No. 4 Group dropped their loads on the target area. Clouds were reported from 3/10 to 9/10 with a few gaps and haze preventing accurate pinpointing. Many aircraft however located their positions by the river and Alster tributary. A number of bursts were seen in the area east-southeast of the station. There were many fires, including a fairly large one in the Altona District as well as in the area between the docks and Alster. Harburg was not spared either. It is estimated that the city received a sharp attack.

Kiel
Eighteen Hampdens identified and attacked the target, Deutsche Werke, Kiel, whilst twenty-one others attacked the town.[20] Many bursts were seen, starting several fires. There was no cloud over the actual target, but 8/10 to 10/10 on the route and in the vicinity with moderate visibility.

Cherbourg
Twelve Wellingtons of Nos 1, 2 and 3 (B) Groups attacked the docks, starting some fires. The weather in the target area, 7/10 cloud, made observation of the results very difficult.
   Three Hampdens successfully laid mines.

Alternative Targets
Wellington Mk IIs (2 × 4,000-lb Brandenburg, 1 × 4,000-lb each Hanover, Rheine, Neustrelitz). Wellington ICs and Whitleys attacked different places in north-west Germany.

We had no thrilling adventures. The only unusual thing was that Vašek Korda was very nervous. He had done forty operations and wasn't his old self any more. He was impatient all the way out. He went so far as to see the coast of the Schleswig again and again when we were somewhere around Emden. We had lots of cloud and haze in the target area, which gave us some difficulty finding the target. The way home was quiet. Our squadron had lots of trouble that night, and the case of Fg Off. Pohlodek's crew is particularly worth noting. This crew's navigator is Plt Off. Macenauer, a strange type. He is a bright fellow and quite capable of doing his work professionally, but he is pig-headed to an extent. This causes him to make the most awful mistakes when he doesn't feel like working or when he refuses to admit to his errors.
   That night they were somewhere east of Texel, the Netherlands, and asked for a QDM, although they were too far from Honington to get a correct one. The

QDM they received led them southwards. Plt Off. Macenauer failed to realise that considering the length of time they had flown for, they couldn't possibly have reached a point to the north of the Wash. The crew had unwittingly flown south, right into the Netherlands. They found an aerodrome with a lit flare path. Taking it to be Honington, they descended to 700 feet and lowered the undercarriage in preparation to land. Had the Germans known to flash a green light, the aircraft would have landed, and they would have captured the plane, crew, codes, and confidential documents. However, they greeted it with a hail of machine-gun bullets. That got the crew thinking. After flying around for a while they encountered a Bf 110 *Zerstörer*, which fortunately did not attack. The crew withdrew to the west under cloud cover and reached England safely. There is a small lake south of Honington, and even though the Zuiderzee is quite a large body of water, some of the crew members expressed doubts about actually being anywhere close to Honington. Macenauer disagreed, making the point that the small lake may have increased in size by the recent heavy rain![21]

The position of Navigation Officer has been authorised on our satellite aerodrome. It calls for someone with the rank of Flight Lieutenant. I have been recommended for the job, effective from 2 December 1940, as I have been *de facto* Squadron Navigation Officer ever since I joined the Squadron. I heard from the Adjutant, Flt Lt Schneider, that Sqn Ldr Ocelka was initially opposed to this nomination. It was not because he holds any grudges against me, but because he was frightened of invoking the wrath of officers more senior than me who are still Pilot Officers and Flying Officers.

Korda, Slánský, Čtvrtlík and I went on our last raid on 5 August 1941. We were flying Wellington T2972/KX-G. This was the Squadron's longest-serving aircraft, flying on its forty-second operation. The rest of the crew comprised Plt Off. Janšta as rear gunner and Sgt Filler as second pilot. The target was Mannheim, Germany. It was a moonlit night, but there were lots of clouds, with a troublesome layer up to 15,000 feet and higher over the Rhine Valley. We were astounded by the inattentiveness of the German night fighters. Flying above a layer of white clouds in bright moonlight must have made us stand out like a sore thumb for many miles, and yet we were not bothered at all.

We ran into quite a bit of flak over the target. Filler, who is good for nothing, had mistaken a black shrapnel burst emerging from the white cloud for a fighter, alarming the whole crew. We felt the last blows of shells bursting nearby and saw the typical balloon-like black smoke puffs all around us. On the way back, I was often in the astrodome. I looked out at the familiar scene of searchlights and flak with a mixture of relief and sadness; it was something that I would not see again for quite a number of months at least. What a glorious night, yet one that also left me unhappy as it signalled an end to my operational flying. We flew into clouds when we were approaching England, and we didn't get below them until we were at 1,000 feet, over East Anglia. The weather was awful, with the cloud stretching to the ground in places; this restricted visibility to perhaps 1,000 yards. We had the misfortune of arriving just a few minutes after an air raid warning, with the flare path switched off. We stooged around in low clouds and rain. We would later learn that we had actually gone over Wretham twice. We finally made the decision to land at an alternate location, which turned out to be Newmarket. There was a marvellous bright flare path that had attracted quite a number of planes from various stations. We got a cup of tea and then waited during the chilly early morning until 6 a.m. Our return to Wretham took thirty minutes. I had bought a bottle of whisky earlier, and I shared it with those of us who were around in these early hours. It did not last very long. After my last flight, I went to bed with a strange feeling in my heart. It was 6 August 1941—ten days short of seven months since I went out for the first time to Emden, Germany, on 16 January 1941.[22]

As I look back on these seven months, I must first admire the energy of the leaders of the RAF, who kept up quite a good offensive with an appallingly small bomber force. Even now, Bomber Command is far from being a strong force. Bomber Command's Order of Battle at the end of June 1941 was as follows:

RAF Bomber Command HQ—High Wycombe, Buckinghamshire

No. 1 (B) Group—Hucknall, Nottinghamshire
Wellington-equipped

No. 12 Squadron, Binbrook	No. 300 (Polish) Squadron, Swinderby
No. 103 Squadron, Newton	No. 301 (Polish) Squadron, Swinderby
No. 142 Squadron, Binbrook	No. 304 (Polish) Squadron, Syerston
No. 150 Squadron, Newton	No. 305 (Polish) Squadron, Syerston

No. 2 Group (B)—Huntingdon, Huntingdonshire
Blenheim-equipped, while No. 101 'Hyderabad' (B) Squadron flew Wellingtons

No. 18 Squadron, Horsham St Faith	No. 105 Squadron, Swanton Morley
No. 21 Squadron, Watton	No. 107 Squadron, West Raynham
No. 82 Squadron, Watton	No. 110 Squadron, Wattisham
No. 90 Squadron, Watton	No. 139 Squadron, Horsham St Faith
No. 101 Squadron, West Raynham	

No. 3 (B) Group—Newmarket, Suffolk
Wellington-equipped, while Nos 7 and 15 (B) Squadrons flew Stirlings

No. 7 Squadron, Oakington	No. 99 Squadron, Waterbeach
No. 9 Squadron, Honington	No. 115 Squadron, Marham
No. 15 Squadron, Wyton	No. 149 Squadron, Mildenhall
No. 40 Squadron, Wyton	No. 214 Squadron, Stradishall
No. 57 Squadron, Feltwell	No. 218 Squadron, Marham
No. 75 (New Zealand) Squadron, Feltwell	No. 311 (Czech) Squadron, Honington

No. 4 (B) Group—York, Yorkshire
Whitley-equipped, while Nos 35 and 76 (B) Squadrons flew Halifaxes and Nos 104 and 405 'Vancouver' (B) Squadrons flew Wellingtons

No. 10 Squadron, Leeming	No. 77 Squadron, Topcliffe
No. 35 Squadron, Linton-on-Ouse	No. 78 Squadron, Middleton St George
No. 51 Squadron, Dishforth	No. 102 Squadron, Topcliffe
No. 58 Squadron, Linton-on-Ouse	No. 104 Squadron, Driffield
No. 76 Squadron, Leeming	No. 405 (Canadian) Squadron, Driffield

No. 5 (B) Group—Grantham, Lincolnshire
Hampdens, Manchesters to be introduced

No. 44 Squadron, Waddington	No. 97 Squadron, Coningsby
No. 49 Squadron, Scampton	No. 106 Squadron, Coningsby
No. 50 Squadron, Lindholme	No. 144 Squadron, Hemswell
No. 61 Squadron, Hemswell	No. 207 Squadron, Waddington
No. 83 Squadron, Scampton	

In total, this amounts to forty-eight squadrons with an operational strength of somewhere around 700 aircraft. This figure corresponds with the current maximum effort of close to 400 aircraft dispatched within a twenty-four-hour period. When I started, No. 1 (B) Group was non-operational and only beginning to convert from Fairey Battles to Vickers Wellingtons. There were no Short Stirlings, Handley Page Halifaxes, Avro Manchesters nor Boeing Fortresses (which have now joined No. 2 (B) Group). Bristol Blenheims were used in a night-time role. In spite of all that, Bomber Command was able to maintain a very good operational tempo with the small force of available Wellingtons, Whitleys, Hampdens and Blenheims. All this was achieved even though they were battling bad weather, with teething troubles in organisation and the inevitable shortcomings and availability of equipment. I am proud to have been 'one of the few' of Bomber Command.

I'll be honest—I admit that I have been pretty lucky to have come out of it unscathed. Our Canadian class came overseas thirty-seven men strong. We have lost Hill, Purser, Acland, Gilmore (still unconfirmed at this time), Rose, Mavor, Webb, Webber, Waldron, Smith, Scott, Heywood, Jepson, Craik, and Easton. That comes to total of fifteen altogether. Pidduck is probably crippled for life. These casualties amount to a 40.5 per cent loss, which is such a staggering and unacceptable attrition rate. Since I have been with No. 311 (B) Squadron, we have lost the following crews on operations: Křivda on 16 December 1940; Kubizňák on 16 January 1941; Cigoš on 6 February; Kráčmer on 17 April; Bufka on 22 June; Helma on 1 July; Nýč on 16 July; and Netík on 19 July. That is eight crews, totalling forty-five airmen, in a squadron that normally operates with eight or nine crews at a time. Twelve crews were our maximum number of sorties for one night. I was lucky to be in a crew with Korda, the Squadron's best pilot, and Slánský, our best W/T operator. I think that we have always done our duty to the best of our abilities, but we have also been careful and have benefitted from good luck, which accounts for more than anything else.

I asked for six weeks' leave and permission to spend it in Canada. The application went up to higher levels, where it was strongly recommended by both squadron and station commanders. There is nothing else for me to do now other than wait and keep my fingers crossed. Plt Off. Černý, from Nýč's crew, has now been reported safe and as a prisoner of war. The only one from the crew who was killed was Sgt Mareš.

On Saturday 9 August, I went with Flt Lt Schneider to Cavenham to see the Homes. RAF Station Mildenhall had made big changes to Cavenham Hall. They had taken over the greater part of the house as lodgings for aircrew officers. A family with three dogs, cats, and a host of other things were housed in a few rooms. I thought the arrangement to be rather homier. Mr Mann, the butler, was the image of the worthy English servant. He was slim, tall, and expressionless. Mann could not stand this unheard state of affairs and made the decision to leave. I had a very good time and decided to stay until Monday morning, while Schneider left on Saturday. Some guests showed up on Sunday, including Miss Lizzy Kirk, a nurse from Newmarket, and Plt Off. Parish, from Mildenhall's Blind Approach Flight.[23] We had a great tennis match and I didn't do too badly, despite not having played for years.

PART II
BIOGRAPHY

16

John Gellner: Solicitor, Mountaineer, Airman, Journalist

On Saturday 18 May 1907, a baby boy was born into the family of a Czech military doctor serving with the Austro-Hungarian Army. His parents, Gustav and Marie, named him Johann. Doctor Gellner came from a wealthy Jewish family. He and his wife were living in Trieste, Italy, at the time of Johann's birth.

Although both parents had Jewish ancestors, Johann's father converted to Catholicism on 22 September 1902. He brought up his children (Johann and daughter Elizabeth, who was born on 7 March 1903) as Roman Catholics too.[1] Johann was given the middle name 'Julius' at his baptism.

John, as he was known from the middle of the war until the end of his life, began school in 1913, attending several schools in Italy, Poland, and France. The constant moving was a result of his father's military postings. After the First World War, the family returned to Czechoslovakia and settled down in Olomouc. His father was Commanding Officer of the Military Divisional Hospital in Klášterní Hradisko between 1927 and 1930.

After moving to Olomouc, John began attending the Imperial and Royal Czech Gymnasium. It was later renamed as 'The State Czechoslovak Real Gymnasium'. He graduated in Professor Ferdinand Kratina's class on 22 June 1925. Later that same year, John began his studies at the Law Faculty of Masaryk University in Brno. He became a Doctor of Law after receiving his degree during a ceremony held on 14 January 1930. He was bestowed the title of *iuris utriusque doctor*, with the abbreviation 'JUDr' written before his name.

Although no official records exist of his pre-war military service, we can make a reasonable assumption based on a number of documents. According to his study materials, he appeared in front of the recruiting board on 20 March 1928. The board declared him fit for National Military Service lasting eighteen months, temporarily deferred to allow him to finish his studies. According to the information he later provided on his enlistment application (Attestation Paper) for service with the Royal Canadian Air Force in 1940, John stated that he carried out the requisite National Military Service between 1929 and 1931. He was released back to civilian life after achieving the rank of Corporal in the Reserves. He went on to complete regular military exercises in 1932, 1934, 1936 and 1938.[2]

After returning to civilian life, John went through the typical experiences in his future chosen profession prior to becoming an articled clerk with JUDr Emil Kostka, a prominent Brno lawyer. In 1937 he decided to tie the knot with Herta Michel, the daughter of a German civil servant with the Pension Institute in Opava. Opava was the provincial capital of the Sudetenland at the time. Their wedding took place on Saturday 26 June 1937 at St Thomas' Roman Catholic Church in Brno. The newlyweds moved into an apartment in a block of flats at No. 135/14 Stojanova Street, in the Brno district of Veveří. They lived there until the German occupation. A milestone event took place in John's life on 5 April 1938; after completing six intense years of practical experience in the legal service and passing the demanding bar exam, his name was put on a registry of practising barristers. John became a junior partner with the aforementioned law office.[3]

In addition to an interest in history—something he inherited from his father—John's biggest passions became mountains and climbing. He became an active mountaineer. He and his climbing companion, František Kroutil, co-wrote a five-volume work entitled *Vysoké Tatry—Horolezecký průvodce* (*High Tatras Climbing Guide*). Each of the first four volumes was published on an annual basis by the Orbis publishing company in Prague between 1935 and 1938. The last volume would remain unpublished due to the German occupation during the Second World War. A second edition, with the complete guide, was published in June 1947.

In his diary, John mentioned a stay in Vienna's Police Investigation Prison at Rossauer Lände, but he gave no further details. His arrest occurred prior to the occupation of Czechoslovakia and after the *Anschluss*—the force annexation of Austria into the Third Reich on 12 March 1938. His uncle, Prof. Arthur Lenhoff—a well-known Austrian Social Democrat—was arrested by the Gestapo, so John lobbied for his release. His endeavours resulted in his own arrest by the Gestapo in the spring of 1938. It took ten days of intervention by the Czechoslovak Consulate in Vienna to facilitate John's release. During John's incarceration, Professor Dr August Miřička, a professor of criminal law at the Faculty of Law at Charles University, Prague, and an internationally recognised expert, also worked hard to ensure his release.

On the night of 24–25 September 1938, during the second mobilisation, John went to Slovakia and joined Infantry Regiment 26 in Banská Bystrica. After the signing of the Munich Agreement on 29 September 1938, the Czechoslovak Army gradually demobilised in four phases. He was demobilised on 11 November 1938, during the third phase.[4]

The turbulent period after the Munich Agreement culminated in the German occupation of the remaining parts of the country on Wednesday 15 March 1939. An extensive preventive arrest action (under the code name *Gitter*, meaning 'Lattice') was carried out immediately within the first few hours of the occupation. It was directed against potential inciters of unrest amongst German immigrants, Jews, active Czech anti-fascists, and communists. John was arrested during this action and imprisoned in a temporary detention camp at an exhibition ground in Brno. He was released, without being questioned, after a few days. This had been a so-called 'preventive custody', similar to the previous cases in 1938. It was ratified by a decree from the Reich Interior Minister on 25 January 1938, when it was stated that political prisoners could be held for up to ten days.

A combination of this experience and further events convinced him that remaining in the *Protektorat Böhmen und Mähren*, which had been officially declared on 16 March 1939 in Bohemia and Moravia, would not be safe. John was a likely target due to his Jewish heritage and his previous experiences with the Gestapo. He found his way into exile one night before the end of March. On foot, he crossed the border into Austria through southern Moravia. It is not known how he managed to make it through Austrian territory. However, his experience as a competent mountaineer was of great benefit as he crossed the Alps in southern Austria into Maribor, Yugoslavia. John made it to his relatives in his native Trieste without any difficulties. Trieste had been a major port during the Habsburg monarchy, and in 1920 it had become part of Italy. At the end of April 1939, John was living in lodging-house Laurana in Ausonia.[5]

According to the records of the Czech Barrister Association, he was deleted from the list of lawyers on 9 May 1939, under the implementation of the Standing Committee No. 284/38 Sb., dated 16 November 1938, and Government Regulation 265/38 Sb. on 4 November. Thanks to his departure, John avoided a governmental regulation published on 4 July 1939 concerning the legal status of the Jews in public life. In the case of lawyers, they were excluded from the profession. They could only act as Jewish legal representatives. Their numbers were restricted to up to 2 per cent of the total number of lawyers registered with the Barrister Association in Prague and Brno.[6]

John Gellner was issued Visa No. 4300 at the American Consulate in the Italian city of Naples on 12 June. It came from unused Italian immigration quotas, as fascist dictator Benito Mussolini's regime did not allow the Italians to travel. John stopped in Paris on his way to the United States via Switzerland and France. He considered joining the French Foreign Legion in order to get to fight against Germany sooner. After the initial interview, he eventually decided to proceed to London and onward to the United States as originally planned.

He bought a ticket for travel on the French Line Company's SS *Champlain*. She provided a service between the ports of Le Havre, France, and New York, in the United States, by way of a stop in Southampton, Hampshire. After a seven-day voyage from Southampton across the North Atlantic, the steamer berthed at the Port of New York City on 30 June 1939.

John travelled on to the city of Buffalo, New York, located on the eastern shore of Lake Erie, where his uncle's family lived. His uncle, fifty-two-year-old Arthur Lenhoff (a fellow lawyer) was married to Clara, a native of Trieste, Italy, and twelve years his junior. They had a six-year-old daughter named Maria. The family had lived in the Austrian capital in the '30s. Because of their Jewish religion and the persecution by the Gestapo, they decided to leave Europe as soon as possible

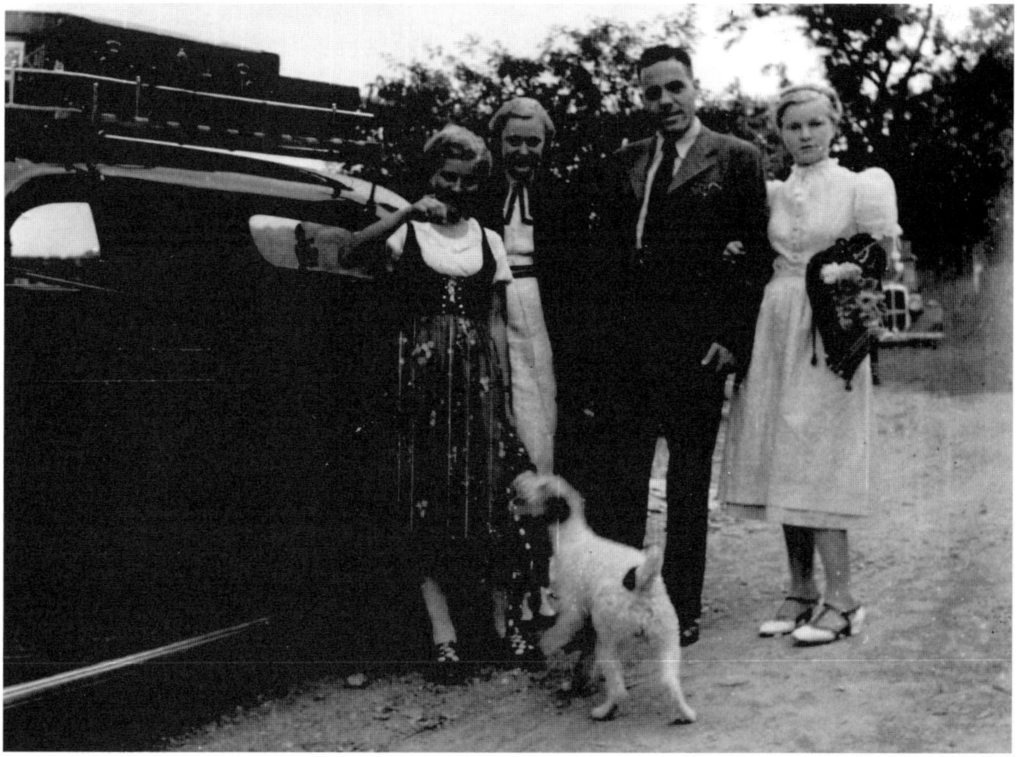

Newly married couple John and Herta Gellner standing by a Praga Lady car just before leaving for their honeymoon. It is believed that this photo of John Gellner is the only preserved example from the pre-war period. (*B. Hull*)

IMMIGRANT IDENTIFICATION CARD
UNITED STATES
DEPARTMENT OF LABOR

Gellner.
SURNAME
Johann Julius.
GIVEN NAME
Italy. May 18, 1907.
COUNTRY OF BIRTH DATE OF BIRTH
Czechoslovakian. Brown.
NATIONALITY COLOR OF EYES
NEW YORK CHAMPLAIN
PORT OF ARRIVAL STEAMSHIP
JUN 30 1939
DATE ADMITTED STATUS OF ADMISSION
IMMIGRANT'S SIGNATURE
ORIGINAL IMMIGRANT INSPECTOR

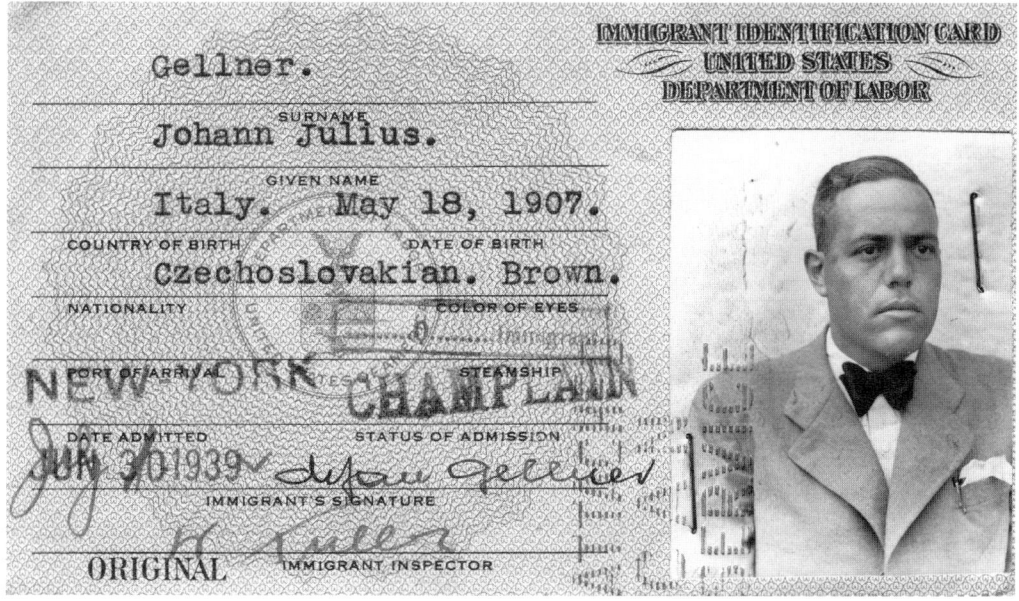

John Gellner's identity card, issued by the Consulate General of the United States in the Italian town of Naples. (*L. Gellner's Archive*)

The control tower of Malton Airport as photographed on 29 July 1940. This airport was the home of the RCAF's No. 1 AOS. (*DND Photo PL#1088*)

A group of student observers is seen preparing for one of their training flights at No. 1 AOS, Malton, on 29 July 1940. LAC J. Gellner is standing on the extreme left, while another Czech LAC, V. V. Havlíček, is standing fourth from the right. (*DND Photo PL#1079*)

Two student observers are seen entering their Avro Anson at No. 1 AOS, Malton, on 29 July 1940. (*DND Photo PL#1080*)

Learning how to operate the Browning .303-calibre machine gun at No. 1 BGS, Jarvis, Ontario, on 26 September 1940. *Left to right*: LACs I. H. Acland, A. H. A. Morris, D. S. Florence, Sgt G. B. Morrell (Instructor), LACs J. G. Flaherty, M. Williams, W. F. Webber, and W. L. Waldron. (*DND Photo PL#2213*)

Photo published in August 1940. The original caption read: 'The first class of pupils to go out from No. 1 Air Observers School, operated by Dominion Skyways (Training) Ltd. at Malton. They completed their course of air navigation at the school on August 16 and have now passed on to the Bombing and Gunnery School at Jarvis to undergo a course there. Another 40 pupils will go out in September, and this number every month from now on.'
Back row, left to right: A. B. MacKenzie, D. S. Florence, D. S. Craik, W. W. Heywood, J. Gellner, J. H. Smith, J. P. Scott, M. Williams, W. F. Webber, W. L. Waldron.
Next row, standing, left to right: J. A. Jepson, J. H. Purser, N. J. Leishman, A. E. Snell, J. R. Gilmore, T. H. Rose, C. D. Noble, J. H. C. Roberts, D. C. Martin, R. A. Mather, I. H. Acland.
Sitting, left to right: G. J. Mavor, L. C. Mansell, H. R. Easton, G. F. King, J. G. Flaherty, J. G. Pidduck, A. H. A. Morris, T. S. Royan, R. W. Alexander.
Front row, left to right: G. T. Webb, L. S. Hill, U. J. Bezaire, T. E. Carter, W. H. Cleaver, B. C. MacNab, P. J. LeBoldus, G. W. Jeffrey. (*L. Gellner's Archive*)

Fresh observers after their wings-presentation parade at RCAF Station Trenton, Ontario, on 24 October 1940. *Left to right*: LACs R. G. Shortried, L. C. Mansell, G. J. Mavor, H. R. Easton, and T. H. Rose. (*DND Photo PL#1776*)

A snapshot from Union Station in Ottawa, just prior to departure to the United Kingdom on 15 November 1940. *Left to right*: Sgts J. H. Smith and W. H. Cleaver, Plt Off. J. G. Flaherty, and Sgts J. P. Scott and M. Williams. (*DND Photo PL#1818*)

A group of Canadian observers who served with No. 42 Squadron posing in front of a Bristol Beaufort Mk I at RAF Station Leuchars, Scotland, on 17 June 1941.
Sitting, left to right: Sgts L. C. Mansell, G. F. King and N. J. Leishman.
Standing, left to right: Sgt D. C. Martin, Plt Off. A. E. Snell, Plt Off. U. J. Bezaire, Sgt A. E. Shaw and Sgt R. S. Irwin.
Except for the last two, all these airmen came from the first observer course in the BCATP. Sadly, only three of the group would survive the war. (*DND Photo PL#4327*)

Wretham Hall, which was used as officer's quarters by No. 311 (B) Squadron while they were based at East Wretham, Norfolk, from 16 September 1940 to 28 April 1942. (*Author's Archive*)

British Liaison Officer Sqn Ldr P. C. 'Pick' Pickard DSO DFC is seen chatting with the first Czechoslovak Commanding Officer of No. 311 (B) Squadron, Wg Cdr K. Mareš-Toman. (*Author's Archive*)

Above and below: Two shots of the King and Queen's visit to RAF Station East Wretham on Saturday 18 January 1941.

Above, left to right: Wg Cdr K. Toman (with back to camera, obscuring the Queen), No. 3 Group Bomber Command AOC AVM J. E. A. Baldwin, King George VI (in the uniform of the Marshal of the RAF), and Grp Capt. J. Berounský.

Below, left to right: Wg Cdr K. Toman, Queen Elizabeth, King George VI, AVM J. E. A. Baldwin, Grp Capt. J. Berounský. (*M. Lambourne*)

Above and below: Wellington Mk IC L7842/KX-T was captured by the Germans after its crew mistakenly landed at Flers airfield in France on 6 February 1941. The undercarriage sunk into the soggy ground, preventing the crew from taking off when they finally realized their mistake. Note that the white ring of the RAF roundel has been partially painted black to reduce the possibility of being spotted by enemy night fighters. (*Author's Archive*)

An unique shot of Heinkel He 111H-3, W. Nr. 3349 'A1 + CM' from 4./KG 53 after crash landing on a field near Ovington, Northumberland, on 18 February 1941. It came down after being hit by the cables of a parachute-and-cable-launcher fired from RAF Station Watton, Norfolk. (*J. Foreman*)

Sgt A. H. A. Morris on 17 June 1941, just four days after his successful torpedo attack on the German pocket battleship *Lützow* in the North Sea. (*DND Photo PL#4324*)

Resting on the stairs to Wretham Hall, spring 1941. *Left to right*: Plt Off. E. Šimon, Sqn Ldr P. C. 'Pick' Pickard DSO DFC with his pet sheepdog 'Ming', Plt Off. K. Bečvář, and Sqn Ldr J. Ocelka. (*Author's Archive*)

Although of poor quality, this is possibly the only known photo of Vickers Wellington Mk IC T2972/KX-G showing its serial number. Gellner completed twenty-five of his thirty-seven sorties aboard this kite. (*V. Kolesa*)

A commemorative picture of No. 311 (B) Squadron flying personnel in front of Wretham Hall, March 1941. Most of them are mentioned in the diary. Sadly, eighteen of the group of fifty-seven would not survive the war. (*Author's Archive*)

Sitting, left to right: Fg Off. MUDr. M. Novák, Fg Off. F. Machálek, Fg Off. J. Breitcetl, Plt Off. A. Kirchstein, Plt Off. J. Vnouček, Plt Off. V. Konštacký, Sqn Ldr J. Ocelka, Wg Cdr K. Mareš-Toman, Sqn Ldr P. C. Pickard, Flt Lt J. Šnajdr, Plt Off. F. M. Doležal, Plt Off. J. Motyčka, Fg Off. J. Gellner, Plt Off. J. Doubrava.

Standing, first row, left to right: Sgt R. Haering, Sgt F. Kráčmer, Sgt F. Radina, Sgt H. Dostál, Sgt J. Doktor, Sgt B. Procházka, Sgt J. Bernát, Sgt K. Truxa, Sgt K. Schoř, Plt Off. K. Bečvář (hidden), Sgt O. Helma, Plt Off. V. Študent, Sgt E. Mikulenka, Plt Off. J. Kostohryz, Sgt V. Kocman, Plt Off. E. Šimon, Sgt M. Čtvrtlík, Sgt P. Babáček, Sgt V. Slánský, Sgt J. Čapka, Sgt O. Langer, Plt Off. J. Liška, Sgt L. Košek, Plt Off. J. Partyk, Sgt M. Mikulík, Plt Off. A. Zimmer, Sgt A. Jedounek.

Standing, second row, left to right: Sgt F. Fencl, Sgt B. Kovařík, Sgt V. Kubalík, Sgt V. Kováč, Sgt V. Kepák, Sgt L. Kadlec, Sgt K. Janšta, Sgt P. Kudláč, Fg Off. J. Fikrle, Sgt V. Korda, Sgt F. Chmura, Sgt V. Cupák, Sgt A. Šedivý, Fg Off. L. Svátek.

Standing, top row, left to right: Sgt L. Anderle, Sgt J. Beneš.

Part of Korda's crew and ground staff in front of Wellington Mk IC T2972/KX-G. *Left to right*: (3.) Plt Off. V. Korda, (4.) FS M. Čtvrtlík, and (5.) Plt Off. K. Janšta. (*V. Kolesa*)

Sgt Anderle's crew at East Wretham in spring 1941. *Left to right*: Plt Off. J. Horák (from Lidice), Sgt J. Filler, Sgt K. Valach, Plt Off. V. Konštacký, Sgt J. Plzák and Sgt L. Anderle. (*Author's Archive*)

Above left: Captain S. Carlin MC DFC DCM, a First World War fighter ace, managed to crew up as an air gunner for one sortie with No. 311 (B) Squadron. (*N. Franks*)

Above right: No. 311 (B) Squadron's 'busiest man', Operations Officer Flt Lt A. Fantl, was awarded an MBE in August 1941. (*V. Zimola*)

Below left: Skipper Plt Off. V. Korda DFC. (*J. Čvančara*)

Below right: Wg Cdr J. Schejbal, the Squadron's second Czech CO, flew two sorties with Korda's crew. (*Author's Archive*)

Above left: A caricature of Gellner by his colleague, navigator Fg Off. S. Dvorský. (*L. Gellner*)

Above right: V. Slánský as a Colonel (Retired) wearing the Order of M. R. Štefánik, 3rd Class. This photo bears the following dedication on the reverse side: 'To Honza Gellner, my "brother in arms" at 311 Sqn, in remembrance from Laďas Slánský'. (*Author's Archive*)

A wartime portrait of wireless operator Sgt V. Slánský. (*Author's Archive*)

Above left: Front gunner Sgt M. Čtvrtlík. (*V. Kolesa*)

Above right: Rear gunner Plt Off. K. Janšta. (*V. Kolesa*)

The funeral of Plt Off. S. Zeinert, Sgt F. Dušek and Sgt M. Stoček at St. Ethelbert Cemetery in East Wretham on 30 May 1941. Padre Sqn Ldr F. Pouchlý is standing in the middle, while pilot Sgt V. Bufka is facing the camera. (*Author's Archive*)

President Dr. E. Beneš talks to No. 311 (B) Squadron airmen on Wretham Hall's terrace, 20 June 1941. *Behind him, right to left*: Minister of National Defence Gen. S. Ingr (turning away from the camera), AVM RNDr K. Janoušek KCB, Gen. A. Nižborský and Minister of Foreign Affairs J. Masaryk. (*J. Foretník*)

A detailed aerial shot of the cruiser *Prinz Eugen* in Brest's dry dock. It was struck in the upper right corner, behind the second gun turret on the port side, during a raid on the night of 1–2 July 1941. (*D. Krakow*)

Plt Off. J. Gellner after he finished his tour of operations. (*L. Gellner*)

```
HONINGTON
3 GP HQ NR  KWY122/28
PASS TO GR20

TO P/O GELLNER RAF EAST WRETHAM NORFOLK
FROM AM  CZECHOSLOVAK INSPECTORATE
P5598 28/8 BLAHOPREJI VAM K JMENOVANI   PODPORUCIKEM LETECTVA =
AVM JANOUSEK===1205
OFC
SW VA+
    R    1515 KWA VA+
```

Congratulations on your being appointed to the rank of Second-Lieutenant of the Air Force.
AVM Janousek

Copy of translation to be passed to Adj! Honington

A cable congratulating Gellner on his exceptional promotion to the rank of 2Lt in the Czechoslovak Army Air Force. It was sent by AVM K. Janoušek KCB. Note the additional handwritten translation into English and the request to return an English copy to RAF Honington's HQ. (*L. Gellner*)

'The Magnificent Seven' with their myriad pipes on display, summer 1941. *Left to right*: Fg Off. J. Fürbach, Flt Lt J. Šejbl, Plt Off. J. Simet, Plt Off. J. Engel, Plt Off. V. Korda, Plt Off. O. Kacíř and Fg Off. F. Machálek. (*Author's Archive*)

No. 1429 Czech Operational Training Flight CO Flt Lt K. Vildomec (on the right), with his successor, Plt Off. A. Šedivý, seen in the cockpit of a dual-control Wellington Mk IC at East Wretham on 16 April 1942. (*K. Vildomec via J. J. Šafařík*)

No. 1429 Czech Operational Training Flight instructors were recruited from former No. 311 (B) Squadron veterans after their tour of operations. *Left to right*: Flt Lt K. Kvapil, Flt Lt K. Vildomec, Plt Off. J. Čapka DFM, Sgt A. Jedounek, and FS J. Filler. This photograph was taken at RAF Station Woolfox Lodge, Rutland, between June and July 1942. (*V. Kolesa*)

This newspaper photo was taken during the ceremony at which Flt Lt Gellner's personal shield was put on display at Malton. *Left to right*: Sqn Ldr E. R. Pounder (No. 1 AOS Chief Instructor), W. W. Woollett (manager of Dominion Skyways Ltd, the civilian organization that aided in the training of observers), and Flt Lt J. Gellner DFC. (*L. Gellner*)

Opposite above: A meeting of 'brothers in arms'. A group of airmen who previously served with No. 311 (B) Squadron are reunited with their former colleague, Flt Lt Gellner, in Canada in early 1942. The Czechs had been posted to the country to assist in ferrying aircraft to the United Kingdom. *Left to right*: FS F. Radina, Plt Off. V. Korda, Flt Lt J. Gellner, H. Gellner, and Plt Off. O. Kacíř. (*S. Liska*)

Opposite below: A newspaper clipping of Flt Lt Gellner's receipt of the DFC. It was awarded to him by Canada's Governor General, Major General The Earl of Athlone, at Rideau Hall, Ottawa, on 3 December 1941. (*True—The Man's Magazine*)

The honour-roll board in the airmen's lounge at No. 1 AOS, Malton, in May 1942. There are observer's half-wings fitted on a two-bladed propeller, each accompanied by the name of the leader of the observer's course. Amongst the ten observers with personal shields below the propellers were three graduates from the first course—Flt Lt Gellner DFC, Fg Off. Florence DFC, and Sgt Martin DFM. The personal shields featured ribbons representing their decorations. (*DND Photo PL#8699*)

Opposite above left and right: Two newspaper photos showing Flt Lt Gellner DFC during his initial pilot training at No. 20 EFTS in Oshawa, Ontario, at the start of 1943. (*L. Gellner's Archive*)

Opposite below left: An official photo of Flt Lt Gellner DFC with his wife, Herta, in Ottowa, Ontario. It was taken on 5 December 1942. (*DND Photo PL#12653*)

Opposite below right: Flt Lt Gellner's official RCAF portrait; he is wearing the ribbons of his DFC, Czechoslovak War Cross 1939, and Czechoslovak Gallantry Medal. The portrait was taken on 5 December 1942. (*DND Photo PL#12654*)

Wg Cdr C. J. H. Holms, CO of No. 5 SFTS, pins pilot's wings on a new graduate, Flt Lt Gellner DFC, at Brantford, Ontario, on 8 July 1943. (*Author's Archive*)

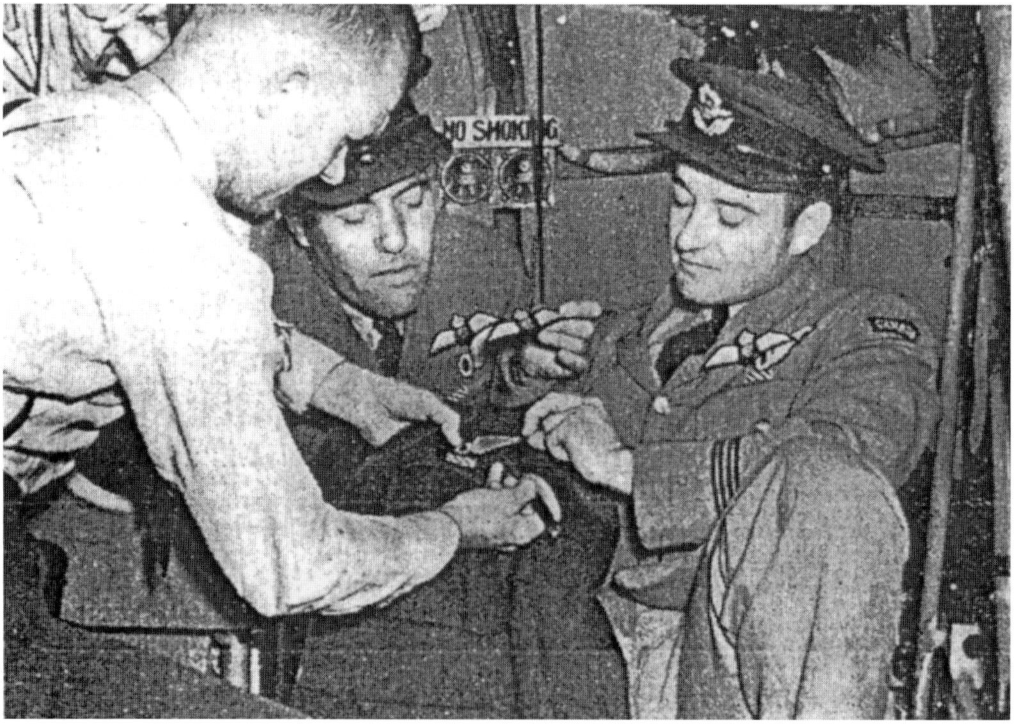

This photo shows three former observers receiving their wings after graduating from pilot training. *Left to right*: Flt Lt W. L. Jennings DFC, Flt Lt J. Gellner DFC and Flt Lt R. W. Alexander DFC. (*L. Gellner*)

A RAF Transport Command Crew Assignment Card belonging to Flt Lt Gellner DFC, containing his basic personal details. (*DHH*)

This Douglas C-47A (former USAAF s/n 42-24354) is shown while in service with the Royal Thai Air Force. It originally served with the RAF as a Dakota Mk III FL541. Flt Lt Gellner DFC ferried the aircraft overseas at the end of September 1943; it initially served with No. 194 Squadron at Basal, India. The aircraft was taken on strength with the Royal Thai Air Force on 29 August 1946. (*S. Promthep*)

Ground crew from No. 429 'Bison' Squadron RCAF admire the bison head presented to the Squadron on behalf of the Canadian National Railway's European manager, Mr. P. A. Clews, at RAF Station Leeming, Yorkshire, on 14 January 1944. (*DND Photo PL#26849*)

Opposite above: Flt Lt Mitchell's crew after he took over command from Flt Lt Gellner DFC.
Sitting, left to right: flight engineer Sgt G. W. Harris, bomb aimer FS R. N. McEachern, and rear gunner FS R. E. Nelson.
Standing, left to right: Mid-upper gunner Sgt C. M. Wert, pilot Flt Lt S. S. Mitchell, and navigator Fg Off. J. H Johnston.
Wireless operator Sgt R. M. Almas is absent. (*J. Pilling-Cormick*)

Opposite below: A group of RCAF personnel who took part in the official opening of No. 1 Air Division Europe's No. 3 (F) Wing at Zweibrücken, West Germany, in February 1953. The wing was formed on 2 February 1953, with Grp Capt. A. C. Hull DFC CD assuming command on 16 February. Pictured in the middle is Grp Capt. A. C. Hull DFC CD, with Wg Cdr J. Gellner DFC CD standing to the left of him. (*A. C. Hull*)

The main entrance to No. 3 (F) Wing at Zweibrücken, with a flight of four Canadair Sabres passing by. (*A. Karcher*)

Grp Capt. A. C. Hull DFC CD, Commanding Officer of No. 3 (F) Wing RCAF from 16 February 1953 to 9 January 1956, poses at the desk in his office (*B. Hull*)

Wg Cdr Gellner's identity card, issued to him upon leaving the RCAF. This card denoted his lifetime honorary membership, which granted him access to all RCAF Officers' Messes. (*L. Gellner's Archive*)

Wg Cdr Gellner DFC CD at the end of his more than eighteen years of adventure in the RCAF. (*L. Gellner*)

Lilo Mattheis and John Gellner with their guide, Hans Hari, after reaching the top of the Swiss mountain Jungfrau (13,642 feet) on 22 July 1977. (*L. Gellner*)

John Gellner is awarded the title of Doctor of Military Science at Royal Roads Military College, Hatley Park, Colwood, British Columbia, on 13 May 1983. (*L. Gellner*)

John Gellner poses with his wife, Lilo, at a reception in Rideau Hall after being appointed as a Member of the Order of Canada on 5 October 1983. (*L. Gellner*)

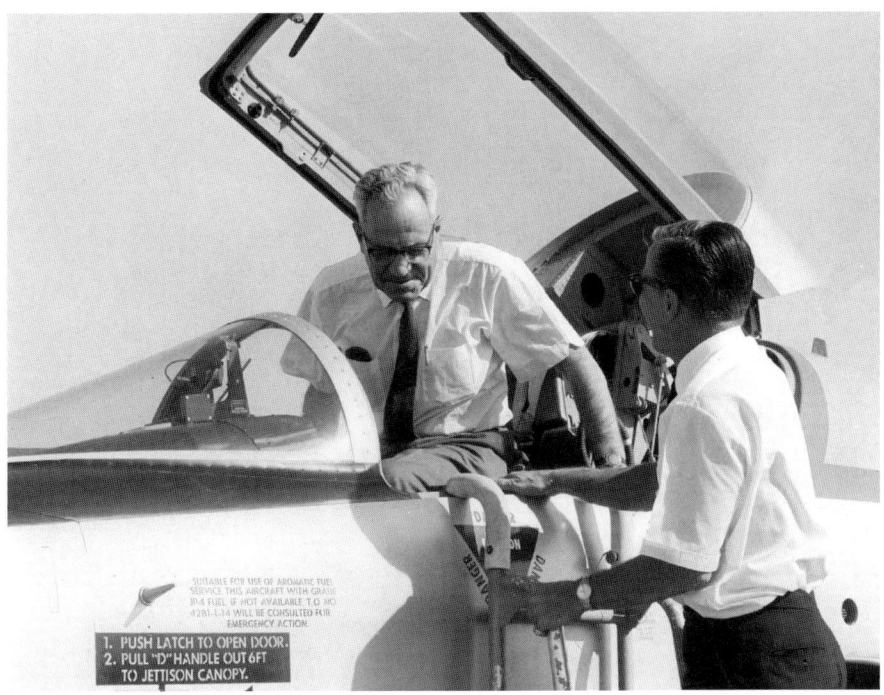

Now a journalist, John Gellner inspects the cockpit of a Northrop F-5 tactical fighter. (*B. Hull*)

Gellner receives a commemorative medal from the Czech Minister of National Defence, RNDr. Vilém Holáň, on 26 November 1994. (*L. Gellner*)

A group of Czech Army officers examine Gellner's flying log book from the war on 9 December 1997. (*L. Gellner*)

John Gellner's resting place at Caledon East Public Cemetery. The cemetery is appropriately located on Airport Road in Caledon. (*E. Murray*)

after the annexation of Austria by the Third Reich. They therefore relocated to neighbouring Switzerland, where they were issued visas by the United States Embassy in Zurich on 20 June 1938. They crossed the Atlantic in the middle of August aboard the steamer SS *Washington*. The family settled down on Lexington Avenue in Buffalo. Arthur found work as an assistant professor and librarian at the Department of Law at the University of Buffalo.

On Thursday 27 July 1939, John Gellner received a multiple-entry visa for the United States—a permit to re-enter the United States that was valid for one year. The beginning of the Second World War found him in New York, where he worked as an assistant gardener. He mainly pushed a wheelbarrow filled with earth or gravel for the gardens of one of the largest blocks of apartments, known as London Terrace. He had originally found employment through the Young Men's Christian Association, in part due to his father being an active member of this international Christian youth organisation back in Czechoslovakia.

John immediately began to consider any possible means of getting involved in the war, as long as it meant he could have a weapon in his hands. The United States was still strictly adhering to its neutrality, but the nearest country that had declared war on Germany was just across the border—Canada (on 10 September 1939). He therefore went to the Canadian Consulate to find information on how he could get into a branch of the Canadian military. The clerk was obviously surprised by such a question; he even thought Gellner might be a mercenary looking for work. While at the consulate, he bumped into two like-minded young Americans who also wanted to fight against Hitler's Germany. They simply decided to go to Canada and enlist at the nearest recruiting office. The pair offered to have him come along. It was not difficult getting across into Canada. The border officials were only asking one thing: 'Where were you born?' It was only a minor problem to find a birthplace that he could pronounce without his accent betraying his Slavic origin. He pretended to be a native of Tampa, Florida. It worked. He crossed the US-Canadian border, without a hitch, on one September afternoon.[7]

Upon his arrival in Canada, John tried to organise volunteers from the Czechoslovak immigrant community and send them to France as civilians. When they got there, they would hopefully join the Czechoslovak Army. The Czechoslovak official authorities decided to have this Czechoslovakian unit form on Canadian soil. Canadian authorities were strictly against this idea, but they did eventually start to accept foreigners into the Canadian military. Due to his continuous efforts, John eventually caught the attention of a frustrated Consul General, Dr František Pavlásek. He mentioned the difficulties associated with the organisation of the resistance in a letter dated 13 February 1940, sent from Toronto to his friend and fellow lawyer JUDr Alois Pražák, who was residing in London:

> I myself have tried from 1 October 1939 to hasten the action so that our people would be in France before foreigners would be accepted into the Canadian Army. This has been hanging above us from the beginning like the sword of Damocles. My insistence was

not liked in our official circles, i.e. the General Consulate in Montreal, my 'devotion to the nation and zeal' was suspicious to them, so they started to look at me as a possible enemy agent. I already tried to send volunteers to France in October, as now do the Finns. It was undisciplined and now is practically forbidden for me to work on this matter. I must say that, personally, I am quite glad I have nothing to do with it anymore, as the way it is being handled there will probably not even be twenty Czechoslovak soldiers sent into battle from Canada. And I do not want to make my name associated with such a debacle. In the early days of the war, there was a lot of enthusiasm to fight for the new Czechoslovakia, perhaps more than now, when those eager for action were disappointed as they found themselves sitting idle for several months.[8]

During almost six months of futile effort, Gellner survived as best he could, particularly thanks to the significant assistance from Professor Marcus Long of McMaster University in Hamilton. Long found him accommodation on campus for a few months and also some short-term work as an assistant teacher. More help was provided to Gellner by a lawyer and the Czechoslovak Honorary Consul in Toronto, Horace Hume van Wart, who engaged him as a temporary auxiliary for a small fee. Van Wart helped many Czechoslovak refugees in 1940, both financially and administratively, with their enrolment process into the Canadian military.

Under Van Wart's patronage, Gellner gave public lectures on Czechoslovakia. Before he was finally allowed to enlist in the RCAF, he and fellow Czechoslovak emigrant Vladimír V. Havlíček both lived practically penniless and served as unofficial Bren-gun instructors in Toronto. John Gellner was sworn into the Royal Canadian Air Force Special Reserve at the Recruiting Centre in Hamilton, Ontario, on Thursday 25 April 1940. He was now at the very bottom of the rank structure, a lowly Aircraftman 2nd Class with enlisted service number R64126. At thirty-three, John was considered quite old to be an aircrew candidate. In spite of this, he was immediately placed in a group of other cadets, slated for air observers' training. That same day, he moved into No. 1 Manning Depot, housed within the Horse Palace, on the grounds of Toronto's Canadian National Exhibition. While there, all recruits received a complete kit of military uniforms. Some received odd-sized uniforms, so they were sent to private tailors to make the necessary alterations. All cadets were required to have mandatory vaccinations. The rest of their time was filled by endless lining up and monkey business.

On Monday 29 April, John went off to No. 1 Initial Training School. No. 1 ITS was housed within the confines of the Eglinton Hunt Club on Avenue Road, Toronto. His stay there was filled with physical training, familiarisation with the RCAF rules and regulations, and endless military drill. At the end of ITS, one would find out what trade they had been selected for. On Friday 10 May, John appeared in front of the Medical Selection Board. The board saw no reason to object to his original aircrew classification. On 23 May, he reported to No. 1 Air Observer School in Malton, just west of Toronto. The AOS was run by the civilian company Dominion Skyways (Training) Ltd. There, he became part of the historic first air observers course, conducted within the British Commonwealth Air Training Plan (BCATP). The day after his arrival, John sewed pair of patches with small propellers onto his sleeves, indicating a promotion to the rank of Leading Aircraftman.

Meanwhile, John's twenty-one-year-old wife, Herta, also left the Protectorate (with a fair amount of luck), and, like him, she also managed to get to Italy. She received a transit visa valid for two weeks at the American embassy in Naples, Italy, on 24 May 1940. On 2 June, she left Genoa aboard the United States Line's SS *Manhattan*. Herta gave her husband's address as 94 Morningside Drive, Buffalo, New York. That was the address of a hotel. Since Buffalo is situated close the border of the Canadian province Ontario, where her husband was undergoing RCAF training, it stood to reason that they should meet there and continue directly into Canada.

Herta initially stayed at Malton House, Malton. Unable to speak a word of English, she attended language classes at a private school. When John was posted to No. 1 Bombing and Gunnery School at Jarvis, Ontario, on 18 August, Herta moved to 95 Homewood Avenue in Toronto. At Jarvis, cadets learned the principles of bombing. They then went from the classroom to flying in Fairey Battles, carrying out practice bombing against floating targets on Lake Erie. Aerial gunnery training was carried out on the same type of aircraft.

After the end of this training period, LAC Gellner was promoted to Temporary Sergeant Paid on 28 September. He was then sent to No. 1 Air Navigation School at RCAF Station Trenton, Ontario, arriving the following day. John distinguished himself by finishing the course with an average of 82 per cent. He was the top graduate amongst his thirty-seven fellow cadets. John was awarded an air observers' badge on 24 October. Thanks to his high standing on the course, he was mentioned in the Canadian press as the first ever Air Observer graduate in the BCATP. The expected commission followed on 27 October, when he was promoted to Pilot Officer and given the new Officer's Service Number J2822.

John and the entire graduating course were posted overseas. He was authorised to take Embarkation Leave between 28 October and 6 November; this was to allow him to arrange his personal affairs and to secure funds for his wife for the period of his absence. On Tuesday 12 November, Plt Off. Gellner reported to No. 3 Manning Depot in Rockcliffe, Ontario, just outside Ottawa. He was transferred to RAF Trainees Pool—Overseas with effect from 14 November. The following day saw him officially attached to No. 1 Depot RAF in Uxbridge, Middlesex. He did not actually arrive until 25 November.[9] John was put in charge of the newly minted air observers on 15 November 1940, prior to embarking on SS *Duchess of Richmond* for Britain. After its arrival, the first group of RCAF air observers was initially sent to No. 1 Depot RAF in Uxbridge. They were split up there and posted to various RAF units. Plt Off. Gellner was posted to No. 311 'Czechoslovak' (B) Squadron on 1 December, at his own request. This was the only Czechoslovak bomber unit in the RAF, and it was equipped with the twin-engine Vickers Wellington Mk I and the ICs medium bomber. The Squadron had conducted raids over the continent from 10 September to 22 October 1940, but unsustainable losses of aircraft and crews had forced the Squadron to temporarily cease operations. The next seven weeks were hectic, with intense training for both veteran and newly-formed crews. The next raid was carried out by two aircraft and their crews from No. 311 (B) Squadron on Monday 9 December 1940. By that time, Plt Off. Gellner was already with the Squadron in East Wretham. He was officially posted to No. 311 'Czechoslovak' (B) Squadron as a navigation instructor, as most of the Czechoslovak navigators had only passed a short refresher course within the Squadron—none had completed an RAF-conducted navigation course. This is confirmed by an entry in the Squadron's Operations Record Book (ORB):

> On 3 December two more crews came to Wretham and were put in Operational Flight. Today Plt Off. Gellner also came from the RCAF. He is a Czechoslovakian, who after the revolution went to the USA and joined the RCAF. He has been attached to the squadron as instructor in astronavigation.[10]

This posting came with a promotion to the rank of Acting Flying Officer, effective from 2 December 1940. At the end of December 1940, John passed the No. 13 Bombing Leaders Course at No. 1 Air Armament School in Manby, Lincolnshire. He did not take any exams at the end of the course, so the only affirmation was this statement by the Chief Instructor, Wg Cdr J. G. Franks:

> This officer, a Czech by birth, has had considerable experience in the Czech Army and in civil flying before joining the Royal Canadian Air Force. He has a very good understanding of bombing equipment, and of bombing theory, but so far has done no operational flight. Apart from some difficulty with the English language he is a very good instructor indeed. While taking a very keen interest in the course, his chief interest is in astronomical navigation, for which he had taught a class and for which he is instructor at his Squadron. He is considered suitable in every way for the post of Bombing Leader in a squadron, but it is felt that he would be far more of value to the service as an instructor in astronomical navigation.[11]

After his return to No. 311 (B) Squadron, John occasionally helped out as Operations Officer. At his own request, he eventually joined an operational crew. Between 16 January 1941 and 5 August 1941, Gellner carried out a total of thirty-seven operations over the territories of occupied France, Belgium, the Netherlands, and Germany.

During an operation on the night of 1–2 July 1941, he flew as the navigator for Wellington Mk IC R1015/KX-L, captained by Plt Off. Václav Korda. It would become a very memorable event in the Squadron's history. Gellner was most likely the one responsible for dropping the bombs that damaged the German cruiser *Prinz Eugen*, anchored in Brest (see Appendix III).

The second period of Gellner's literary activity took place while he served with No. 311 (B) Squadron. He contributed to the magazine *Čechoslovák*, which was issued periodically in London. John also penned six stories about No. 311 Squadron for the book *Wings in Exile*. English and Czech-language versions of this book were published in London in 1942. They were all signed by a simple cipher—'G.'—and by his own pen.

On 31 July 1941, Gellner was officially appointed to the post of Station Navigation Officer at East Wretham. To fulfil this position, John was given the temporary rank of Acting Flight Lieutenant. A short time later, during an interview with reporters about his completed tour of operations, he recalled his further service with the Squadron:

> I started my rest-cure by being a kind of 'Jack-of-all-trades' in my squadron. I was Squadron Navigation Officer, Bombing Leader, and, for almost three weeks, even Adjutant.

Gellner finished off his tour on 5 August 1941 by flying an operation against Mannheim. He became the third navigator in the Squadron's history to finish a tour of 200 operational hours. His thirty-seven trips placed him among forty members of No. 311 (B) Squadron who flew the most sorties within RAF Bomber Command. Among the navigators, he was tied for fourth place after Plt Off. Josef Motyčka (who had flown forty sorties), Plt Off. Karel Lanczik (with thirty-eight), and Plt Off. Herbert Němec (who also flew thirty-seven sorties, but recorded more operational hours). Of Korda's crew, wireless operator Sgt Vladimír Slánský was ahead of him with forty-five sorties, as was air gunner FS Miroslav Čtvrtlík with forty-two sorties. Even the skipper, Plt Off. Václav Korda, recorded forty-one sorties.[12]

Plt Off. Gellner's departure meant that No. 311 (B) Squadron's Commanding Officer now had to deal with the vacant positions of Squadron Bombing Leader and Squadron Navigation Officer for an undetermined period of time. No replacement had been trained—an example of poor planning on someone's part. On 4 August 1941, a British Liaison Officer attached to the Squadron, Wg Cdr Kenneth Stewart Batchelor, asked the headquarters of No. 3 (B) Group RAF to give Plt Off. Emil Palichleb a seat on the earliest-available Bombing Leaders Course, as 'Plt Off. Gellner is at present the only member of the operational squadron trained and he will be going on rest from operations this week'. Two days later, a letter arrived informing headquarters that Plt Off. Palichleb could not attend the course due to his poor knowledge of English, and that Fg Off. Jaroslav Kula would replace him. This was one of the reasons why Plt Off. Gellner stayed with No. 311 Squadron until mid-September 1941, even after he finished his operational tour. According to the report submitted by the Commanding Officer on 13 September, 'Plt Off. Gellner now fills the vacancy of Squadron Navigation Officer and Bombing Leader'.

Even as late as August, No. 311 (B) Squadron's Commanding Officer, Wg Cdr Ocelka DFC, had to explain the situation to No. 3 (B) Group RAF:

> It is pointed out that in this squadron, it will be necessary to combine the duties of Squadron Bombing Leader and Squadron Navigation Officer. These duties will

be carried out by a single officer for the time being. The officer who will attend No. 26 Bombing Leaders Course, Fg Off. Kula, has been chosen mainly for his fair knowledge of English and will, after completion of the course (about 15 September 1941), be employed firstly as Flight Bombing Leader until he gets more operational experience. (Up to the time he has done nine operations.) At present, there is only one observer in the squadron who has completed operational flying and who now fills the vacancy of both Squadron Navigation Officer and Squadron Bombing Leader, Plt Off. J. Gellner. It will, however, be possible to divide the two functions in accordance with No. 3 Group's letter ref: 3G/S8139/Armt at a later date.

In August and September 1941, Plt Off. Gellner finally received awards for his operational service. Firstly, he was promoted to his equivalent officer's rank in the Czechoslovak Army, as shown by the *Sborník důvěrných výnosů a nařízení* (SDVN) (Volume of Confidential Issues and Orders) No. 26/1941 on 25 August 1941:

Commissioned with seniority and effect on 1 August 1941, particularly for excellence in combat as Second Lieutenant of Air Force in Reserve, Corporal in Reserve GELLNER John JUDr, currently in the Royal Canadian Air Force.

The following SDVN No. 27/1941, dated 1 September 1941, showed Gellner's name on a list of Czechoslovak airmen to be awarded the Czechoslovak Gallantry Medal. The citation stated that he would be awarded this honour 'for outstanding and successful acts of personal bravery against the enemy on the battlefield'. Subsequent SDVN No. 28/1941, dated 22 September 1941, announced his receipt of the Czechoslovak War Cross 1939 from the President of the Czechoslovak Republic for a 'successful executive act, during which he was personally exposed to the risk of life'.[13] Despite the fact that in both cases these were Czechoslovak state decorations awarded to a person with Czechoslovak citizenship, Gellner's service in the RCAF meant that it would take eight months for the complicated approval process to be completed (see Appendix II).

In addition to these decorations, on 17 September 1941 No. 311 (B) Squadron Commanding Officer Wg Cdr Josef Ocelka DFC submitted a recommendation for the award of the British Distinguished Flying Cross to Acting Flight Lieutenant John Gellner. The recommendation (see Appendix I) was approved by Commanding Officers at all levels, and Britain's King George VI approved the award with effect from 15 November 1941. Acting Flight Lieutenant Gellner was the fifth Czech (and only the third member of No. 311 (B) Squadron) to be awarded the DFC. He also had the distinction of being the Squadron's first navigator to receive this honour. Before he left for Canada, Gellner had the opportunity to personally meet the Czechoslovak President, Dr Edvard Beneš. There was still quite a lot of bitterness towards the President due to his acceptance of the Munich Agreement in 1938. A meeting between Gellner and Beneš took place at the President's residence at Aston Abbotts, Aylesbury, in Buckinghamshire. During the meeting, the President presented Gellner with the Czechoslovak War Cross 1939. This was followed by a short private conversation:

> After the ceremony, during a stroll in the gardens, he asked me why I was serving in the Royal Canadian Air Force and not in the Czechoslovak forces that were fighting on the Allied side. I told him frankly that I was so shattered by what had happened in that September two years earlier and so suspicious of the nation's leadership that I just did not want to risk having to go through the same experience once more. The President shook his head and said that history would prove him right. It hasn't.[14]

According to the King's Regulations & Air Council Instructions, flying personnel were entitled to take sixty-one days of leave per year. Gellner used only eighteen of those during his three leave periods during 1941. After the end of his operational tour, he was still entitled to forty-three more days. It is clear from his diary that the rest of the leave, which began on 29 September, would be spent in Canada. After it was over, he would return to flying operations with No. 311 (B) Squadron.

John once again set sail from Liverpool to return to Canada. However, this trip would be different. He later recalled that the ship he was on was part of a convoy with an armed escort. Neither his memoirs nor the official RCAF Service Records indicate the date of his departure; however, it is known that he landed at the Canadian port of Halifax on Saturday 11 October. Nine days later, on 20 October, Gellner began ten days of Disembarkation Leave. It is very likely that the ship he returned to Canada on was part of Convoy ON 20. This convoy departed Liverpool on 25 September, and on 9 October it was scattered in the North Atlantic. On 11 October, four of convoy's ships—the tankers *British Resource* and *Solør*, along with the cargo ships *Empire Rainbow* and *Fernmoor*—anchored in Halifax.

After his arrival, several newspaper articles were published that celebrated his return to Canada. The first one was printed in *The Hamilton Spectator* on Friday 17 October, under the banner headline 'First Graduate of Empire Plan now in Canada', with the sub-title 'Flt Lt Gellner Is RAF Hero of Many Raids'. He was the subject of another, more comprehensive article, which told his life story and included an interview with him; in the interview, Gellner amusingly remarked that he had 'visited' Cologne so many times he should have been made an honorary citizen. The article also mentioned how his wife had covered up his escape from the Protectorate. She was released after five hours of questioning by members of the Brno Gestapo, only just managing to convince them that her husband had left her for another woman.

Gellner was posted to the RCAF's No. 7 Manning Depot in Rockcliffe, Ontario, and was promoted to the rank of Acting Flight Lieutenant with effect from 27 October. He was to report back to No. 311 (B) Squadron at East Wretham on 11 November 1941, upon completion of his leave. However, he did not make it back on the assigned date.

On Monday 1 December 1941, *The Hamilton Spectator* published an article about the first awards ceremony to be held in Canada with the King's approval. It was to take place on Wednesday 3 December in Ottawa. Of the sixty-five people decorated that day, forty-five were airmen—including Gellner. The ceremony was held at Rideau Hall, the official residence of the Governor General of Canada, with the participation of Canadian high officials and military dignitaries. The decorations were clipped on uniforms by the Governor General, The Earl of Athlone, Major-General Sir Alexander Augustus Frederick William Alfred George Cambridge, Prince Alexander of Teck and the uncle of King George VI.

Meanwhile, Gellner was attached to the RCAF Headquarters in Ottawa, which had a special assignment for him. He was to visit BCATP navigation schools and give lectures to the students about his combat experiences; this would give them a realistic idea of what to expect when they reached operational units overseas. His speaking engagements would take him across almost the entire country. Gellner made the first of his visits on 19 January, beginning with the Central Ontario schools of No. 1 Training Command. On 30 January, Gellner toured the two schools in Eastern Ontario administered by No. 3 Training Command. He began visiting the schools of No. 2 Training Command, which had headquarters in the provincial capital of Winnipeg, Manitoba, on 18 February. They were responsible for training schools throughout the province, as well as Fort William in north-western Ontario and the northern part of the province of Saskatchewan. The No. 4 Training Command schools were Gellner's focus of attention from 10 March. No. 4 TC looked after all the schools in the southern region of Saskatchewan and the provinces of Alberta and British Columbia.[15]

The job itself was simple enough, but the travelling took a toll on him physically. The trip was also interrupted by an odd incident; immediately after arriving at No. 2 TC in Winnipeg, the OC, Wg Cdr John L. Walmsley, thought that Gellner could perhaps be an enemy spy. His suspicions were aroused after hearing John's heavy accent and seeing the ribbons of his two Czechoslovak medals, which he did not recognise. Walmsley then diplomatically ordered Acting Flight Lieutenant Gellner to have a 'rest' in the hotel while he was thoroughly investigated. It took a few days before confirmation of his innocence arrived from RCAF HQ.[16]

During his promotional work, he wrote an article addressed to all future airmen:

> There is no greater honour than to be an aircrew member and I for one wouldn't barter my stripe on my light blue uniform for a commission in the Coldstream Guards.[17] As you are looking forward to your first spell of operations, I am hoping to get my second crack. Let all of us keep our fingers crossed for a chance to meet high up over Germany.

John did not get a chance to briefly settle down somewhere until 23 March 1942, when he became a navigation instructor at No. 1 Air Navigation School at Rivers, Manitoba. The school underwent a reorganisation while he was an instructor there. On 11 May, it was re-designated as the 'Central Navigation School'. By the end of June, Gellner had flown a total of seventy-six hours as an instructor. He also focused on theoretical navigation training with aid of classroom simulators. On 15

July 1942, Gellner finally received a promotion to Temporary Flight Lieutenant. He continued instructing students and training his replacements until 21 December 1942, when was posted to the Air Force Headquarters in Ottawa.[18]

After almost one year of service at the navigation school, he was asked how he envisaged his future military service. His answer was definite—he wanted to fulfil his life-long dream and become a pilot.

In all probability, his request for pilot training was approved due to his exemplary previous combat service and the considerable and very positive media attention he received, which also reflected quite well on the RCAF. Gellner's age did not present an obstacle as he celebrated his thirty-fifth birthday on 18 May 1942. A humorous story pertaining to his pilot training was later recalled by one of his friends:

There were three officers in the Directorate of Air Training—two of whom were Squadron Leaders, each responsible for Elementary and Service Schools, as well as filling accident reports. We were able to keep track of John's progress through the accident reports. He had one at each stage![19]

Gellner was posted to Ontario to start his elementary flying training. He was accompanied by two other former navigators; all three were Flight Lieutenants who had finished an operational tour and had been awarded a DFC. They became darlings in the media, who fell in love with them and dubbed the trio 'The Three Musketeers of the Air'. However, both of his colleagues were much younger than him. Flt Lt Robert W. Alexander, aged twenty-three, was from the same course as Gellner, and twenty-four-year-old Flt Lt Warring L. Jennings was a graduate of the third course of air observers in the BCATP.

Flt Lt Gellner commenced his *ab initio* pilot training on 22 January 1943 at No. 20 Elementary Flying Training School in Oshawa, Ontario. Training at the school was conducted under the supervision of civilian instructors in the two-seat, Canadian-built de Havilland DH82C Tiger Moth. The bi-plane was powered by a 140-hp D.H. Gipsy inline engine. This Canadian license-built version of the famous British aircraft had a few features that took the freezing cold and snowy winters into account. The most obvious difference was the addition of a sliding canopy. A cockpit heater was also a welcome addition on chilly flights. The main landing gear was moved forward and it was fitted with a different instrument panel.

The first of John's aforementioned accidents took place on Monday 1 March 1943. He was overjoyed at having survived the ordeal and was not afraid to let people know it. While touching down in Tiger Moth Mk I s/n 8872, Gellner had experienced a cross-wind. He bounced the aircraft and instinctively advanced the throttle. Unfortunately, the engine failed to respond—most likely because it was opened too quickly. The Tiger Moth touched down again, ground looped, and overturned. Gellner was harnessed properly, and this certainly prevented him from suffering any injury. His aircraft fared far worse. The engine was only slightly damaged, but the airframe suffered more serious Category 'B' damage. The extent of the destruction would normally necessitate transfer to the manufacturer for repairs; however, owing to the fact that No. 20 EFTS would receive the new Fairchild PT-26 Cornells by the end of 1942, the repairs were abandoned. Authorisation to scrap the aircraft was requested on 26 March, and permission was granted on 28 April 1943. It is quite surprising that this crash had no consequences for Gellner—it was not even recorded in his log book.[20]

At age thirty-six, Flt Lt Gellner DFC became one of the oldest pilots trained within the BCATP. Deep down, he knew that he was too old to be a fighter pilot, as he noted in an interview with the Canadian press:

> A fellow begins to lose that elastic quality when he gets into his thirties. But I think I have enough elastic left in me to handle a four-motored bomber on a few more visits to Germany.

After finishing his elementary pilot training, John was posted to No. 5 Service Flying Training School in Brantford, Ontario, on 20 March 1943. He was there to learn to fly multi-engine aircraft. On Monday 29 March 1943—only a week since Gellner's arrival at Brantford—he crashed again. It was exactly four weeks since his previous accident. At 9.15 a.m., Gellner was taking off in an Avro Anson Mk III (s/n 6360) for a solo training flight when the aircraft begin to swing. He over-corrected with throttle and the aircraft subsequently ground looped. As in his previous accident, the airframe suffered serious damage. The pair of Jacobs L-6MB engines fared much better, suffering only slight damage. Gellner managed to walk away from the Anson without any injury except for a bruised ego. The cause of the accident was determined as 'misuse of controls', with 'inexperience' cited in his Log Book. The Anson also sustained Category 'B' damage; it was handed over to the Central Aircraft Manufacturing Co. in London, Ontario, for repairs, becoming airworthy again on 30 September 1943.[21]

An afternoon Wings Parade at Brantford was held on Thursday 8 July 1943, and the school's CO, Wg Cdr C. J. H. Holms, pinned coveted pilots' wings onto fifty-seven graduates from course No. 77. The 'Three Musketeers of the Air', side-by-side, led the graduates during a rousing march past. The trio also became the first student pilot graduates among veterans who had already completed an operational tour. The following day, Flt Lt Gellner was transferred to No. 5 Manning Depot in Lachine, Quebec, where his original trade, Air Observer, was amended to 'Pilot General' in his RCAF Service Record.

His first posting was as a multi-engine pilot with RAF Transport Command. On 24 July 1943, he left Lachine for No. 45 Air Transport Group at Dorval Airport, Montreal. There he began to prepare for the role of a transport pilot, which involved ferrying new aircraft across the Atlantic Ocean. In early August, Gellner was scheduled to ferry an aircraft to North Africa. He took the train from Montreal to Miami on 11 August; from Miami, Gellner continued on to Nassau, in the Bahamas. Nassau was the home of No. 113 (South Atlantic) Wing. After Gellner's arrival on 14 August, he was assigned to the Transport Conversion Unit for training.

Flt Lt Gellner's first transatlantic crossing was on 3 September 1943, when he acted as the second pilot on a Martin B-26 Marauder (s/n FB424) (see Appendix IV). The crew's 4,040-mile route took them from Nassau to Piarco, Trinidad, to Belém, Brazil, to Natal, also Brazil, to Wideawake, Ascension Island, and then to Accra. They landed on 7 September at the Gold Coast's Accra Airport. The country is now known as Ghana. The crew boarded Liberator Mk III s/n FL914 as passengers for a lift back to Nassau. They arrived there on 10 September.

During another ferry flight, he was the second pilot aboard Dakota FL541 (see Appendix IV). The crew followed the same route, and it took them from 19 to 22 September to reach Accra.[22] During the final stages of this crossing, an amusing incident occurred:

> I was the second pilot on a transport aircraft, but I was in the captain's seat as he had found a nook in which he retired and took a rest. The aircraft was filled with war materials, but there were also half a dozen VIP passengers. One of them, an Army Colonel, came into the cockpit and saw me reading a book. He was obviously taken aback. 'You are reading?' he asked. I told him the aircraft was on automatic pilot and that the Flight Engineer was watching the instruments. 'What are you reading?' he asked. I showed him—it was recent edition of Edward Gibbon's classic *The History of the Decline and Fall of the Roman Empire*. The Colonel withdrew, but he was back in no time. He told me that the passengers were finding it bad enough that a pilot could read and write, but to learn that he was reading a history of Ancient Rome was just too much. It convinced them that they were being flown by a madman. I asked him to tell them that the captain would probably take over when we were nearing Accra, but that in any case I would then lay aside my book and do my part, whatever it would be, in landing the aircraft.[23]

After flying from Accra on 24 September aboard an aircraft from the USAAF's Air Transport Command, Gellner made a brief stop in the United States. They landed in Miami on 26 September. On 2 October, Gellner travelled to Montreal by train, where he applied for a new passport at the Czechoslovak Consulate:

> Consul General in Montreal reports by note ref. 3363P43, dated 24 October 1943, that an Air Force Captain Dr John Gellner reported the loss of his passport. This passport was destroyed in a plane crash in Nassau in the Bahamas, completely burned together with the plane in which it was stored. The passport was issued by Police Headquarters in Brno on 2 July 1935 and extended to 25 July 1945. The Consul General of the Czechoslovak Republic in Montreal issued new passport No. 229305 on 21 October 1943 to the named, who was born on 18 May 1907 in Trieste and is domestic in Brno.[24]

USAAF Martin B-26C Marauder s/n 41-35485 was transferred to the Royal Air Force under the Lend and Lease Act and re-serialed as FB457. The Flying Accident

Card (AM Form 1180) provides more details about the accident. The aircraft was captained by Canadian pilot J26915 Plt Off. F. R. McGill. Up to the time of the accident at 11.43 a.m. on 1 October 1943, McGill had flown 454 hours solo and thirty-nine on the type. Marauder FB457 crashed during take-off on the runway at Windsor Field in Nassau. The Flying Accident Card reads:

> Co-pilot retracts U/C on take-off run, mistaking movement of captain's hand for signal to do so. U/C collapsed, A/C bursts into flames. AOC: Captain of A/C FB457 had run of 400 yards when U/C was raised by co-pilot who mistook sign from first pilot, A/C went on belly, fire broke out, completely burning A/C. Co-pilot thought he saw signal and acted promptly. Group OC: Unfortunate error of co-pilot. ACM Transport Command: Concurs.

No. 45 Air Transport Group's ORB confirms that it was indeed Flt Lt Gellner DFC who, while carrying out second-pilot duties, mistakenly raised the landing gear prematurely. The entire crew—consisting of the aircraft's captain, Plt Off. F. R. McGill, co-pilot Flt Lt J. Gellner, navigator WO J. T. D'Altray, and W/T operator Plt Off. G. D. Boyd—survived after escaping from the burning aircraft before it was consumed by fire.[25]

With new travel documents in hand, Flt Lt Gellner would make another ferry flight by the end of October 1943. On Tuesday 26 October, he took off from Dorval airport aboard a North American B-25 Mitchell (s/n FW119) (see Appendix IV). This was to be his third and final ferry flight while serving with RAF Transport Command. Gellner was the second pilot again. He and the crew flew the aircraft to Gander, Newfoundland. From there, they continued on directly to Prestwick, Scotland, arriving on 30 October, after travelling a distance of over 2,110 miles in one leg.

Gellner's career as a transport pilot ended rather abruptly. There are still unanswered questions as to whether the RCAF Headquarters approved his request to return to operations, or whether his transfer from RAF Transport Command was simply accelerated by his recent accident. Gellner's posting with RAF Transport Command was cancelled after his arrival in Britain. He now found himself unattached to any unit and, even worse, with no aircraft to fly. He was ordered to proceed to No. 3 (RCAF) Personnel Reception Centre in Bournemouth, Hampshire, on 1 November 1943. This was where all RCAF airmen were posted to upon their arrival from Canada. From there he was sent to a course at No. 1534 Beam Approach Training Flight in Shawbury, Shropshire. It ran from 12–24 November. On the course, he practised flying blind approaches and landings using Airspeed Oxford Mk IIs that were specially equipped with the Beam Approach Beacon System and the Standard Beam Approach System.

Gellner then returned to No. 3 (RCAF) PRC, where he waited until 14 December 1943 for his new posting. It would be off to No. 24 Operational Training Unit at Honeybourne, Worcestershire, where night bomber crews were trained. The practice of forming new five-man crews was actually quite simple. The new crop of airmen in December 1943 comprised twenty-two pilots, twenty navigators, twenty bomb aimers, twenty-two wireless operators, and forty-six air gunners. Prior to crewing up, they usually gathered in a large hall or hangar. There, they were greeted by the Commanding Officer, who gave a typical welcoming speech. Then the selection process would begin. For the most part, airmen were picked by the pilots for any number of reasons. When a crew was formed, teamwork was the optimum word. Training consisted of numerous cross-country flights, air-bombing practice, and aerial gunnery. All crew positions would be under scrutiny—not only from the 'skipper', as the pilot was affectionately known as, but also from the instructors of the OTU.

The flying training was usually carried out in obsolete and 'clapped-out' kites like the Armstrong Whitworth Whitley bomber. These war-weary aircraft were usually on their last legs after having been withdrawn from operational units during 1942. Many were maintenance nightmares, with a number lost in training accidents.

The highlight of operational training was a night training exercise called 'Bullseye'. This was a raid on a target over 'enemy territory'. For the purposes of training, a major city in the United Kingdom would substitute for an actual enemy location. To make the exercise as real as possible, searchlights units with anti-aircraft artillery were engaged, as well as night fighter squadrons. This gave the crews first-hand experience of what they could encounter in the field while remaining in a controlled environment. Crews from Operational Training Units were also given an opportunity to get a taste of operational flying with a 'trip' over enemy territory. A Nickel raid—more commonly referred to as 'Nickelling'—was the dropping of propaganda leaflets over German territory and occupied countries. Crews under training were restricted to targets only in continental coastal countries.

Gellner's crew completed all the required training flights without any serious mishaps or emergencies. It was not until Exercise Flashlight Bullseye on Friday 11 February 1944 that bad luck reared its ugly head—this time, in the form of technical failures. Of the eight Whitley Mk Vs that took part in the exercise, only five were able to complete it successfully. One aircraft crash-landed at Church Broughton, Derbyshire, with a defective airspeed indicator, while another returned early due to an SBA failure. Flt Lt Gellner was forced to return early while flying Whitley Mk V T4236. He gingerly nursed his aircraft back to a successful landing on one Merlin engine. This was not the first time this particular aircraft had had trouble while in flight. On 19 December, Sgt Elsley and his crew were forced to land at Enstone, Oxfordshire, due to an unserviceable SBA and wireless radio.[26]

From 10 January 1944, Gellner had more than his operational training to worry about. After being offered a position by Minister Ján Lichner and accepting it, he sat as a member of an advisory committee for aviation under the Czechoslovak Ministry of Agriculture and Public Works in Exile. The entirety of the ministry's activities consisted solely of theoretical planning for the country's post-war agricultural recovery and development after being exhausted by the war. It was the same for the future of air transport.

Flt Lt Gellner finished his operational training course on 26 February 1944. This was followed by two weeks of leave. On 10 March, he was transferred to the RCAF's

No. 61 (Training) Base, which was headquartered at Topcliffe, Yorkshire. This parent unit served as a training centre for No. 6 Group RCAF, and it was responsible for all units based at Dalton, Dishforth, and Wombleton in Yorkshire. Later that same day, he reported to Dalton to undergo a course at the No. 6 (RCAF) Group Battle School.

This special school was founded on 1 September 1943, with 95805 T/Maj. P. M. S. Gegde (from the British Army's Green Howards Regiment) becoming its Chief Instructor. The unit's primary objective was to prepare airmen for escape and evasion, both in theory and in practice, in the event of having to abandon their aircraft over enemy territory. The school ran each course with several tens of airmen from all ranks participating. They learned basic French and German phrases, camouflage techniques, orientation in unfamiliar areas, and how to destroy various objects. As part of the practical training, all underwent pistol and rifle training and basic demolition with explosives. Non-swimmers were put through a course at the pool in Ripon Spa Baths, located in the nearby Yorkshire town of Ripon.

Thirty officers from Nos 22, 24, and 82 OTUs had arrived at Dalton alongside Gellner on 10 March 1944. They would all take part in Battle School Course No. 25. The course's final night exercise, 'HOMER', started on the evening of Monday 20 March. Instructors dropped off participants in small groups from buses, on the line between Pickering and Malton, about 23 miles east as the crow flies from the base at Dalton. Members of the Home Guard and 'Bobbies' (as British civil policemen were affectionately known) were involved in this training. Their only task was to arrest any 'suspicious persons'. Airmen were restricted to travelling most of the way back to base on foot. This was for a good reason; participants in the first courses had 'borrowed' so many civilian vehicles to make it back to Dalton that their use was now prohibited by request of the police. Nevertheless, by mid-morning next day all the participants had successfully returned to the base. They were all congratulated for their efforts as each of them had managed to return—unlike in some previous courses.

Battle School Course No. 25 ended on 23 March. The participants were sent for advanced operational training to either Nos 1659, 1664, or 1666 Heavy Conversion Units. Flt Lt Gellner passed the next stage of his training at the RCAF's No. 1659 (Canadian) Heavy Conversion Unit in Topcliffe. He completed four weeks of flying training on the four-engine Handley Page Halifax heavy bomber, a type that was being used by RCAF bomber squadrons for operations at the time. The course covered all the aircraft's systems in great detail, in addition to familiarisation with the cockpit. The practical flying training included numerous take-offs and landings, aborted landings, and coping with emergencies such as the loss of an engine (or even two) and three-engined landings.

While at the HCU, Gellner's crew was complemented by two final members—the flight engineer and mid-upper gunner. Now a complete crew, they carried out navigation flights by both conventional means and by the use of the H2S airborne ground-scanning radar system. The bomb aimer was kept busy by simulating bombing runs, including Bullseye exercises. The air gunners honed their skills by simulating firing at aircraft from fighter affiliation units, which undertook mock attacks at them from all quarters.

After the final phase of training at No. 1659 (RCAF) HCU, the crew were certified as combat-ready, which meant a posting to an operational squadron. They were assigned to the RCAF's No. 429 'Bison' (B) Squadron at Leeming, Yorkshire. The Squadron's history dates back to 7 November 1942, when it was formed at East Moor, Yorkshire, as the RCAF's tenth overseas bomber unit. It was initially equipped with the venerable Vickers Wellington Mk IIIs and would be supplemented by the Wellington Mk Xs in January 1943. The Squadron's first sorties were flown on 21 January 1943, when three Wellington Mk Xs were sent out to lay sea mines around the island of Terschelling, in the northern part of the Netherlands. One aircraft aborted its sortie, while another failed to return. The Squadron relocated to Leeming on 13 August 1943. It would take the fight to the Germans using the four-engined Handley Page Halifax B Mk IIs. This Rolls-Royce-powered version was joined by the Halifax B Mk Vs in November and would no longer be in service with the Squadron by the following January. The Halifax B Mk V was superseded by the very capable Halifax B Mk III from March 1944. One year later, in March 1945, the Avro Lancaster B Mk Is and IIIs joined the Squadron. By the end of April 1944, No. 429 'Bison' (B) Squadron was temporarily commanded by C4801 Delford Harold Kenney DFC AFC, who handed over command to twenty-one-year-old J10503 Wg Cdr Allan Frederick Avant DFC, from Hughton, Saskatchewan, on 1 May.[27]

No. 429 (B) Squadron gained seven new crews during April 1944. The penultimate crew, which arrived at Leeming on Tuesday 25 April, consisted of one officer and six non-commissioned officers: the pilot—J2822 Flt Lt J. Gellner DFC; the flight engineer—871553 Sgt G. W. Harris (an RAF chap in his forties, making him the oldest in the crew); the navigator—R161385 Sgt W. H. Devine; the bomb aimer—R171540 Sgt R. N. McEachern; the wireless operator—R161274 Sgt R. M. Almas; the first air gunner—R196866 Sgt C. M. Wert (aged twenty, the youngest of the crew); and the second air gunner, R212423 Sgt R. E. Nelson.

The primary reason for the sole RAF member in the otherwise entirely Canadian crew was that the RCAF did not start to train their own flight engineers until the formation of No. 1 Flight Engineers' School, Aylmer, Ontario on 1 July 1944. Therefore, prior to the establishment of the flight engineer trade in the RCAF, the FE would invariably be from the RAF—a graduate from No. 4 School of Technical Training at RAF Station St Athan, Glamorgan.

On 30 April 1944, No. 429 (B) Squadron had 241 aircrew on strength. It was a mixed bag of 174 Canadians from the RCAF, two US citizens from the RCAF, a further sixty-three RAF British airmen, one Canadian serving in the RAF, and one USAAF airman.

Before the new crews were sent into action for the first time, they had to complete more ground and flying training. Flt Lt Gellner's crew therefore sat in on intelligence lectures held in the station cinema on 28 April. They were airborne the following day, taking part in a cross-country flight as well as mock attacks by fighters. All seven new crews were required to pass a special navigation lecture held in the afternoon by the Station Navigation Officer, Sqn Ldr Craig. Saturday 29 April 1944 went by with further training in a peaceful setting; however, this was all about to change the next day. The ORB stated:

> The squadron was required for an operation tonight. Sixteen aircrews were detailed and briefed to carry out a bombing attack on the marshalling yard at Somain. All took off. Weather over the target was clear with slight haze. Visibility was fair to good. Pathfinder Force were late and the 'Master of Ceremonies' had considerable difficulty in deciding which markers should be bombed. Some crews had to make a second run owing to this fact. The bombing seen appeared well-concentrated and accurately placed on and around the markers. A terrific explosion took place at 11.34 p.m., with an orange flash followed by a mushroom of black smoke rising to 3,000–4,000 feet. Defences over the target were negligible. A few enemy aircraft were sighted. This appeared to have been a successful raid. All our aircraft returned safely to base.

The following squadrons from No. 6 (RCAF) Group represented a combined force of some 114 bombers sent out to bomb marshalling yards at Somain, northern France, near the Belgian border: Nos 420 'Snowy Owl', 424 'Tiger', 425 'Alouette', 427 'Lion', 429 'Bison', 431 'Iroquois', 432 'Leaside', 433 'Porcupine', and 434 'Bluenose'. Halifaxes from No. 429 (B) Squadron took off from Leeming at intervals of a few minutes between 9.37 and 10.53 p.m. Halifax B Mk III LW694/AL-Z—with a crew consisting of pilot Flt Lt Gellner, flight engineer Sgt Harris, navigator Sgt Devine, bomb aimer Sgt McEachern, wireless operator Sgt Almas, mid-upper gunner Sgt Wert, rear gunner Sgt Nelson, and supernumerary air gunner Sgt J. V. Sheardown—was the last aircraft to leave. On the night of 30 April–1 May 1944, Flt Lt Gellner completed the first combat sortie of his second operational tour. The Squadron ORB recorded his operation as follows:

> Attacked primary at 11.33 p.m. from 8,000 feet. No cloud, slight ground haze, visibility unlimited. Bombed on red Target Indicator covering green spot fire on ground as instructed by the 'Master of Ceremonies'. The markers were well-concentrated. Bomb load: 9 × 1,000-lb MC, 6 × 500-lb GP.

All the aircraft from No. 429 (B) Squadron returned safely to the home base, landing between 1.45 and 2.54 a.m. Flt Lt Gellner's Halifax landed at 2.48 a.m., one of the last to return.

Flt Lt Gellner and his crew took the part in another operation on the following night, 1–2 May. The RCAF's No. 6 Group dispatched a force of 105 bombers made up of twenty-six Lancaster B Mk IIs & Xs (Nos 408 'Goose', 419 'Moose', and 426 'Thunderbird' Squadrons) and eighty-nine Halifax B Mk IIIs & Vs (Nos 420 'Snowy Owl', 425 'Alouette', 427 'Lion', 429 'Bison', 431 'Iroquois', 432 'Leaside', and 434 'Bluenose' Squadrons). Their target was the marshalling yard in the Belgian town of

Saint-Ghislain. Fifteen Halifaxes from No. 429 (B) Squadron took off between 9.43 and 10.16 p.m. Halifax LW694, piloted by Flt Lt Gellner and with the same crew as the night before, was the twelfth to depart, at 10.13 p.m.:

> Attacked primary at 00.07 a.m. from 7,500 feet. 3/10–4/10 scattered cloud, visibility good. Bombed on red Target Indicator on the instruction of the 'Master of Ceremonies'. The markers were well-concentrated and the bombing was well-placed on and around the markers. One large explosion occurred at 00.05 a.m. This should be a successful attack if the markers were accurate. Bomb load: 9 × 1,000-lb MC, 6 × 500-lb GP.[28]

On this night, the attacking force lost two bombers that were brought down by enemy night fighters. They were Lancaster Mk X KB711/VR-C, from No. 419 'Moose' (B) Squadron, and Halifax B Mk III LW415/AL-K, from No. 429 'Bison' Squadron. Therefore only fourteen of the Squadron's bombers returned to Leeming. They started to arrive home at 1.19 a.m. Flt Lt Gellner's Halifax LW694 was the last to touch down, arriving at 2.52 a.m. Everything was shaping up to be another successful sortie until the undercarriage made contact with the runway; the aircraft lost directional control, causing it to ground loop and subsequently end up on a pile of gravel adjacent to the runway. As recorded in the entry for RAF Station Leeming's ORB on 2 May:

> On return from operations last night aircraft Z-429 LW694 ground looped and suffered damage to the port wing, undercarriage and propellers. It was necessary to use the station's salvage equipment for the first time since January to remove the aircraft from the runway.

During first half of May 1944, three Leeming-based Halifax B Mk IIIs sustained varying degrees of damage, ranging from Category 'AC' to 'B', according to an entry in the Station's ORB dated 15 May. The first to prang his kite was Flt Lt Gellner:

> LW691 [sic.] of 429 Squadron swerved off the runway on landing and ended up on a pile of crushed stone used for road surfacing. This presented a rather difficult salvage problem in that the aircraft had gone right up on top of the rock pile and then the undercarriage collapsed. Under the circumstances, it was felt best to let No. 60 MU carry out the salvage operations.[29]

However, neither of aforementioned sources state the actual cause of the accident. The Flying Accident Cards, which provide information on any RAF aircraft involved in an accident not caused by enemy action, have not survived.[30] Whatever the cause may have been, the accident had dire consequences for Flt Lt Gellner. He was subsequently grounded and withdrawn from operational flying. This meant not only an abrupt halt to his second operational tour, but also the end of his very

short career as a pilot. The Canadian government apparently had no desire to see him behind the controls of an expensive bomber again (the average cost of a new, four-engined Handley Page Halifax being £23,354).[31]

Gellner's accident was recalled by one of his squadron's pilots, although his memories differ slightly from the official accounts:

> John was aware that he wasn't the most proficient pilot and always had the crew in 'ditching' position for every landing. I think he had been on three operations when he taxied into another Halifax (*sic.*). He appeared before the CO and was told that Bomber Command couldn't afford to lose any more aircraft, so he was sent to London.[32]

This event was undoubtedly one of the lowest points in his RCAF career. It could be put down to the cards fate dealt him, or perhaps it was simply that his luck ran out; either way, his days of being shot at were over. Thankfully, his name would not appear on the Squadron's roll of honour, which listed the seventy-seven airmen who fell in combat between mid-May 1944 and the end of the war. That list would include the names of five of his former crew mates. They were posted back to No. 61 Base, where they went through operational training again. They crewed up with their new pilot, Flt Lt S. S. Mitchell, and new navigator, Fg Off. J. H. Johnston. A posting to No. 429 'Bison' (B) Squadron followed on 18 September. They flew their first operation together on 25 September. The crew met their fate on the night of 21–22 November 1944, when Halifax B Mk III MZ377/AL-D failed to return from a sortie against a refinery near Castrop-Rauxel, Germany. All but the skipper and the rear gunner were killed. On a more positive note, former navigator Sgt Devine and air gunner Sgt Sheardown continued their operational flying with the 'Bisons' and survived the war. Flt Lt Gellner's name appeared for the last time in No. 429 'Bison' (B) Squadron's ORB at the end of June. The list of airmen posted in and out simply noted that he left the Squadron for a Repatriation Depot on 23 June.[33]

Flt Lt Gellner spent the three weeks at the RCAF Repatriation Depot in Houghton Green, Warrington, Lancashire. It was responsible for the allocation of incoming RCAF airmen to overseas units and for those going back to Canada. On 14 July he reported to RCAF Overseas Headquarters, where he served out the last ten months of the war in Europe. He worked as a Staff Officer during this time. His knowledge of the German language was beneficial because he was occasionally called upon to interrogate prisoners of war. On 1 September 1944, Gellner was promoted to the rank of Temporary Squadron Leader.

As people throughout Europe celebrated VE Day on 8 May 1945, marking the cessation of hostilities, John did not experience the same joyous feeling that victory had provided others:

> As the war progressed and ultimate victory became a certainty, my thoughts turned more and more to the day that I had so much hoped for, and, when the opportunity had offered, I had strived for. I envisioned myself in front of my

parents, my sister and her family, in uniform, pilot's wings and medal ribbons on my chest, at the happy ending of a long, difficult and often adventurous journey. It was not to be. It all came crumbling down after a note was delivered to me about a week after VE-Day. From that note, I learned that my parents, my sister, and my brother-in-law had perished. Of how it happened, I was informed later.[34]

During the war, John's parents lived on Vratislavova Street in Prague XI-Žižkov. His father, Gustav, devoted himself to the history of Czechoslovak medicine. Most of his time was taken up working on the life of university master Adam Zalužanský of Zalužany. It focused primarily on the period after the Battle of White Mountain. When the Protectorate of Bohemia and Moravia was established, it began a series of anti-Semitic persecutions. Gustav applied for the cessation of anti-Jewish measures. It may have been his strong conviction as a Roman Catholic and his professional activity that drove him to make the request.

The police headquarters in Prague were initially positive about his request, but this would be short-lived. On 21 April 1942, he and his wife, Maria, were arrested by members of the No. 3 (Counterintelligence) Department of the Prague Gestapo. The reason given was 'suspicion of espionage and violations of the anti-Jewish measures'. John's parents were taken to Pankrác Prison on Monday 21 September. This detention facility was under the control of the Prague Gestapo at the time. While there, they were registered under prison numbers 11393 and 11394. The two were then transferred on Tuesday 24 November 1942 to the Prague Gestapo's police prison, which was located in The Small Fortress at Terezín. Gustav Gellner died in Terezín on 8 January 1943 as a result of his imprisonment and brutal torture. He was cremated, without his real identity being known, in the local crematorium on 15 or 16 January 1943. The crematorium records stated nothing more than 'unknown man from The Small Fortress'. His ashes probably ended up in a ditch next to the crematorium.

In January, Maria Gellner left Terezín aboard one of the many transports heading east, to the notorious Auschwitz concentration camp. She would survive her husband by only three weeks. On Saturday 30 January 1943, she died an agonizing death after the inhalation of Cyclon B gas in one of the gas chambers. Her death certificate number, 4438/1943, clearly indicated how many people died in Auschwitz during the first month of 1943.[35] Gellner's sister, Elizabeth, and her husband, Mojmír Dvořák—a former Lieutenant in the Czechoslovak Army—both met the same, sad fate. John's young niece, Gabriela, was the only survivor from the entire family.

The last known official movement of Sqn Ldr Gellner while in the United Kingdom was his attendance at an air–sea-rescue course held at RAF Station Calshot, Hampshire. It ran from 23 July to 4 August 1945. Gellner then left England and flew back to Canada. On 5 August, he reported to the No. 1 Repatriation Depot at RCAF Station Lachine. It was located at Dorval Airport. Gellner immediately requested dispensation for a period of special leave, and this would be authorised by the Station's Commanding Officer two days later, on 7 August.

Gellner's special leave lasted from 7 to 26 August 1945. This would be the only three-week leave he took between 1945 and 1947. It is believed that while on this break, he visited Czechoslovakia in order to organise his personal affairs. He probably departed Dorval for Prestwick, Scotland, on 7 August 1945. From there, he would have travelled by train to London. Gellner arrived in Prague on 11 August 1945. During this visit to his homeland, he sought out his sister-in-law and mother-in-law, who thankfully survived the war. However, because of their Sudeten German origin, they were now being held in an internment camp in Záluží, near Most, awaiting deportation to Germany. He managed to have the pair released from the camp and then helped them to get to Salzburg, Austria. Gellner also went to Prague to meet his now nineteen-year-old niece, Gabriela. He then spent the rest of the three-week stay in Brno.[36]

The end of the war meant Gellner was faced with a difficult decision. He had to weigh the pros and cons of returning to his native country. His family had been exterminated and the family property had been looted, not to mention the strong anti-German sentiment in the newly liberated country. The latter would surely pose a threat to his wife. She was a native Sudeten German who spoke Czech poorly and with a strong German accent. Moreover, after he returned to Canada, he found that his wife, Herta, was very upset and confused. At first, Gellner thought it was a result of her long isolation and living in a foreign country. However, the cause would turn out to be much more serious; Herta was diagnosed with schizophrenia. She received treatment with varying degrees of success, but she never recovered completely. His indecision about where to go was relieved; on 23 August 1945, he was granted Canadian citizenship. Canada became Gellner's second home for the rest of his life.

During his absence, he had been transferred from No. 1 RD in Lachine, Quebec, to RCAF Station Yarmouth, Nova Scotia, on 8 August. It was followed by another move on 1 October—this time to No. 1 Y Depot in Moncton, New Brunswick. It was re-designated as No. 10 Release Centre, and he was posted there on 25 October.

Gellner elected to pursue a post-war career in the RCAF. On 20 November 1945, he became an Administration Officer and was posted to Eastern Air Command Headquarters in Halifax, Nova Scotia.

The year 1946 brought major changes to the RCAF. Its ranks were drastically reduced to a peacetime level; the RCAF would now have a strength of 16,000 Regular Force airmen, 4,500 airmen organised into auxiliary units, and 10,000 reservists. For many airmen who wanted to stay in the RCAF, this meant a reduction in rank. Many were officers one day and enlisted the next. However, this did not concern Gellner. The transition was smooth, from RCAF Special Reserve on 30 September 1946 to RCAF Regular Force the following day. With this change came a new Officer's Service Number—19540. Gellner remained a Squadron Leader. At the same time, his classification changed from Aircrew to Administrative Branch.

On 15 February 1947, he was posted No. 1 Air Command, headquartered at RCAF Station Trenton, Ontario. He stayed there for two weeks, during which time No. 1 Air Command underwent reorganisation, becoming Central Air Command, effective from 1 March. Gellner departed Trenton the following day for the Air Force Headquarters in Ottawa, Ontario. He worked there for more than two years. Gellner was temporarily posted to RCAF Staff College at Armour Heights in Toronto, Ontario, on 7 September 1949; this was the place to go if you were looking at reaching loftier positions in the Air Force. His academic studies ended on 26 July 1950. With that, he returned to Ottawa as a Staff Officer assigned to the Directorate of Air Intelligence, Air Force Headquarters. On 16 August 1950, Gellner received his first post-war assignment outside of Canada. He reported for duty at the Canadian Joint Staff in Washington, DC. Gellner spent less than three months in the US capital before returning to Air Force Headquarters in Canada on 5 November 1950.

On 1 June 1952, after more than five and a half years of service in the post-war Royal Canadian Air Force, he was promoted to the rank of Wing Commander. His promotion would come with a posting at a later date. The posting message came on Christmas Eve 1952—a truly great present. Gellner was off to RCAF Air Division Europe, to No. 3 (F) Wing at Zweibrücken, Germany. The reason for his transfer was very simple—very few other RCAF officers had the command of the German language that he did.

Shortly thereafter, he sailed overseas for the third time in his widely varied RCAF career. On 27 December 1952, he departed from the Port of Halifax, Nova Scotia, on the ship RMS *Samaria*. It steamed for Southampton, Hampshire, England, with a stop in France. Gellner was accompanied by his wife as well as her mother, who had taken up residence with them. The ship docked in the French port of Le Havre on 7 January 1953. From there, the trio continued by train to the city of Grostenquin, home of the RCAF's Canadair Sabre Mk 2-equipped No. 2 (F) Wing RCAF. On 16 February 1953, Gellner travelled by himself to the air base at Zweibrücken, Germany, located 2 miles south-east of the town bearing its name. It was in the southern part of France's occupation zone. Today, it forms part of the federal state of Rhineland-Pfalz. In 1950, the Canadian government submitted an application to the French government to have an airbase built near the town. The site was intended to be the future home for the RCAF's No. 3 (F) Wing. After approval was granted, French engineers drew up plans, and it was built by German construction companies. The new air base was handed over to the RCAF on 6 January 1953, although the official transfer would not be until 27 April. The first CO of No. 3 (F) Wing was Grp Capt. Allan Chester Hull DFC CD, who assumed command on 16 April 1953. He personally requested that Wg Cdr Gellner DFC CD to be posted to his staff.

They had met for the first time in 1942, when both were working with the Directorate of Training at RCAF Headquarters. Hull served overseas from 1943. He was initially with No. 420 'Snowy Owl' (B) Squadron before being posted to No. 428 'Ghost' (B) Squadron as a Flight Commander, with effect from 21 July 1944. Wg Cdr Hull DFC assumed command of the No. 428 (B) Squadron on 8 August 1944. He relinquished his command to Wg Cdr M. W. Gall on 1 April 1945, after his tour of operations expired. Wg Cdr Hull DFC then became the Senior Operations Controller with No. 6 (RCAF) Group, RAF Bomber Command. He and Gellner met again after the war and formed a close friendship while working together in Halifax. This relationship would become even stronger while they served together in Germany. The bond of friendship was only broken with Gellner's death.

Between 1953 and 1955, while Wg Cdr Gellner served as Chief Administrative Officer in Zweibrücken, the station was home to Nos 413 'Tusker', 427 'Lion', and 434 'Bluenose' (F) Squadrons. They were initially equipped with the Canadair Sabre Mk 2, followed by the Mk 5 in May 1953 and the Mk 6 in September 1955. The Canadair Sabre was a license-built version of the North American F-86 Sabre. The RCAF operated from Zweibrücken for more than sixteen years during the so-called 'Cold War'. The RCAF left the base on 27 August 1969.

In 1953, the RCAF Flyers (Europe), known as Canada's skating ambassadors, was formed at No. 3 (F) Wing. It comprised airmen serving with No. 1 Air Division Europe's four fighter wings, which were split between France and Germany. Gellner took part in the organisation of this team. On the occasion of Canada's departure from Zweibrücken in the summer of 1969, he mentioned the team in an article—'John Gellner Takes a Glance Back at Those Busy Hectic First Days at 3 Wing'—for the October issue of *Sentinel Magazine*:

> I acted as a kind of general manager. As such, I acquired an undeserved reputation for ruthlessness in the Air Division. Once, when I came to Grostenquin on perfectly legitimate Air Force business, I found a sign on the headquarters building: 'To Wing Commander Gellner: No point coming in. We have no more hockey players.'

In addition to his service and other related activities, his pre-war education in law meant he was destined to become involved in disciplinary court martials. During the Second World War, Gellner only got involved in two. The first was in England, and the second took place in Canada a year later. Between 1945 and 1953, he attended sixteen disciplinary court martials, at six of which he sat as a Judge advocate, one as an associate judge, and nine others as the president. The busiest month was January 1946, when he presided over four courts at various stations. The final disciplinary court martial he attended took place on 1 September 1953, at No. 2 (F) Wing in Grostenquin, France.

June 1955 would be Wg Cdr Gellner's last month as the Administrative Officer of No. 3 (F) Wing RCAF in Zweibrücken. Two articles in the German press, which were published on the occasion of his departure, undoubtedly bear testimony to the popularity and respect had built up over the past years.

After holidaying in Switzerland, Wg Cdr Gellner DFC CD and his wife, Herta, drove to the French port of Le Havre on 26 July. There, they boarded the ship SS *Homeric* of the Italian company 'Home Lines', based in Genoa. The couple shared cabin M-41 in the first class section, paid for by the RCAF. Including port charges, it cost 208,600 French francs at the time. Gellner said goodbye to the first class luxury on Monday 1 August, when they reached the port of Quebec and stepped onto Canadian soil for the first time in two years and seven months.

On his return to Canada, Wg Cdr Gellner took two weeks of disembarkation leave. He then took up his new posting with the RCAF Staff College in Armour Heights, on 17 August 1955. He served as a member of the Directing Staff until his retirement. Gellner's last day in uniform was on Wednesday 25 June 1958. This fifty-one-year-old, six-foot-tall, brown-eyed and grey-haired officer received his discharge certificate, which stated: 'Wg Cdr John Gellner DFC CD is released from the RCAF as of 14 November 1958 for the reason of the achievement of the mandatory age of retirement'. He had spent eighteen years, six months, and twenty days serving his adopted country—including combat flying during the Second World War. It is truly amazing that he came through everything unscathed. The next day, he was administratively processed and placed into a non-effective category at Air Force Headquarters. Gellner then took leave; he firstly used up his annual leave, which took him up to 26 July, before subsequently withdrawing 110 days of rehabilitation leave, which took him up to 14 November.[37]

Herta's schizophrenia was treated with various medications, but they were not very successful, and her mental condition did not improve. In the end, therefore, she resorted to undergoing electroconvulsive therapy. Herta's medical condition did not allow her to participate in her husband's active lifestyle. Despite his age, Gellner still retained his youthful passion for mountain-climbing; it was this hobby that would eventually lead to him meeting his future second wife, Lilo Mattheis from Essen, Germany. They first met in 1958 in Kandersteg, Switzerland, where he was on a climbing expedition with his friend and was accompanied by Swiss guide Hans Hari. Two years later, Lilo joined the trio during their tours in the mountains of Austria and Switzerland. Ever since then, whenever they went to Europe over the summer they would go to the Alps. In 1974, Gellner reached the summit of one of the peaks of the Hoher Dachstein, Austria. Three years later, on his seventieth birthday, Gellner reached the 4,158 metre peak of the Jungfrau, in the Bernese Alps of Switzerland. He celebrated the momentous occasion with a glass of champagne.

Gellner's post-military career saw him working as a reporter for the Toronto *Globe and Mail* newspaper and *Saturday Night* magazine. He also served as a correspondent for a number of other domestic and European newspapers, including the prestigious German national daily *Die Welt*. Gellner particularly liked to write about military conflicts around the world. For a number of assignments, he found himself right in the middle of warzones. Gellner's passport reflected his global reportage with exotic stamps. The first time he reported from a 'hot spot' was during the spring of 1960, in Algeria. He also travelled to the United Arab Republic in 1961 and visited the embattled island of Cyprus several times in 1966 and 1967.

During the first half of 1968, the political situation in Czechoslovakia became less strict; this was dubbed the so-called 'Prague Spring'. Gellner was doubly motivated to visit his former homeland, both on a personal and professional level. He was issued a visa to the Eastern-Bloc country by the Czechoslovak Consulate in Montreal on 9 February. Gellner only made the one visit in the following months.

The Vietnam War is undoubtedly one of the most famous conflicts in all of history. Gellner spent two weeks in the Vietnamese capital city, Saigon, in May 1968. While there, he watched the Viet Cong's activities from the relative safety of the Eden Roc Hotel's rooftop. He also had the opportunity to go on a reconnaissance patrol into the jungle with American troops—this is quite an admirable feat, considering he was sixty-one years old.

Due to his advancing years, Gellner stopped touring as a reporter at the end of the '60s. Despite this, he still remained involved in journalism; he worked as the editor of the Canadian *The Commentator* from 1964 to 1970. There was a crossover period from 1967 to 1969 when he was also the president of the Canadian Institute of International Affairs. From 1970 onwards, he began a twelve-year stint teaching as a visiting professor of Political Science at York University, Toronto. Today, in honour of his memory, York University awards the John Gellner Graduate Scholarship in Strategic Studies.

Gellner was also one of the founders of the magazine *Canadian Defence Quarterly* in 1971. The periodical was a forum for the Canadian military and public to openly express their points of view on wide range of military and scientific topics. He held the post of Chief Editor until 1987. The magazine ran for sixty-five issues.

Over this period, the health of Gellner's wife, Herta, had steadily declined. Eventually, in the early '70s, she went to Salzburg, Austria, where she would spend the last years of her life with her sister. She was buried there after her death on 15 April 1977 from heart failure.

Almost a year later, John Gellner married his second wife, Lilo Mattheis. The ceremony was held in Toronto on 14 March 1978. She moved to Canada to join him in August 1978, after serving as a director of an elementary school in her hometown of Essen. Gellner left his residence in Toronto that same year, and the couple settled in the small town of Caledon East.

Gellner was awarded several decorations for community service in his new homeland. Firstly, he was awarded an Honorary Doctorate of Military Science at Royal Roads Military College, Victoria, British Columbia, in May 1983. That same year, he received the lowest grade of the Member of the Order of Canada (CM), which is awarded for an outstanding lifetime contribution to the development of society and the nation. He accepted the decorations from Governor General Edward Schreyer during a ceremony in Ottawa, Ontario, on 5 October.

Gellner had every intention of publishing his memoirs. A contract with the Stoddart Publishing Company Ltd in Toronto, Ontario, had already been signed. The book's title was to be *A Front-Row Seat to History*. However, John had developed Alzheimer's, and the disease progressively worsened. It prevented him from finishing the manuscript.

Sadly, John Gellner—lawyer, mountaineer, navigator and pilot with the Royal Canadian Air Force, journalist, editor, and writer—lost his battle with Alzheimer's disease three years later. He passed away in the Vera M. Davis Community Care Centre in Bolton, Ontario, on 27 April 2001, at the ripe old age of ninety-three. The man had certainly led a full life. He was buried on 30 April 2001 and now peacefully rests in the Caledon East Public Cemetery.[38]

APPENDIX I
Decorations Awarded to John Gellner

Czechoslovak Gallantry Medal

The order of the Czechoslovak government in exile stated:

> It is a visible decoration to commemorate the fight for the liberation of the Czechoslovak Republic from an enemy occupation to those who have demonstrated an act of personal bravery against the enemy on the battlefield on the home front or abroad.

The recommendation was submitted in April 1941 (see Appendix II), but the official publication of the award was released in SDVN No. 27/1941 on 1 September 1941. The date of the award is also given differently in his RCAF Personal Record, where it is mentioned as being given in April 1941 or 23 June 1941, but in both cases reference is made to the Air Force Routine Orders (AFRO) 385/42 of 13 March 1942.

Czechoslovak Military Cross 1939

The order of the Czechoslovak government in exile stated:

> It is a visible decoration to commemorate the fight for the liberation of Czechoslovak Republic from an enemy occupation to Czechoslovak citizens in the homeland, units and members of the Czechoslovak Army abroad, as well as units and members of the allied forces who took part in the fight blazed out in 1939, and who proved an excellent and successful act of the executive or command, during which they personally risked their lives or they sacrificed their life.

The recommendation was submitted in June 1941 (see Appendix II), but the official publication of the award was released in SDVN No. 28/1941 on 22 September 1941.

The date of the award in his RCAF Personal Record is given as July 1941 or 1 July 1941, but in both cases with reference to the AFRO 385/42 of 13 March 1942.[1]

Distinguished Flying Cross (DFC)

This decoration for RAF officers was established by King George V on 3 June 1918, in recognition of 'an act or acts of valour, courage or devotion to duty whilst flying in active operations against the enemy'. The silver cross hung below a white ribbon with broad, purple, diagonal stripes.

The recommendation for John Gellner to receive the award was submitted in September 1941, and the decoration was awarded on 15 November 1941 (see AFRO 385/42, 13 March 1942).[2] The decoration was presented to him during a ceremony held in Ottawa on 3 December 1942. The recommendation reads as follows:

RECOMMENDATIONS FOR HONOURS AND AWARDS

Christian name: John
Surname: GELLNER
Rank: Acting Flight Lieutenant
Service number: CAN/J2822
Command or Group: No. 3 Group (Bomber)
Unit: 311 (Czech) Squadron
Total hours flown on operations: 194 hours 45 min since outbreak of war
Number of sorties carried out: 37 since outbreak of war
Recognition for which recommended: Distinguished Flying Cross
Appointment held: Navigator, Squadron Bombing Leader and Navigation Officer

On the night of 1–2 July 1941, he was Navigator of Wellington R1015, captained by Pilot Officer V. Korda, detailed to attack the German cruiser *Prinz Eugen* at Brest. Though conditions were good and the docks visible, the cruiser could not be seen due to darkness. It was then decided to drop a stick across its position, endeavouring to get the first bomb on the jetty. Despite intense flak, four runs across the target were carried out and a determined attack made on the last run. The heaviest bomb and another hit the jetty, lighting up the area, and it was estimated the remainder of the stick straddled the position of the cruiser. Intelligence reports later stated that two direct hits were obtained on that night, severely damaging the cruiser and killing many of the crew. These hits were credited to either 9 or 311 Squadrons, and it is highly probable that one of their hits was obtained by Pilot Officer Gellner.

Since January 1941, this officer has taken part in thirty-seven major operations, and his skill as a Navigator has been exceptional throughout. His precision and accuracy, particularly in astro navigation, would be difficult to exceed. He has had a log published in the August Bomber Command Monthly Navigational Summary under the heading of 'Meritorious Flights'.

He has shown conspicuous courage and devotion to duty in his determination to hit his target. He frequently carried out three or four runs to satisfy himself as to his target, and often dropped at least two sticks of bombs. His splendid example and instruction have been of the greatest asset in raising the standard of navigation and bombing in 311 Squadron.

Jos. Ocelka
Wing Commander, Commanding No. 311 (Czech) Squadron RAF
Date: 17 September 1941

Covering Remarks of Station Commander:

As outstanding Navigator and a most gallant officer, whose work and example has been of the greatest value in building up No. 311 (Czech) Squadron, he is strongly recommended for the award of the Distinguished Flying Cross.

J. A. Gray
Group Captain, Commanding RAF Station Honington
Date: 23 September 1941

List of Operations

No.	Date 1941	Target	Hours
1.	16/01	Emden	4.25
2.	12/02	Bremen	1.35 returned with bombs—engine trouble
3.	21/02	Wilhelmshaven	4.25
4.	23/02	Boulogne	2.25
5.	26/02	Cologne	4.30
6.	12/03	Berlin	7.50
7.	18/03	Bremen	5.10
8.	23/03	Berlin	7.45
9.	15/04	Kiel	5.20
10.	17/04	Berlin	7.05
11.	20/04	Cologne	5.30
12.	23/04	Brest	6.05
13.	26/04	Hamburg	6.35
14.	28/04	Brest	5.00

Appendix I

15.	11/05	Hamburg	5.40
16.	15/05	Hanover	5.35
17.	27/05	Cologne	4.50
18.	02/06	Düsseldorf	4.35
19.	11/06	Duisburg	4.55
20.	12/06	Essen	5.15
21.	16/06	Aalter aerodrome	2.40 last resort target—engine trouble
22.	17/06	Düsseldorf	4.40
23.	19/06	Cologne	5.35
24.	22/06	Bremen	4.55
25.	01/07	Brest	5.50
26.	05/07	Münster	4.55
27.	07/07	Cologne	4.50
28.	08/07	Münster	4.30
29.	10/07	Cologne	4.40
30.	12/07	Bremen	5.25
31.	14/07	Bremen	5.20
32.	15/07	Hamburg	6.15
33.	19/07	Hanover	6.05
34.	23/07	Mannheim	5.40
35.	25/07	Hamburg	6.20
36.	02/08	Hamburg	6.25
37.	05/08	Mannheim	6.10
		Total	**194.45**

Covering Remarks of Air Officer Commanding:

It is submitted that the action on the night of July 1–2, taken in conjunction with this Navigator's consistent record of successful sorties, entitles him for consideration for a Non-Immediate Award.

J. Baldwin
Air Vice-Marshal, Commanding No. 3 Group
Date: 28 September 1941

Bomber Command Headquarters were informed about the approval of Flt Lt Gellner's DFC by a telegram from the Air Ministry dated 18 November 1941 and marked as 'SECRET':

DFC to Acting Flight Lieutenant John GELLNER (CAN/J.2822) approved STOP Award will not be published STOP DFC will be presented at an investiture STOP.

As was the case with other Czechoslovaks who received British honours (and other Allied airmen from countries occupied by Germans), the award was not published in *The London Gazette*. This was to protect family members left behind in the occupied homeland. This is clearly indicated by a 5 February 1942 letter from F. E. Sheppard, of the Air Ministry, to the RCAF Headquarters in the UK:

> Referencing the telephone conversation with your department on 3 February, it is confirmed that the DFC was awarded to Acting Flight Lieutenant John GELLNER (CAN/J.2822), Royal Canadian Air Force, with effect from 15.11.41. This Officer is a Czech serving in the RCAF, and as the publication of citations relating to awards to foreigners is prohibited, no details of the services rendered in connection with this award are referred. Such details could, however, be supplied if required solely for record purposes at your headquarters.[3]

The 1939–45 Star

The star was established as the first of eight star decorations awarded for participation in combat across various theatres of war in the Second World War. The criteria for flying personnel in the European theatre were active service in the operational zone for sixty days and participation in operational flights against the enemy over the period of 3 September 1939 to 8 May 1945.

He was awarded by the 1939–45 Star ribbon on 13 December 1943, while he was with No. 3 PRC. The ribbon consisted of three equally broad stripes representing the individual components of the British Armed Forces (dark blue for the Navy, red for the Army, and light blue for the Air Forces). The full decoration was sent to him by post after the war.

Air Crew Europe Star

This was another of the eight stars awarded for participation in combat across various theatres in the Second World War. This star was awarded exclusively to flying personnel after sixty days of active service with an operational unit, operating over the European continent from bases on the British Isles, over the period from 3 September 1939 to 4 June 1944. Moreover, the person concerned had to perform at least one operational flight in this period, and the claim could be made only after the 1939–45 Star had previously been awarded.

The three-colour ribbon had a light-blue stripe in the middle that represented day operations, surrounded on both sides by equal black stripes representing night operations. The blue and black stripes are divided by narrow yellow stripes representing enemy searchlights.

Appendix I

Canadian Volunteer Service Medal 1939–1947 (CVSM) & Clasp

This decoration, established on 22 October 1943, was granted to members of any rank in the Naval, Military or Air Forces of Canada who voluntarily served on Active Service and completed eighteen months (540 days) of voluntary service from 3 September 1939 to 1 March 1947.

A silver clasp with a maple leaf at its centre was awarded for sixty days' service outside Canada. A silver maple leaf was worn on the ribbon. The ribbon has a royal-blue centre flanked by two equal stripes of scarlet and dark green, the dark green being on the edges. The ribbon was issued during the war, while the medal was issued after the war. Claims were made for 1,183,000 medals; 650,000 medals and 525,000 clasps were awarded.

Gellner was awarded the CVSM ribbon with the clasp on 27 March 1944, while on training with No. 24 OTU.[4]

Defence Medal

The Defence Medal, established on 16 August 1945, was usually awarded to Canadians for six months of service in the United Kingdom between 3 September 1939 and 8 May 1945. The exact criterion was service in the forces in non-operational areas subjected to air attack or closely threatened, providing such service lasted for three or more years. The medal could be awarded for service overseas or outside the country of residence, provided that it lasted for one year—except in territories threatened by the enemy or subject to bomb attacks, in which case the medal could be awarded for service carried out for six months prior to 2 September 1945.

The light-green ribbon had a central stripe of orange and a narrow black stripe in the middle of each green stripe. The orange represents the enemy attacks on the green land of England, and the black represents the blackouts. Some 325,000 of these medals were awarded to Canadians.

War Medal

This medal was established on 16 August 1945 and awarded to all full-time personnel of the Armed Forces and merchant marine for a minimum of twenty-eight days of service between 3 September 1939 and 2 September 1945. The ribbon consists of seven coloured stripes—red, dark blue, white, narrow red (in the centre), white, dark blue, and red. Around 700,000 silver Canadian medals were issued (the British-issue medals were made of cupro-nickel).

The aforementioned five decorations (The 1939–45 Star, The Air Crew Europe Star, The Canadian Volunteer Service Medal 1939–1947 and Clasp, The Defence

Medal, and The War Medal) were not available *in natura* at the time they were awarded to John Gellner; they were sent to him via post after the war, with some not reaching him until 1949.[5]

Operational Wings

Operational Wings were awarded for completion of the operational tour. There are no known exact criteria for this award, such as number of sorties or operational hours flown during the tour. However, there are some known cases of when Operational Wings were not awarded after a very small number of sorties. The following conditions meant that Operational Wings would be awarded regardless of the number of sorties completed:

a. Death before completion of a tour.
b. Wounds severe enough to prevent completion of a tour or required hours or sorties.
c. Termination of hostilities.

A small, metal, winged 'O' was accompanied with a brevet with the following dedication:

> This is to certify that Flight Lieutenant J. Gellner has been awarded the Operational Wings of the Royal Canadian Air Force in recognition of gallant service in that he has completed a tour of operational duty in action against the enemy.[6]

In the case of a particular airman who finished more than one operational tour, a small bar was attached under the original badge for the second tour, or two bars in case of three tours.

Flt Lt Gellner received his Operational Wings according to his RCAF Service Record in the spring of 1944 during his service with No. 429 'Bison' (B) Squadron RCAF. Unfortunately, there are no known photos showing him wearing his Operational Wings.

War Service Badge

The War Service Badge 'General Service Class' was the original name for the honour today known as the 'General Service Badge'. It was established by the Canadian government on 29 March 1940, and was dedicated to the following:

> … members of the Naval, Military or Air Forces of Canada who have declared their willingness or who have engaged to serve in any of the said forces on active service beyond Canada and overseas during the present war, and who have honourably ceased their active service:

1. After no less than three months of continuous paid service.
2. By reason of physical disability.

The button-sized badge consisted of a silver-coloured shield with three maple leaves joined on one stem, surmounted by a crown, and underneath, on a scroll, the words 'GENERAL SERVICE'.

War Service Badge 'General Service Class' No. 1464378 was awarded to Sqn Ldr Gellner DFC in 1946.[7]

Canadian Forces Decoration (CD)

This medal was established on 15 December 1949, and it is awarded to officers, men, and women in the Canadian Forces who have completed twelve years of service. The medal is awarded to all ranks, but they must have a good record of conduct during the final eight years of their claimed service. This award supersedes all other awards for members joining the Canadian Forces after 1 September 1939.

Gellner was awarded the CD in 1952, after twelve years' service in the RCAF (according to AFRO 406/52 A-127 of 13 June 1952).

Member of the Order of Canada (CM)

The Order of Canada was established in 1967 by Queen Elizabeth II to recognise 'a lifetime of outstanding achievement, dedication to the community and service to the nation'. The order has three classes—Companion (CC), Officer (OC), and Member (CM). The Member of the Order of Canada recognises 'a lifetime of distinguished service in or to a particular community, group, or field of activity'. The CM was awarded to John Gellner on 20 June 1983, and he was invested on 5 October 1983:

> After escaping the Nazis in Czechoslovakia during the invasion, Mr Gellner served in the Royal Canadian Air Force during and after the Second World War. On his retirement twenty-five years ago, he turned to editing political and defence periodicals and introduced strategic studies at Toronto and York Universities. Through his teaching and writing he has helped to make Canadians more aware of the need for critical thought on strategic matters.[8]

Doctor of Military Science (DMS)

John Gellner received an Honorary Doctorate in Military Science at the Royal Roads Military Academy on 13 May 1983.

APPENDIX II

Correspondence Regarding the Award of Czechoslovak Decorations to John Gellner

The Czechoslovak government in exile was faced with an unfamiliar situation with regards to awarding Czechoslovak decorations to Czechoslovak citizens who served with the Commonwealth air forces. The Office of the Czechoslovak President informed the British Foreign Office of their intention to allow Czechoslovak government officials to present a decoration, and a proposal outlining this was then submitted to the Air Ministry. This set a precedent that allowed any other British airman to be awarded Czechoslovak decorations.

This was a landmark case—the first of its kind. The intended recipient was a serving member of the RCAF. The Air Ministry requested the permission of the Canadian government via the High Commissioner of Canada in London. London's National Archives contains correspondence showing the miles of official 'red tape' that piled up over an eight-month period of discussions regarding nothing more than the award of two decorations to one officer.

The official 'roundabout' was started by a letter from Jaroslav Šejnoha, Chief of Protocol in the Czechoslovak Presidential Chancellery. It was addressed to the Foreign Office on 3 April 1941:

Dear Mr Dunbar,

I write to inform you that the Czechoslovak government is contemplating proposing the decoration with the Czechoslovak Medal for Valour[1] of those members of the RAF who are attached to Czechoslovak Bombing Wing No. 311:

Plt Off. John Gellner
FS Patrick Leo Hennigan DFM
Sgt Leo Joseph Judson
Sgt Ernest James Linley Robb

Appendix II

Plt Off. John Gellner is a Czechoslovak subject who, after escaping from his country to Canada, joined the RCAF. He was sent to England as a Plt Off. and was attached to the Czechoslovak Air Force at his own request.

The Air Ministry was informed of the developments by the Foreign Office in a letter on 11 April 1941. In turn, the Air Ministry forwarded the information on to the Canadian Ambassador in London on 16 April:

Sir,

I am directed to inform you that the Foreign Office has intimated that the Czechoslovak government are contemplating the award of the Czechoslovak Medal for Valour to Plt Off. John Gellner, Royal Canadian Air Force, in recognition of services rendered in connection with the training of Czechoslovak Air Force personnel in this country. Plt Off. Gellner is said to be a Czechoslovak subject who, after escaping from his country to Canada, joined the Royal Canadian Air Force, was posted to England and, at his own request, was attached to the Czechoslovak Air Force. He is at present serving with No. 311 (Czech) Squadron. I am to request that you will be good enough to ascertain whether the Canadian authorities are willing to permit this officer to accept and wear the distinction in question.

In the case of the three British airmen who were to be awarded a Czechoslovak decoration alongside Plt Off. Gellner, the Air Ministry sent an approval letter to the Foreign Office on 21 April. The Air Ministry later received a letter informing them of the decorations for FS Hennigan DFM, Sgt Judson, and Sgt Robb. At 11.00 a.m. on 7 May 1941, the Czechoslovak Gallantry Medals were presented to them by No. 311 (B) Squadron Commanding Officer Wg Cdr Josef Schejbal at their headquarters at RAF Station East Wretham.

The Air Ministry waited until 19 May for a reply from the Canadians with regards to Plt Off. Gellner:

Sir,

I am directed to reply to your letter of April 16, reference A.1330000/40/S.10.a, stating that the Czechoslovak government contemplate the award of the Czechoslovak Medal for Valour to Plt Off. John Gellner of the RCAF, at present attached to the Czechoslovak Air Force, and asking whether the Canadian authorities would be willing to permit this officer to accept and wear the distinction in question.

I have today received a cabled communication from the Canadian government stating that the award by the Czechoslovak government of the medal to Plt Off. Gellner has been approved by the Minister of National Defence for Air and by the Prime Minister.

> I am directed to state that the general policy with regard to Foreign Decorations is under consideration by the Canadian government and that it is expected that a submission will be made shortly to His Majesty to approve the rules with regard thereto. There is, however, no objection to the acceptance of this award by Plt Off. Gellner pending the settlement of a general policy.

The Air Ministry immediately forwarded this information to the Foreign Office on 20 May:

> Dear Mr Dunbar,
>
> Further to my letter of 21 April (in reply to your T.2322/82/372 of 11th idem), I write to let you know that the High Commissioner for Canada has now informed us that the Canadian authorities approve of the award of the Czechoslovak Medal for Valour to Plt Off. John Gellner, Royal Canadian Air Force.

The Foreign Office delayed forwarding the information to the Czechoslovak President's Office until 5 June. They added the following amendment:

> I shall be glad if you will very kindly let me know when the distinctions have actually been conferred, in order that arrangements may be made to enable the recipient to wear them.

The proposal to decorate John Gellner with the Czechoslovak Gallantry Medal was finally submitted to the Military Office of the Czechoslovak Presidential Chancellery by the Czechoslovak Ministry of National Defence on 16 June, with the following citation:

> Plt Off. John Gellner, RCAF, is of Czechoslovakian nationality and citizenship. He is a member of the Royal Canadian Air Force attached to No. 311 Czechoslovak Bomber Squadron. He is a member of the operational crew and also the astronavigation instructor. As a navigator, he has carried out six sorties over enemy territory by the end of this March. He always fulfilled his tasks successfully despite bad weather and heavy enemy anti-aircraft fire, whereby he showed courage and bravery.

An unknown Lieutenant-Colonel wrote a comment in red on the proposal—'Is he authorised to serve in the RAF according to the Military Act?' It was necessary for him to check in order to award the decoration, and therefore the Head of the Military Office of the Czechoslovak Presidential Chancellery, Gen. Nižborský, sent the following letter to the Czechoslovak Ministry of National Defence on 27 June:

Appendix II

In your letter (reference number 9757-I/1.part 41) of 16 July of this year, you propose the award of the Czechoslovak Medal for Valour to Plt Off. John Gellner RCAF, who is of Czechoslovak nationality and citizenship.

I would like to ask you if the named was given the approval to enter the RCAF in accordance with Military Act No. 193 of 19 March 1920, as amended by Act 29/1934 and the Military Order par. 5. If this has not yet happened, I find it necessary to resolve this particular question in order to fulfil Czechoslovak law, and then to act on the proposed decoration.

During the exchanging of diplomatic correspondence, Plt Off. Gellner was made aware of the delicate situation. The Commanding Officer of No. 311 (B) Squadron, Wg Cdr Josef Schejbal, was also notified. On 23 June, the Commanding Officer drafted an official letter and mailed it to headquarters at RAF Station Honington:

Enclosed is the application of Plt Off. J. Gellner, RCAF, to be granted permission to join the Royal Canadian Air Force.

It is pointed out that this is a purely formulary matter, but the above mentioned Officer must obtain permission from the Czechoslovak Ministry of National Defence as he is a Czechoslovak subject.

Plt Off. Gellner joined the RCAF at a time when the Czechoslovak government had not yet received official recognition in the United Kingdom, and could therefore not ask for permission to join a foreign military formation.

The letter and the application caused some confusion, and the next day it was returned from Honington—unsigned—by a British Adjutant:

Your letter dated 23.6.41 regarding an application from the above named Officer is returned, as the reason for the application is most obscure. The first sentence asks for permission for an application to join the RCAF, whilst in the third sentence it is stated that 'Plt Off. Gellner joined the RCAF at the time'.

The copies of the application for Plt Off. Gellner are also returned.

Flt Lt MacNicol, the Adjutant of No. 311 (B) Squadron, took matters into his own hands by sending a well-thought-out letter to Honington on 26 June, which explained the situation with Gellner in great detail:

Plt Off. J. Gellner

With reference to your HON/C/601/294/P1, dated 24 June 1941, the following is the explanation of the above named officer's application.

It appears that before a Czechoslovakian subject may join a foreign air force, permission has to be granted by the Czechoslovak Ministry of National Defence, and before submitting an application to the Ministry it should be approved by the commander of the station on which the officer is serving. In the case of Plt Off. Gellner, the application is purely a formal matter as he is in fact already in the Royal Canadian Air Force, and the application is being submitted merely to regularise the position as far as the Ministry of National Defence is concerned.

The application, therefore, is returned, and it would be appreciated if the Station Commander could sign both the Czech application and the translation as 'Approved' and return them to this unit.

At this point, it is necessary to note that East Wretham did not have a Commanding Officer during the summer of 1941. That forced No. 311 (B) Squadron to deal directly with Grp Capt. J. A. G. Gray, CO of RAF Station Honington, who was also in charge of the East Wretham satellite. It was only after the matter was thoroughly explained that Plt Off. Gellner was able to forward his official request for transfer to the RCAF to the Czechoslovak Ministry of National Defence on 12 July:

I would like to request subsidiary permission for me to join the Royal Canadian Air Force and I am providing the following reasoning.

I was in New York when the war broke out. It was at a time of strict neutrality for the United States of America, and it was immediately clear to me that there would be hardly any Czechoslovak military action there. When Canada entered the war on 10 September 1939, I went there with the expectations of enlisting with the Czechoslovak Legions, which hopefully would be formed. I found that even in Canada things had still not progressed very far. I could not count on any Czechoslovak military action in the foreseeable future. It was before the fall of France. I felt there would be a quick victory by the Allies and I feared that if I will waited too long, it would be too late for me to fight the Germans. Therefore, I joined the Royal Canadian Air Force (RCAF) as an Aircraftman 2nd Class (AC2) in April 1940. I was trained as an observer and I was commissioned at the end of October 1940. I was sent to Europe on 15 November 1940. On my own request in England, I was posted to Czechoslovak Bomber Squadron (No. 311), where I am currently a navigation instructor and a member of the crew. So far, I have done twenty-nine operations against targets in Germany and in German-occupied territories, and I was selected for a decoration. Soon after my arrival in England, I reported to Gen. Nižborský and explained my proceeding to him. It was reinforced by the situation and especially by the distance between Canada and the assembly point of Czechoslovak troops in France. I would like to ask for approval of my proceeding, especially in view of the fact that I was only driven by the desire to get into the fight against the Germans as quickly as possible.

Plt Off. John Gellner, RCAF
No. 311 (Czech) Squadron

Appendix II

The Ministry sent the request to the Military Office of the Czechoslovak Presidential Chancellery on 21 July with the following comment from the Minister of National Defence, Gen. Ingr: 'I recommend a positive acknowledgement due to the reasons mentioned in the request.'

The requested subsidiary approval by the Commander in Chief of the Czechoslovak Armed Forces, President Dr Edvard Beneš, bears the date 26 July:

> I am granting to G E L L N E R John, born 18 May 1907 in Trieste, resident in Brno, Moravia-Silesia, permission to join the Royal Canadian Air Force for the duration of war, in accordance with Military Act of the Czechoslovak Republic No. 193 of 19 March 1920, as amended by Act 29/1934 Paragraph 5 of the Military Order.

After nearly four months, all the requirements had been met, and approval was granted by the President and the Cabinet Council. Plt Off. Gellner could now finally be awarded his well-deserved Czechoslovak Gallantry Medal.

However, the whole 'bureaucratic carousel' was started again on 25 June 1941 by another letter from the Czechoslovak Presidential Chancellery to the Foreign Office:

> Dear Mr Dunbar,
>
> I write to inform you that the Czechoslovak government is considering a proposal to the President of the Republic concerning the awarding of the decoration of the Czechoslovak Military Cross 1939 to:
>
> Plt Off. John Gellner, Royal Canadian Air Force, attached to No. 311 Czechoslovak Squadron.
>
> This officer is a Czechoslovak subject. He is a member of an operational squadron and has undertaken operations as a navigator up to the end of May 1941, including sixteen operational bombing flights over enemy territory. On these occasions he has carried out his tasks very successfully and displayed resolution and bravery.

The Foreign Office withheld the application until 17 July, before forwarding it to the Air Ministry. There was some confusion as to the actual name of the decoration. Was it the one already approved, or was it another award?

> With reference to your letter No. A.133000/40 on 20 May, I enclose a copy of a letter from the Director of Protocol in the Czechoslovak Presidential Chancellery regarding the proposed award of a further distinction to Plt Off. John Gellner of the Royal Canadian Air Force. In case you should think that we have taken a long time to pass this nomination on to you, I would explain that as originally received,

M. Sejnoha's letter again specified the Czechoslovak Medal for Valour and we had to confirm from him that a second award was in fact contemplated.

Would you kindly let me know whether we may inform M. Sejnoha that there is no objection to the bestowal of the 'Military Cross' now contemplated?

As in the case of the previous decoration, the Air Ministry approached the office of the High Commissioner for Canada in London on 21 July:

With reference to your letter of the 15 May, relative to the award of the Czechoslovak Medal for Valour to Plt Off. John Gellner, Royal Canadian Air Force (attached to the Czechoslovak Air Force), I am directed to inform you that the Foreign Office has intimated that the Czechoslovak Government are contemplating the award to this officer of the Czechoslovak Military Cross. This further award is in recognition of his having participated as a navigator in sixteen operational bombing flights over enemy territory and of the success, resolution and bravery attending the performance of his tasks on these occasions.

I am to request that you will be good enough to ascertain whether the Canadian authorities are willing to permit this officer to accept the above award.

A positive reply was sent by the Canadian authorities on 12 August, as it had been in the first case:

With reference to your letter of 21 July, A.133000/40/S.10(a), regarding the further award of the Czechoslovak Military Cross to Plt Off. John Gellner, Royal Canadian Air Force (attached to the Czechoslovak Air Force), I am directed to inform you that the general position with regard to Foreign Decorations is still unchanged since Mr Hudd wrote you on May 15 on this subject and that the general policy if the Canadian government in now under consideration.

Under these circumstances, there is no objection on the part of the Canadian government to Plt Off. Gellner's acceptance of this further award pending the settlement of a general policy.

The Air Ministry therefore confirmed the approval to the Foreign Office in a letter dated 15 August:

Further to my letter of 21 July, I write to let you know that the High Commissioner for Canada has now informed us that the Canadian authorities approve of the award of the Czechoslovak Military Cross to Plt Off. John Gellner, RCAF.

The next day, the same information was passed on to RAF Bomber Command:

Further to this department's letter on 19 June, numbered as above, relative to the award of the Czechoslovak Medal for Valour to Plt Off. John Gellner, Royal Canadian Air Force, of No. 311 Squadron, I am directed to inform you that the Czechoslovak authorities have now expressed their intention of awarding a further distinction to this officer, namely the Czechoslovak Military Cross 1939. This additional award is in recognition of resolution and bravery displayed as navigator whilst engaged on bombing flights over enemy territory.

It has been ascertained that the Canadian Government has no objection to the acceptance of this second award and I am to request that you will report when it has been presented.

RAF Bomber Command Headquarters sent a reply on 12 September:

Award of Foreign Decorations

I have the honour to refer to Air Ministry letter A.133000/40/S.10a, dated 16 August 1941, and to state that the following awards were presented to Plt Off. J. Gellner by Air Vice-Marshal Janoušek, the Inspector General at the Czech Inspectorate, on 2 August 1941:

Czechoslovak Medal for Valour—w.e.f. 23.6.41
Czechoslovak Military Cross 1939—w.e.f. 1.7.41

This information is apparently inaccurate, as Plt Off. Gellner was on an operation on the night of 2–3 August—so there was no way he could have been in London at the same time. However, the date roughly corresponds to an undated entry in his diary that indicates when he learned about the award, sometime between 25 July and 2 August.

Under the established practice, it can be assumed that after the information about his two decorations reached No. 311 (B) Squadron Headquarters, he just picked up ribbons for his uniform and was decorated later *in natura*.

On 2 December 1941, when Flt Lt Gellner had already been back in Canada for several months, the Czechoslovak Presidential Chancellery informed the Air Ministry about the approval of his award:

With reference to your kind letter No. T 4858/82/372 of 22 August 1941, I beg to inform you that on 24 August 1941 the President of the Czechoslovak Republic conferred the Czechoslovak Military Cross 1939 to Plt Off. John Gellner of the Royal Canadian Air Force.

The bureaucratic 'red tape' thankfully came to an end on 15 December, in the form of a letter from the Foreign Office to the Czechoslovak Presidential Chancellery:

Dear Monsieur Sejnoha,

I am much obliged to you for your letter No. 2118/41 of 2 December, in which you kindly informed me of the bestowal of the Czechoslovak Military Cross 1939 upon Plt Off. John Gellner. We are communicating this information to the authorities concerned in order that necessary steps may be taken to enable this officer to wear his decoration.

Yours sincerely,

R. Dunbarn.[2]

APPENDIX III

Air Raid on the Cruiser *Prinz Eugen* in Brest Harbour, Night of 1–2 July 1941

The Krupp Germania shipyard, in the northern German city of Kiel, began constructing the hull of the *Kriegsmarine*'s third heavy cruiser—under the provisional name *Kreuzer J* (Cruiser J)—in 1936. The cost of building this mighty ship escalated to the princely sum of 104.5 million Reichsmarks. Under the name *Prinz Eugen*, it was finally launched on 22 August 1938 by the wife of the Hungarian governor, Admiral Miklós Horthy. It was named after the Austrian commander of French origin, Prince Eugene of Savoy, who became famous in the eighteenth century for his campaign against the Turks.

The cruiser was commissioned on 1 August 1940 under the command of *Kapitän zur See* Helmuth Brinkmann. On the night of 1–2 July 1940, it had sustained light damage after being hit by a pair of bombs dropped by RAF bombers during a raid on Kiel Harbour. No one envisioned this event as a foretaste of worse things to come the following year.

As 1940 ended and 1941 began, crew training was conducted, including a test cruise around Kiel and the Baltic Sea. On 8 April 1941, the cruiser sailed from Kiel to Gotenhafen (the German name for the Polish port of Gdansk in 1939–45). The cruiser struck a sea mine while returning to Kiel on 22 April, but it only suffered minor damage and returned to Gotenhafen. The ship was repaired there and declared as seaworthy on 2 May 1941. It then set sail for the wide-open Atlantic Ocean on 18 May 1941, accompanied by the giant battleship *Bismarck*, commanded by *Kapitän zur See* Ernst Lindemann.

On Friday 23 May, at 8.22 a.m. CET, south-west of Iceland, both German ships were sighted by the Royal Navy heavy cruisers HMS *Suffolk* and HMS *Norfolk*. After a brief exchange of gunfire, the British ships lost contact with the Germans during the night. The following morning, the British fleet regained contact with both German ships. Between 6.53 and 7.13 a.m. CET, the German ships fired on the battle cruiser HMS *Hood* and the battleship HMS *Prince of Wales*. At 7 a.m. CET, HMS *Hood* exploded after one hit from *Prinz Eugen* and five others from *Bismarck*. The HMS *Hood* sank immediately, taking 1,415 sailors to a watery grave. After HMS

Prince of Wales was hit seven times by the heavy guns on *Prinz Eugen* and *Bismarck*, she broke away and continued to shadow the enemy ships from a safe distance.

Prinz Eugen came away from the gunfight unscathed. During the subsequent escape, the German ships split up. This eventually proved to be a fatal decision. *Bismarck* was sunk on 27 May, after a battle with the British fleet. *Prinz Eugen* refuelled from three tankers over the next few days and prepared to start attacking Allied merchant ships in the Atlantic alone. An engine failure on 29 May forced *Kapitän zur See* Brinkmann to return to Brest, France. He anchored the *Prinz Eugen* on 1 June 1941.

At the end of March 1941, an RAF pilot carried out a photo-reconnaissance sortie over Brest. A close look at the film showed the sister battleships *Gneisenau* and *Scharnhorst* hidden in the harbour. The RAF drew up plans for a bombing offensive against the ships.

A British Intelligence summary describes the total RAF deployment:

Between 28 March and 31 August 1941, the Royal Air Force has delivered forty-seven attacks on Brest, despatching 1,688 aircraft, making 1,392 effective sorties and dropping 8,371 bombs weighing 1,899 tons. In addition, the photographic reconnaissance unit have flown 552 sorties, and 360 sorties have been despatched to lay mines, of which 291 have completed their task.

RAF losses on these raids totalled fifty-one aircraft, of which twenty-eight were lost during daylight operations.

The British recorded the arrival of the cruiser *Prinz Eugen* and her being berthed in dry dock No. 8, which was located on a promontory at the eastern part of the Port de Commerce on Wednesday 4 June 1941 (the RAF report records the port as 'Dry Dock Grand Bassin Du Nord Est Port Du Commerce de Porstrein'). The cruiser was covered with camouflage nets, and the masking was assessed as very effective as the British had difficulties finding the ship's outline in the dry dock. An RAF intelligence report also includes a summary of events relating to the cruiser:

- 7.6.41 Heavy camouflage netting completely covered the cruiser and a boom was in position at the dock entrance.
- 18.6.41 The dock was seen to be dry.
- 27.6.41 Clouds of smoke were seen issuing from two chimneys at the side of the dry dock. No further developments have been noticed apart from the movements of a floating crane to and from the Dock Gates.[1]

At 10 p.m. on Tuesday 1 July 1941, Brest issued a warning for an imminent air raid. The ships and docks had been targeted many times over a three-month period. The German monitoring service was able to track a number of RAF bomber squadrons from the time they took off. Over a ninety-minute period, from 9.30 to 11 p.m., a force of fifty-two bombers from RAF Bomber Command's No. 3 Group took off from airfields located in eastern England. The sole objective was to cause as much damage as possible to the German warships in the harbour. Forty minutes after midnight, Brest was confirmed as the target for the air raid. The third-highest level of air raid warning—*Hoechstalarm*—was broadcast around the harbour. Unfortunately for Brest, its seaside location gave it little or no time to prepare, as the air raid warning arrived too late. The first bombs hit just a few short minutes after the warning was sounded.[2]

Nine Vickers Wellington Mk ICs from No. 101 (B) Squadron (based at Oakington, Cambridgeshire) were tasked with bombing the port docks. Ten Wellington Mk ICs from No. 99 'Madras Presidency' (B) Squadron, taking off from Waterbeach, Cambridgeshire, would attack the battleship *Gneisenau*. *Scharnhorst*, her sister ship, would be attacked by fourteen Wellington Mk ICs from No. 149 'East India' (B) Squadron, based at Mildenhall, Suffolk. The greatest attention was to be given to the cruiser *Prinz Eugen*, which would be attacked by eleven Wellington Mk ICs from No. 9 (B) Squadron, Honington, Suffolk, along with eight aircraft of the same type from No. 311 (B) Squadron, East Wretham, Norfolk. A total of forty-one aircraft reached their target, dropping 65 tons of bombs in the harbour area.[3]

An overview of how the particular crews got along during the raid is provided in the individual squadron ORBs. It is clear that crews either dropped their bomb loads in the target area (without attaining the precise location of a particular ship due to an effective smokescreen) or brought bombs home, regardless of the defined objectives. Only four aircraft captains reported bombs dropping in the close vicinity of No. 8 Dock.

Sgt Moore (No. 149 Sqn) reported one stick (240°) to have fallen just north of No. 8 Dry Dock. A burst was seen, but no other results were observed. Haze and probable smokescreen made the identification of the target impossible.

Sqn Ldr Cruickshanks (No. 9 Sqn) reported seeing the jetties and the inland smokescreen. Bombs were dropped at the end of the jetty, in the vicinity of Dock 8. The bursts were not seen.

Sgt Peatfield (No. 9 Sqn) attacked the target, identifying the docks, coastline, and river. His bombs were dropped immediately north of the position of the cruiser, and three bursts were seen.[4]

For No. 311 Sqn, Plt Off. Korda's individual bombing report has survived to the present day:

Aircraft No. and Letter:	R1015/KX-L
Captain:	Plt Off. V. Korda
Take-off time:	21.45
Bombing time and height:	00.50, 14,000 feet
Type and number of bombs dropped:	1 × 1,000 GP
	4 × 500 GP
	1 × 250 GP

Results observed:	No fires on arrival.
	Bombed on 090° M, saw five bursts.
	1,000 lb on root of Dock 8, end of stick should have hit ship.
Weather:	Clouds 1/10, temperature -2° at 14,000 feet.
Date and time landed:	2. 7. 03.25[5]

Dry Dock No. 8 still exists today. Its orientation towards the sea is from the south-west to the north-east. According to aerial photographs, *Prinz Eugen* was docked at the east pier, with its bow facing the mainland. After the air raid warning had been sounded in Brest harbour, sailors aboard the cruiser took up their posts, manning the anti-aircraft guns and machine guns. The silence of the harbour had not been broken yet. The artificial fog generators worked hard, progressively shrouding the harbour under a protective veil of fog.

The book *The Story of the Prince Eugen* is based on the original cruiser's log, which recorded that night's events on board in detail: however, exact times are not given for the individual events. The first event recorded after the air raid warning was a British bomber flying in from the north-west. A battery of anti-aircraft artillery subsequently opened fire, while the guns on the cruiser remained silent so as not to betray its position to the attackers. Then the first attackers arrived:

'Do you hear? There are the first bombs falling!' said Paulus, looking at the flame-striped eddies of mist and listening to the bomb bursts.

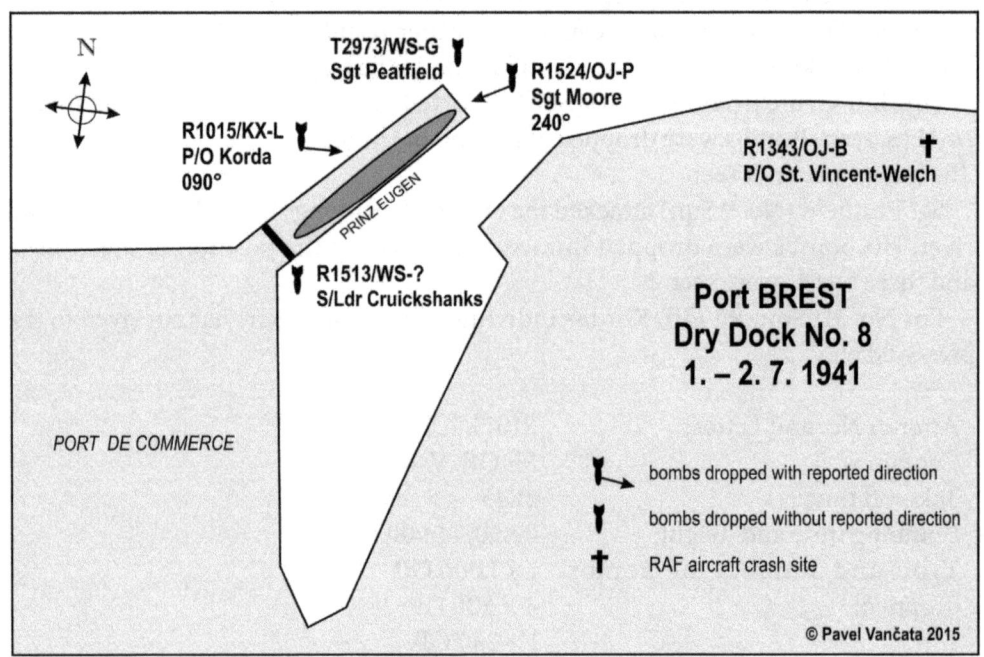

Ravoom-roomroom! Water spouted mast-high and stones whizzed over the action control platform and clattered against the mast and guard-rail.

'That was on the port quarter and starboard bow,' declared the Gunnery Commander in a matter-of-fact tone.

'It was damnably close, I thought!' was the Second Gunnery Officer's comment.

'Yes, indeed! That was certainly indeed for us, Herr *Kapitänleutnant*!' came the voice of Ordinary Seaman First Class Domnitz from the port direction.

Bomb explosions and flak gradually dwindled until there was silence all around the harbour once again. Initially, it appeared that the ship had come through another raid unscathed. All stations subsequently reported to the bridge but one—the control centre. The presumption of a temporary disconnection was short-lived. Soon, a seaman posted to check the situation noted smoke coming from a half-open hatch leading down to the control centre. The rescue team, in asbestos suits and respirators, found several wounded sailors who were immediately transported to the ship's hospital. There were no survivors in the control centre.

The explosion killed forty-seven men, including the First Officer, *Fregattenkapitän* Otto Stooss. Over the next few days, another thirteen sailors died as a result of injuries sustained in the attack. They were originally buried in the Kerfautras Cemetery in Brest. Their bodies were later exhumed and transferred to the German war cemetery in Lesneven, about 15 miles to the north-east of Brest.

The Story of the Prince Eugen also describes the curious manner in which the cruiser was hit:

> The bomb, a heavy armour-piercing bomb with a wall thickness of up to 2 inches, had hit the ship on the port side, on the upper deck, in the waterway somewhat below the aft edge of the bridge. The hole through which it had entered measured only 12 inches. If it had been released only one hundredth of a second sooner, the bomb would have landed, ineffectually, on the dock, which was filled with thirteen feet of water. As it was, however, it slid inside, down the sloping ship's side, forced its way through several vertical ribs, was deflected at a traverse rib, penetrated the armoured deck and the floor of the upper platform deck, and did not explode until it reached the lower platform deck. The explosion had taken place right among the heavy guns, in the forward directing and calculation position. As only these two compartments were equipped with this apparatus and they were totally destroyed, the heavy guns were put right out of action. The repair work, under the brilliant direction of the Naval Engineer Dr Strobusch and Naval Staff Engineer Flemming, went on until the end of the year, and was frequently interrupted by enemy air attacks.[6]

The bomb struck the cruiser *Prinz Eugen* on the port side, right behind Gun Turret 'B' (second from the bow) on the windward deck in front of the bridge. It then penetrated the interior of the ship. The explosion completely destroyed the front repeater station, which was using thyratrons— gas-filled tubes used to amplify electrical current and voltage. The electricity was used for powering various items of artillery equipment, like a lift for the projectiles, engines, and gun-barrel elevation. It also seriously damaged the mechanical artillery computer in the fire control centre. This was used to enable the ship to fire its guns at low elevation; the main control station also sustained damage. This was where the First Officer could watch all the ship's systems and direct rescue and repair teams during the fight if necessary. Other damaged areas included the compass room, which contained the main gyrocompass—the data from which was transmitted throughout the ship, including to the bridge. Damage was also done to the switching room, where distribution panels were located; these distribution panels connected the fire control station and the computer rooms, and allowed different stations to share gun control in order to maintain continuous fire from all turrets against different targets. All the electrical and communication lines within the radius of the explosion were also destroyed or damaged.

In addition, several fragments pierced the inner and outer bottom of the hull, so some sections were also flooded to a height of about 3 feet. A certain amount of water remained in the dry dock for cooling purposes and as a supply of water in case of fire. It took until 11 November 1941 to repair the damaged hull, and the replacement of the damaged cable networks took until 16 December.[7]

The British were unable to verify that the cruiser had been damaged, and therefore the RAF intelligence reports contained only estimates:

As a result of the attack made on the night of 1–2 July, *Prinz Eugen* received three direct hits [*sic*.], one of which was made near the funnel and is believed to have caused considerable internal damage. As this vessel has been in dock since her arrival to Brest and there has been no attempt to move her, it is probable that serious damage has been caused, although exact particulars are not available.[8]

The extent of the cruiser's damage can be found today from official German sources, but to say which of the RAF crews scored the lucky hit is very difficult. While the war records attributed this unique hit to a crew either from No. 9 (B) Squadron or No. 311 (B) Squadron, some later publications indicated the possibility that the cruiser was hit by a bomb from an aircraft of No. 149 'East India' (B) Squadron which was shot down and crashed near its target.[9]

Likewise, the French publication *La Bretagne dans la bataille de l'Atlantique* attributes the hit to the downed Vickers Wellington Mk IC R1343/OJ-B:

The uncontrollable aircraft crashed at the rocky shore of the cargo port, where its ruins remained for some time on view to the public. However, before it crashed, the crew managed to drop bombs that hit the cruiser, broke through the upper deck, and exploded in front of the radio room [*sic*.] ... The explosion was so powerful that its shockwave lifted the steam locomotive standing on the tracks leading to the port within a few hundred yards from the ship. A pair of engine drivers miraculously survived the blast wave, just being knocked down for a few seconds.[10]

Author Roger Huguen gathered information from the eyewitness testimony of his father, Jean Huguen, one of the engine drivers mentioned above. He also wrote a letter to a relative of one of the crew members of the downed bomber:

> My father worked at the station on the north end of the dock and he was close to the ship at the time of the air raid. He saw Wellington R1343 ... descending towards the *Prinz Eugen* after being set on fire by a parachute flare dropped by another aircraft. He recalled seeing the aircraft dropping bombs before being shot down, and shortly afterwards he was knocked down by the explosion's shockwave. A nearby concrete canteen was levelled by the explosion. The aircraft crashed on rocks near to the ship and was left there for some time.[11]

According to other testimonies, Vickers Wellington Mk IC R1343/OJ-B actually fell into the sea about half a mile to the east of the dock. It impacted a few-dozen yards from a place called Tritschler Beach. The crew, Plt Off. S. L. St Vincent-Welch, Sgt W. M. Symmons (both RAAF), Sgt W. J. Megran, Sgt R. H. Crafts (both RCAF), Sgt C. C. Reidmuller, and Sgt A. R. J. Harrison, were buried at the Kerfautras Cemetery in Brest.

In addition to Plt Off. Vincent-Welch's crew being lost, the RAF bomber force lost another aircraft from No. 149 'East India' (B) Squadron. Vickers Wellington Mk IC R1408/OJ-J, piloted by Plt Off. J. E. Horsfield, crashed at Plouzané, about 6 miles to the west of Brest. All except one of the aircraft from No. 311 (B) Squadron landed at their home base. That night, Fg Off. František Pohlodek and his crew had steered too close to the balloon barrage; it was only by sheer luck that they escaped after colliding with one of the steel balloon cables. Until now, most Czech books have reported that the incident occurred over Brest. This would be nothing unusual, as the Germans used captive balloons (as the British did) to protect their towns and other important potential targets from Allied bombers. However, Gellner's diary brings new information to light, indicating that the aircraft collided with a balloon cable over the English city of Coventry, near the heart of the country, approximately 100 miles to the west of the East Wretham aerodrome! None of the records describing this operational flight give the location of the incident; the air raid timetable produced by the ground wireless operator from No. 311 (B) Squadron simply states: 'landed at Grantham with wing damaged by balloon barrage'.[12]

A Flying Accident Card (AM Form 1180) at the RAF Museum at Hendon reveals the full details of this accident, including the assessment of the cause by the Officers Commanding at all levels:

> Hit balloon cable in Rugby, Coventry area. After obtaining QDMs from Abingdon, failed to get QDMs from Honington owing to wireless congestion and static. CO—Navigation faulty, completely lost. AOC—Bad navigation.[13]

Let us now return to the question of who hit the *Prinz Eugen*. RAF Bomber Command intelligence summaries for the night's raid in Brest present the total number and types of bombs that were dropped on the harbour:

Place and Target	Sent	Attacked	Number and type of bombs dropped
Brest—Docks	9	9	90 × 250-lb
Brest—*Gneisenau* & *Scharnhorst*	24	14	3 × 2,000-lb, 3 × 1,000-lb, 69 × 500-lb, 7 × 250-lb
Brest—*Prinz Eugen*	19	17	7 × 1,000-lb, 109 × 500-lb, 11 × 250-lb[14]

The bomb punctured a hole in the deck of the ship which according to the publication *The Story of the Prince Eugen* had a diameter of 12 inches [304.8 mm]. The Vickers Wellingtons carried the following types of bombs:

Bomb type	Bomb dimensions (diameter / length)
1,000-lb GP	440 mm / 2,150 mm
500-lb GP	326 mm / 1,660 mm
250-lb GP	260 mm / 1,400 mm
2,000-lb AP	343 mm / 2,870 mm
500-lb SAP	335 mm / 1,560 mm[15]

It is unlikely that it was a small GP bomb weighing 250 lbs that penetrated the ship's deck, though its diameter fits with the measurements of the cavity. It is necessary to consider that it could have been either a 500-lb GP or 500-lb SAP bomb, even if their diameter does not appear to fit. This observation may simply be due to a lack of actual measurements of the cavity. However, in terms of penetrative ability, the 500-lb SAP seems to be the only marginal possibility.

When assessing the attack during the war, the possibility of the hit coming from a lost aircraft piloted by Plt Off. Vincent-Welch was not taken into account; at the time, it was unknown whether the aircraft had dropped its bombs before being shot down. Moreover, the records from No. 149 'East India' (B) Squadron did not indicate what types of bombs the plane was carrying.

Meanwhile, Plt Off. Gellner's statement that he dropped his bombs at an orientation of 90 degrees corresponds to *The Story of the Prince Eugen*'s statement that the series of bombs fell crossways, left to right, and from behind in relation to the ship's heading. However, there will never be 100-per cent certainty about whether or not it was Plt Off. Gellner who actually hit the *Prinz Eugen* on the night of 1–2 July 1941.

APPENDIX IV

Aircraft Flown by John Gellner

Most Frequently Flown Aircraft Within No. 311 'Czechoslovak' (B) Squadron

Vickers Wellington Mk IC T2972, powered by a pair of 1,050-hp, nine-cylinder, air-cooled radial Bristol Pegasus XVIIIs engines, was manufactured by Vickers Armstrongs Ltd at the company's works at Weybridge, Surrey, as one of 300 aircraft ordered under contract No. B38600/39. After a lengthy series of test flights, this aircraft was assigned to No. 9 Maintenance Unit (MU) at RAF Station Cosford, Shropshire on 11 December 1940. The aircraft went through a series of installations of new equipment and armaments systems from Christmas Eve. It was allotted to No. 311 (B) Squadron on 15 January 1941.

While with this unit, it carried the code 'KX-G'. 'KX' was the squadron code, while 'G' was the individual aircraft letter. Between February 1941 and September 1941, this 'Wimpy'—as the Wellington was affectionately known—flew fifty sorties over enemy territory, with Plt Off. Gellner flying half of them. It flew the third-highest number of sorties of any aircraft during its time with the Squadron.

On 11 September 1941, the aircraft was transferred to No. 43 (Maintenance) Group. It was then ferried to No. 30 MU at RAF Station Sealand, Flintshire on 22 September. While there, the aircraft went through a thorough overhaul. Work was completed on 14 February 1942 and the aircraft was given the status of 'Repaired and Awaiting Allocation'.

On 15 March 1942, the Wellington was returned to No. 9 MU. On 10 June 1942, it was ferried to RAF Station White Waltham, Berkshire, the headquarters for the Air Transport Auxiliary. The aircraft was modified for service with the ATA and ready for operations by 3 October 1942; it was assigned to ATA HQ from 9 October.

Between 28 January and 13 February 1943, more repairs were carried out on Wellington T2972. The aircraft sustained minor damage that was repaired at White Waltham between 28 September and 9 October. The aircraft was flown to No. 8 MU at RAF Station Little Rissington, Gloucestershire, on 2 November 1943. It sat there for a year before being given a Category 'E' designation and subsequently scrapped.[1]

The Handley Page Halifax from No. 429 'Bison' (B) Squadron RCAF

Handley Page Halifax B Mk III LW694/AL-Z was powered by four Bristol fourteen-cylinder, air-cooled radial, sleeve-valve Hercules XVI engines, each one producing a maximum of 1,675 hp. It was one of 260 airframes built at the English Electric Company's Preston Works, Lancashire, between October 1943 and March 1944, under Contract No. A/C 1807. The aircraft parts were then transported to the company's 'shadow factory' and airfield at Samlesbury, Lancashire, where they would be assembled and test-flown.

This bomber began serving with No. 429 'Bison' (B) Squadron at Leeming, Yorkshire, on 5 March 1944. This Halifax sustained damage to the port wing, landing gear, and both port propellers as a result of a ground loop while returning from an operation over Saint-Ghislain, Belgium, on 2 May 1944. After the accident, it would not take to the skies for almost a year. It is interesting to note that the crash record in the Squadron ORB was amended by a handwritten note: 'Aircraft damaged Category 'B' on landing'. This conflicts with the information given on the form of the Aircraft Movement Card (AM Form 78), which states that the damage was less serious (Category 'AC').

Between 1941 and 1952, the Royal Air Force designated seven categories of damage:

Category	Damage
U	No damage
A	Damaged but repairable on site by nearest RAF unit
AC	For repair by contractor's working party
B	Damaged but repairable at MU or contractor's works
C	Destroyed but of salvage value
D	Burnt out but of salvage value
E	Complete write-off, no value except metal salvage

As the aircraft was taken to Handley Page Ltd, it is clear that it was, in fact, Category 'B' damage. After repairs were finished on 1 September 1944, the aircraft was flown to No. 44 MU in Edzell, Kincardineshire, on 11 September. It was transferred from there to No. 620 (SD) Squadron in Great Dunmow, Essex, on 17 April 1945.

While serving with this unit, the aircraft was damaged once again—this time on 28 May 1945. The damage was assessed as Category 'AC', and it was repaired by the manufacturer. Halifax LW694 was back flying with the Squadron on 26 June 1945, when it was used to transport soldiers between the United Kingdom and Europe.

By 21 March 1946, the aircraft was in service with No. 1385 (Heavy Transport Support) Conversion Unit in Wethersfield, Essex. Its final transfer came in early April 1946, when it served very briefly with No. 1 Ferry Unit at RAF Station Pershore, Worcestershire. The aircraft suffered Category 'B' damage on 15 April 1946, and it was struck off charge with the RAF the same day. The aircraft was re-classified to Category 'E' in January 1947 and was sent for scrapping on 18 January 1947.[2]

Aircraft Flown During Service with RAF Transport Command

Martin Marauder Mk IIB FB424

The Martin B-26 Marauder (Model 179), which was built by the Glenn L. Martin Company, was a twin-engine medium bomber crewed by five to seven airmen (although this number was six in service with the RAF). Construction of the high-speed aircraft was split between two plants—Middle River, Maryland, and Offut Field in Omaha, Nebraska.

The Marauder would go on to see action in the Pacific, Mediterranean, and European theatres of war. Of 5,157 produced, 521 were acquired by the Royal Air Force through the Lend-Lease Act. They were flown operationally by three RAF squadrons—Nos 14, 39, and 231. They also saw wide service with the South African Air Force, serving in Nos 12, 21, 24, 25, and 30 Squadrons.

Martin B-26C-25-MO Marauder (USAAF s/n 41-35324) was one of 100 bombers (reserialed FB400–FB522 for service in the RAF) taken on strength with the RAF as the Marauder Mk II. The aircraft entered service with the RAF *circa* July 1943. Marauder s/n FB424 was ferried to North Africa on 7 September 1943, and three days later it was assigned to No. 70 (Middle East) Operational Training Unit at Shandur, Egypt. The OTU, which was part of No. 203 (Training) Group, Middle East Command, was the only Marauder training unit in the RAF.

On 14 October 1944, the undercarriage of Marauder FB424 collapsed while landing at LG211 (Fâyid), located just west of The Great Bitter Lake, Egypt. After languishing in heat of the desert, the damaged aircraft was relegated to instructional airframe status on 28 February 1945. Scrapping would seem to be the likely fate of this aircraft.[3]

Dakota Mk III FL541

The twin-engine Douglas C-47 Skytrain and C-53 Skytrooper were military variants of the highly successful pre-war commercial DC-3 airliner. The United States Army Air Corps ordered their first C-47s in 1940. The USAAF (as the USAAC was now known) purchased ninety-two commercially-operated aircraft in May 1942 to be used for troop-carrying and VIP duties. Of the 10,123 C-47s and C-53s built at Long

Beach, California, and Oklahoma City, Oklahoma, more than 1,200 were supplied to the RAF through the Lend-Lease Act. The C-47 is one of the most iconic symbols of the Second World War, having provided sterling service across all the theatres. It became legendary for flying dangerous supply drops over the Burmese jungle and dropping airborne troops over Europe.

Douglas C-47A-60-DL Skytrain, USAAF s/n 42-24354 was delivered to the RAF on 9 September 1943 as a Dakota Mk III; it was reserialed 'FL541'. It arrived to Accra, Gold Coast, on 22 September, and from there it travelled eastwards over the African continent. Dakota FL541 was accepted through No. 317 MU at Mauripur (Karachi), India (now Pakistan), and entered service with No. 194 (T) Squadron on 8 October 1943. They began flying operations in February 1944 over the dense jungle of Burma, where they dropped large groups of airborne troops and countless tons of supplies. The Squadron flew these highly dangerous sorties from a number of bases, including Comilla, Agartala, Imphal, and Basal (all in India), and Maunubyin and Akyab Main (both in Burma).

Dakota FL541 was transferred to No. 31 (T) Squadron, arriving in Agatarla, India, on 24 August 1944. While at Agatarla, the Squadron flew supply flights from there and its detachments at Dinjan, Kharagpur, and Tezpur. No. 31 (T) Squadron pioneered the use of a unique method of aerial delivery that had been developed in May 1942; they would fly their Dakotas through narrow valleys in a dangerous zigzag pattern while dropping supplies behind Japanese lines. The Squadron's pilots would also land on small, confined areas in order to supply Allied units.

Between 21 June and 1 July 1944, another former No. 311 (B) Squadron officer, Sqn Ldr Vladimír Nedvěd MBE DFC, found himself flying with both the Agartala-based No. 31 (T) Squadron and No. 194 (T) Squadron. Nedvěd flew a number of adventurous supply flights, but he never got a chance to fly Dakota FL541.

Dakota FL541 next served with No. 353 (T) Squadron, arriving in Palam, India, on 24 August 1943. The Squadron maintained a detachment at Dum Dum, India. As the war came to an end, they were primarily tasked with flying long-range transport flights to the east, over the Himalayan Mountains, to Kunming, China, southwards to Colombo, Ceylon (now known as Sri Lanka), and westwards to Mauripur, India (which later became part of Pakistan). After the war, Dakota FL541 was one of fifty-five selected for transfer to the Royal Thai Air Force.[4]

The North American Mitchell Mk II FW119

The twin-engine B-25 Mitchell medium bomber was produced by North American Aviation at two plants. It had the distinction of having been the only American aircraft named after an historic figure—Gen. William L. 'Billy' Mitchell (1879–1936). Mitchell is considered as 'a father of the United States Army Air Force'. A total of 9, 816 bombers of all versions were built, giving outstanding service in all theatres of war.

Appendix IV

The Royal Air Force acquired Mitchells through the Lend-Lease Act under Requisition Number 4617. A total of 164 B-25Cs and 314 B-25Ds were transferred to the RAF and re-designated as the Mitchell Mk II. Mitchells were used by RAF Squadron Nos 98, 180, 226, 681, and 684. They were joined by several Allied units—Polish No. 305 'Ziemia Wielkopolska' Squadron, Dutch No. 320 'Netherlands' Squadron, and Free French No. 342 'Lorraine' Squadron.

North American B-25D-25 Mitchell USAAF s/n 42-87331 was handed over to the RAF as a Mitchell Mk II and reserialed as 'FW119'. It was ferried overseas, arriving in the United Kingdom on 30 October 1943. The aircraft was fitted with equipment and armament systems at No. 12 MU, Kirkbride, Cumberland; the installation was carried out from 5 November 1943 into January 1944. On 19 January 1944, the Mitchell was transferred to No. 13 OTU, located at RAF Station Bicester, Oxfordshire. This unit was founded on 8 April 1940 with the initial role of training light bomber crews using Bristol Blenheims. Mitchells were taken on strength with the OTU in May 1943. Mitchell FW119 continued to serve at No. 13 OTU, which relocated to RAF Station Harwell, Berkshire, on 12 October 1944. It remained there until 2 July 1945, when it was ferried back to Kirkbride; the aircraft sat there until 5 June 1947, when it was sent to be scrapped.[5]

APPENDIX V

Graduates of the British Commonwealth Air Training Plan's First Air Observers Course

The group shot of the first air observers to graduate was taken in August 1940. It shows the class of thirty-seven receiving their air observers' brevet. Sadly, twenty-five of these thirty-seven men would die while serving with the RAF or in RCAF units overseas or in Canada. This gives a terribly high loss rate of 68 per cent. The following table shows that by the end of 1941, a year after they commenced their operational tours, less than half of the graduating course remained alive.

Year	Deceased	
1940	1	3%
1941	19	51%
1942	2	5%
1943	1	3%
1944	2	5%
Total	25	68%

Author's note: unless a membership of a particular air force (RAAF, RCAF, RNZAF) is mentioned in brackets after their name, the following airmen were members of the RAF.

J2827 Pilot Officer Ion Huge Acland

† Age twenty-six, born in Victoria, British Columbia. He was posted to No. 2 School of Army Co-operation at RAF Station Andover, Hampshire. On 18 March 1941, his Bristol Blenheim Mk IV, T2443, crashed in Penton Mewsey, Wiltshire, as a result of the pilot losing control shortly after take-off from Andover. The entire crew perished. Pilot Plt Off. J. L. Baines is buried at the Oadby Cemetery

in Leicestershire, navigator Plt Off. I. H. Acland is buried at the local Andover Cemetery, and wireless operator Sgt V. Moore is buried at the Tunstall Cemetery in Stoke-on-Trent, Staffordshire.

J2833 Squadron Leader Robert Wilfred Alexander DFC

† Age twenty-four, born in Norwich, Ontario. He served with No. 148 (B) Squadron RAF at Luqa, Malta and Kabrit, Egypt. Alexander was awarded the DFC on 7 April 1942:

> As an air observer this officer has carried out fifty-one operational sorties against the enemy, involving 456 flying hours. He has participated in many attacks against objectives in Libya, Syria, Greece, and in the whole Mediterranean area. He also took part in mine-laying and supply-dropping operations in Greece. Flight Lieutenant Alexander is a fine bomb aimer and an exceptionally good navigator. He has carried out the duties of Squadron Navigation Officer with great success over a long period, and his experience as an observer, combined with his ability as an instructor, have enabled him to attain a very high standard of navigation in the squadron. This officer has displayed consistent keenness, coolness and determination, and has set a fine example to all.

Alexander returned to Canada in August 1942 after finishing a tour of operations lasting fifty-five sorties. He then successfully completed pilot training, graduating on 8 July 1943. Alexander began his second tour with the Douglas Dakota-equipped No. 437 'Husky' (T) Squadron RCAF. He failed to return from a supply-drop flight on 21 September 1944. His aircraft, Dakota Mk III KG387/Z2-UF, took off at 1.14 p.m. from Blakehill Farm, Wiltshire. Alexander and his crew were tasked with dropping supplies in the Arnhem area of the Netherlands to assist Allied ground units taking part in 'Operation Market-Garden'. His aircraft was shot down by a Luftwaffe fighter from I./JG 26. At 4.30 p.m., the Dakota crashed onto Sonniushoeve Farm near Esp, which is located close to the town of Son, Noord-Brabant. Sqn Ldr R. W. Alexander DFC (RCAF), Fg Off. W. S. McLintock (RCAF), Cpl A. E. Hall, Driver H. Woodward, and Driver F. G. W. Yeo (all three from the Royal Army Service Corps) were killed. FS A. McHugh, Fg Off. J. Rechenuk and L/Cpl O. R. Jones were able to bale out. The Provisional American Military Cemetery in Son became a temporary resting place for the dead crewmembers. Unfortunately, only Woodward was identified. The remains of the ill-fated crew were later transferred to the British War Cemetery in Bergen-op-Zoom. It was not until 1995 that the remaining aircrew were positively identified, allowing their graves to be properly marked.

J2829 Flying Officer Ulysse Joseph Bezaire

Born on 15 June 1918 in River Canard, Ontario. He served with No. 42 (TB) Squadron RAF, flying Bristol Beaufort Mk Is in the anti-shipping role. He completed an operational tour while with this unit. Bezaire was sent back to Canada in November 1941; he would remain there for the rest of the war, acting as an instructor with the BCATP. He left the RCAF on 17 August 1945.

J15007 Flying Officer Thomas Edward Carter

Born on 16 September 1916 in St Thomas, Ontario. He served with No. 22 (TB) Squadron RAF, flying anti-shipping strikes with Bristol Beauforts. Carter finished his operational tour while with this unit, returning to Canada on 25 April 1943. Carter started his pilot training on the Fleet Finch at No. 7 EFTS in Windsor, Ontario, in June 1943. On 19 December 1943, he finished his service-flying training course; he received his 'wings' at the North American Harvard-equipped No. 6 SFTS in Dunnville, Ontario. On 31 December 1943, Carter was posted for further training to No. 1 General Reconnaissance School in Summerside, Prince Edward Island. Between 27 March and 14 July 1944, he served with No. 9 (BR) Squadron RCAF in Bella Bella, British Columbia. The Squadron was equipped with Supermarine Stranraers and Consolidated Catalinas. By the end of July 1944, he had left Canada for his second overseas tour; he returned on 5 September 1945. He was demobbed on 19 October 1945.

J15326 Flying Officer William Herbert Cleaver

Born on 31 March 1913 in Toronto, Ontario. He served with No. 22 (TB) Squadron RAF and later with No. 404 'Buffalo' (Coastal Fighter) Squadron RCAF. Cleaver flew a combined seventy-two sorties (shared between both squadrons) during his tour of operations. One of his most adventurous exploits took place on 27 December 1941. 'Operation Archery' was the combined-operation naval landing by commando forces on the Norwegian islands of Vaagso and Maaloy. One of the aircraft involved was Blenheim Mk IV Z6181/EE-B from No. 404 'Buffalo' (CF) Squadron. It was crewed by Sgt McCutcheon, Sgt Cleaver, and Sgt Cruickshanks. Another Blenheim, piloted by Plt Off. E. W. 'Teddy' Pierce, accompanied them. Both crews were carrying out a fighter patrol for the convoy. While they were doing this, two Messerschmitt Bf 109s from I./JG 77 appeared in the area and were subsequently attacked by the Blenheims. The Germans broke off contact and left the area in a hurry, with one Bf 109 trailing smoke from its engine and rapidly losing altitude. When the crews made it back, they submitted claims for one probable and possibly shot down. After his return to Canada in July 1942, Cleaver served as an instructor at RCAF Station

Trenton, Ontario. He commenced his pilot training in April 1943 at No. 20 EFTS in Oshawa, Ontario, and finished it on 29 October 1943 at No. 5 SFTS in Brantford, Ontario. Cleaver would go on to serve as a pilot in the post-war RCAF.

R61304 Sergeant David Stewart Craik

† Age twenty-six, born in Caron, Saskatchewan. He was serving with No. 22 (TB) Squadron RAF when he went missing in action on 15 January 1941. Beaufort Mk I W6489/OA-W took off at 6.10 p.m. from RAF Station North Coates, Lincolnshire, for a 'Gardening' sortie on the Weser River Estuary near Bremerhaven, in northwest Germany. Nothing was heard from the aircraft after take-off. Another crew from the same squadron later reported that at 7.15 p.m., about 120 miles from base, a brilliant white light was seen in the sky and appeared to lose height. The crew believed it might be an aircraft on fire and falling. The entire crew—Flt Lt J. R. Fishwick, Sgt D. S. Craik (RCAF), Sgt T. Wareing and Sgt A. T. Smith—are commemorated on the Runnymede Memorial, which honours those with no known grave. Craik Island (coordinates 55°36'N and 105°24'W), in the Canadian province of Saskatchewan, is named in his memory.

R56846 Sergeant Herbert Robinson Easton

† Age twenty-two, born in Winnipeg, Manitoba. He served with No. 214 'Federated Malay States' (B) Squadron RAF. Easton went missing during a raid against Kiel on the night of 7–8 April 1941. His Wellington Mk IC, R1380/BU-K, took off from Stradishall, never to be heard from again. As there are no known graves, the entire crew—Sgt R. A. Williams, Sgt K. Manson (RNZAF), Sgt H. R. Easton (RCAF), Sgt R. A. Chatfield, Sgt R. C. Plummer, and Sgt C. H. R. Mercer—are commemorated on the Runnymede Memorial.

J2826 Squadron Leader James Gerard Flaherty

† Age thirty, born in Toronto, Ontario. He returned to Canada in the middle of 1941 after overseas service with No. 22 (TB) Squadron RAF. On 25 June, Flaherty was posted as an instructor to No. 31 Air Navigation School in Port Albert, Ontario. He subsequently received a posting notice to No. 32 Operational Training Unit, Patricia Bay, British Columbia, and reported there on 2 October 1942. Flaherty was promoted to Squadron Leader on 1 April 1943. He was part of the crew of Beechcraft Expeditor Mk III HB100 when it went missing on a flight from RCAF Station Rockcliffe, Ontario, to RCAF Station Patricia Bay, British Columbia, on 16 January 1944. The

entire crew—Fg Off. H. W. Donkersley DFC & Bar (RCAF), Sqn Ldr J. G. Flaherty (RCAF), and Plt Off. E. Sowerby (RCAF)—and their passenger, Sqn Ldr T. A. Pringle, are commemorated on the Air Force War Memorial in Ottawa, Ontario.

J2834 Squadron Leader David Stewart Florence DFC

Born on 14 February 1912 in Edmonton, Alberta. Florence served with No. 75 'New Zealand' (B) Squadron RAF. He completed thirty operational sorties between March and July 1941, culminating in a total of 170 hours. He was awarded the DFC on 9 September 1941:

> This officer has shown great enthusiasm for night photography and has secured no less than twenty photographs, many of which contained valuable information. Despite weather conditions and enemy opposition, the courses given to his captain were invariably accurate. He is a very through and persevering navigator who has done much to raise the standard of photography and navigation throughout the unit. As a bomb aimer he has been equally successful.

Florence returned to Canada on 19 November 1941 with the rank of Flying Officer. On 13 April 1942, he was posted to the Central Air Navigation School at Rivers, Manitoba. Florence was promoted to Squadron Leader on 1 March 1943. On 1 November 1943, he was posted to No. 168 (HT) Squadron RCAF at RCAF Station Rockcliffe, Ontario. This Squadron operated the Boeing Fortress Mk IIA and the Douglas Dakota Mk I, III and IV, along with the Consolidated Liberator GR Mk VIT. They were used to ferry mail between Canada and United Kingdom. Florence was later posted to No. 9 (Transport) Group at RCAF Station Rockcliffe, Ontario. He left the RCAF on 20 March 1946.

J2822 Wing Commander John Gellner DFC

See 'Part II: Biography'.

J2831 Squadron Leader John Russell Gilmore

Born on 26 March 1909 in Rock Island, Quebec. He finished his tour of operations with the RAF and returned to Canada in the autumn of 1941. Gilmore began serving as an instructor with No. 1 ANS at Rivers, Manitoba, on 30 November 1941. He was promoted to the rank of Squadron Leader on 1 March 1943. Gilmore retired from the RCAF on 22 February 1945.

R52038 Sergeant Wray William Heywood

† Age twenty-one, born in Rouleau, Saskatchewan. He served with No. 150 (B) Squadron RAF. Heywood failed to return from a raid on St Nazaire, France, on the night of 7–8 May 1941. Wellington Mk IC R1374/JN-G took off at 10.30 p.m. from Newton, Nottinghamshire. It was later hit by flak and crashed near Nantes, France. The entire crew—Flt Lt F. H. Savage, Sgt J. M. Fulford, Sgt W. W. Heywood (RCAF), Sgt L. F. Harris, Sgt P. V. Read and Sgt J. L. Hart—are buried at Pont-du-Cens Communal Cemetery.

J2823 Pilot Officer Lawrence Stanley Hill

† Age twenty-six, born in Weyburn, Saskatchewan. He served with No. 42 (TB) Squadron RAF. Hill went missing on 28 December 1940. Beaufort Mk I N1162/AW-G took off at 1.50 p.m. from Wick, Scotland, for a 'Rover Patrol'. Their task was to attack a tanker off Trondheim, Norway. The aircraft was last seen off Sumburgh, the Shetland Islands, on the return leg. Parts of the wreckage and a log book were later recovered on the coast near Kirkwall, Orkney. The entire crew—Flt Lt M. R. Baillon, Plt Off. L. S. Hill (RCAF), Plt Off. J. H. Gow and Sgt C. F. Young—are commemorated on the Runnymede Memorial.

R53751 Sergeant George Wilbert Jeffrey

† Age twenty-four, born in Ottawa, Ontario. He served with No. 15 (B) Squadron RAF. He and his crew failed to return from the raid on Essen on the night of 8–9 August 1941. Stirling Mk I N3658/LS-E took off from Wyton, Huntingdon, and was later shot down during the return leg by a Messerschmitt Bf 110. It would be the only Short Stirling shot down on that night. At 2.33 a.m., N3658 fell victim to the guns of *Leutnant* Kurt Loos from 2./NJG 1. The Stirling crashed at 2.37 a.m. at Overasselt, Gelderland, 5 miles south-southwest of Nijmegen, in the Netherlands. The entire crew—Plt Off. F. J. Needham, Sqn Ldr J. Vivian, Sgt G. W. Jeffrey (RCAF), Sgt S. H. Broyd, Sgt J. T. Corbett, FS R. A. Ross and Sgt K. L. Rowley—are buried at Uden War Cemetery.

R53752 Sergeant James Alton Jepson

† Age thirty, born in New Bedford, Massachusetts, USA. He served with No. 22 (TB) Squadron RAF. Jepson went missing in action on 11 February 1941. Beaufort Mk I N1109/OA-I took off at 6.44 p.m. from North Coates, Lincolnshire, on a 'Gardening' sortie against the area of Borkum Island, East Frisian Islands, in the North Sea. On

the return leg, the Beaufort was plotted by Fighter Command radar near Harwich, flying northwards. They were last heard from at 9.56 p.m. The message indicated that the crew assumed that they were near the Wash; in fact, the aircraft was far to the south, almost over the Dutch coast. The Beaufort was shot down by naval flak guns and crashed into the Western Scheldt, near Flushing, in the Netherlands. The entire crew—Fg Off. R. C. Greenlees, Sgt J. A. Jepson (RCAF), Sgt W. Haywood and Sgt F. W. Smith—are commemorated at Runnymede Memorial.

J15525 Pilot Officer George Frederick King

† Age twenty-five, born in Toronto, Ontario. He served with No. 108 (B) Squadron RAF. King was killed on 16 March 1942 in a flying accident. Consolidated Liberator Mk II AL577/N, from the Overseas Aircraft Delivery Unit, was carrying No. 108 (B) Squadron personnel from Fâyid, Egypt, to RAF Station Hurn, Dorset. During the last leg of the trip, the wireless set malfunctioned. Strong winds also forced the aircraft off-course. They eventually found themselves over Dublin, Ireland. Realizing their mistake—which could have seen them interned—the decision was made by the skipper and No. 108 (B) Squadron CO Wg Cdr R. J. Wells DFC to fly to RAF Station Aldergrove in Northern Ireland. Unfortunately, the Liberator crashed into Slievenaglogh Mountain at 7.45 a.m. The mountain is located about 2 miles east of Jenkinstown, Louth. Only five of the nineteen airmen survived this violent crash. Some of them sustained serious injuries, and one would succumb to his injuries and pass away at Dundalk Hospital on 19 March. The deceased airmen are buried in several different cemeteries scattered around the British Isles. All the crew members not native to the United Kingdom—including Plt Off. G. F. King (RCAF)—are buried at Belfast City Cemetery.

J15034 Flying Officer Peter John Leboldus

† Age twenty-five, born in Vibank, Saskatchewan. Leboldus was a navigator with No. 418 'City of Edmonton' (I) Squadron RCAF. He failed to return from a sortie on the night of 12–13 February 1943. Douglas Boston Mk III AL766/TH-(?), took off at 11.57 p.m. from Bradwell Bay, Essex, for a sortie that would see them dropping leaflets over Nantes, France. They were last plotted approaching the coast of France. The aircraft subsequently crashed in the vicinity of Saint-Riquier-ès-Plains—most likely as a result of German flak. Wireless operator Sgt T. S. McNeill was captured, while pilot FS R. R. Jackson and navigator Fg Off. P. J. Leboldus (RCAF) were killed. Both were originally buried at the Communal Cemetery in St Riquieres-des-Plaines; however, they were later exhumed and reburied at Grandcourt War Cemetery.

There were four brothers in the Leboldus family who fought during the Second World War. Sadly, only one would survive. Two other brothers serving in the RCAF were also killed in action, within just three months of each other. R155568 FS John Anthony Leboldus served in the Middle East as an air gunner with No. 142 (B) Squadron RAF. He was killed during a raid to Turin, Italy, on the night of 24–25 November 1943, when his Wellington Mk X (LN566/QT-D) struck a hill in fog. The middle brother, R61333 Sgt Martin Benedict Leboldus, a flight engineer, went missing in action during a raid on Leipzig, Germany, on the night of 19–20 February 1944. He was part of the crew of Halifax Mk II JD114/VR-V, from No. 419 'Moose' (B) Squadron RCAF.

J15965 Pilot Officer Noel John Leishman

Born 28 December 1912 in Brantford, Ontario. He served with No. 40 (B) Squadron RAF. Leishman's operational tour expired with the Squadron, and he was repatriated to Canada in October 1942. On 7 October 1942, he assumed his new role as an instructor with No. 31 General Reconnaissance School at Charlottetown, Prince Edward Island. Leishman was commissioned on 25 July 1943 and continued to serve until he left the RCAF on 10 April 1944.

J10947 Flight Lieutenant Angus Blake MacKenzie

Born on 7 August 1914 in Edmonton, Alberta. He served with No. 42 (TB) Squadron RAF until he finished his tour of operations. MacKenzie returned to Canada in October 1941. On 25 October 1941, he commenced duties as an instructor with No. 32 OTU at Patricia Bay, British Columbia. MacKenzie was selected for pilot training, beginning his course in April 1944 with No. 5 EFTS at Lethbridge, Alberta. He finished pilot training at No. 32 SFTS in Moose Jaw, Saskatchewan, on 3 November 1944. His later flying assignments included duties with No. 3 SFTS in Calgary, Alberta, and No. 7 B&GS in Paulson, Manitoba. MacKenzie left the RCAF on 23 November 1945.

R51633 Sergeant Lloyd Colley Mansell

† Age thirty-two, born in Sault Ste Marie, Ontario. He was serving with No. 42 (TB) Squadron RAF when he was killed in action on 30 August 1941. Beaufort Mk I L9834/AW-V took off at 2.10 a.m. from Leuchars, Scotland, for a sortie. Just two short minutes later, the aircraft crashed into a hill near Craigfootie, Fife, killing the entire crew. Sqn Ldr G. S. P. Rooney DFC and Sgt L. C. Mansell (RCAF) were buried at Leuchars Cemetery, while Fg Off. Grand and FS R. S. Knott were buried at Wellsill Cemetery in Perth and Milton Cemetery in Portsmouth respectively.

J15312 Flight Lieutenant Douglas Christopher Martin DFM

Born in 1920 in Brantford, Ontario. He began serving with No. 42 (TB) Squadron RAF on 9 January 1941. Martin was awarded the DFM on 29 October 1941:

> Sergeant Martin has participated in twenty-three operational missions. In October 1941 he was observer of an aircraft which carried out an attack at dusk on enemy shipping off the Norwegian coast. A successful attack was carried out, but in the heavy gunfire encountered, Sergeant Martin was wounded in the leg. He did not inform the pilot of his injuries, however, and successfully navigated the aircraft back to base without the aid of the air speed indicator, which had been put out of action. This airman's courage in navigating the aircraft under difficult conditions and in spite of the pain from his wounds has set a magnificent example.

After the end of his tour of operations, he was commissioned and repatriated to Canada. Martin underwent pilot training and went on to attain the rank of Flight Lieutenant by the end of his service. On 7 July 1945, he was mentioned in dispatches for his service with Eastern Air Command Meteorological Flight:

> Flight Lieutenant Martin has been navigation leader of Eastern Air Command Meteorological Flight since its inception in October 1943. His perseverance and devotion to duty have made him one of those instrumental in the carrying out of the original plan and development of this unit. The organization ability he has displayed ensured the very high standard of navigation required to cope with the adverse weather conditions encountered. Flight Lieutenant Martin has contributed materially to the high unit morale, and in addition to his other duties has compiled a great number of hours on meteorological flights.

J2830 Pilot Officer Robert Addison Mather

† Age twenty-eight, born in Vancouver, British Columbia. He was serving with No. 405 'Vancouver' (B) Squadron RCAF when he went missing in action during an operation against Hamburg, Germany, on the night of 30 November–1 December 1941. Wellington Mk II W5476/LQ-H took off at 5.21 p.m. from Pocklington, Yorkshire. The last radio message from the aircraft was received at 6.35 p.m., stating that it was returning to base. The Wellington disappeared without a trace. It is believed to have either ditched or crashed into the North Sea. The entire crew—Sqn Ldr R. C. Bisset DFC and Bar, FS A. J. Knight (RCAF), Plt Off. R. A. Mather (RCAF), Sgt W. L. Evans, FS C. E. Hillmer (RCAF) and Sgt R. P. Mann (RCAF)—are commemorated on the Runnymede Memorial.

R56873 Sergeant Grant John Mavor

† Age twenty-four, born in Winnipeg, Manitoba. He was serving with No. 9 (B) Squadron RAF when he failed to return from an operation against Cologne, Germany, on the night of 17–18 April 1941. Wellington Mk IC N2745/WS-O took off at 8.23 p.m. from Honington, Suffolk. The last message from the aircraft was received at 11.43 p.m., stating that the crew was preparing to bale out. The Wellington crashed at Neuwied, located 7.5 miles north-west of Koblenz, Germany. The skipper—Sgt G. E. Heaysman—and navigator—Sgt G. J. Mavor (RCAF)—were killed and later buried at the Rheinberg War Cemetery. The remaining four crew members—Sgt S. F. Whitlock, Sgt T. Lancaster, Sgt B. Hanlon and Sgt G. C. Balch—were captured and became prisoners of war.

R53756 Warrant Officer Alan Hubert Andrew Morris

† Age twenty-two, born in Nokomis, Saskatchewan. He served with No. 42 (TB) Squadron RAF. On 13 June 1941, he was the navigator of Beaufort Mk I L9939/AW-W, piloted by Sgt R. H. Loveitt. Their torpedo hit the German Pocket Battleship *Lützow* out in the North Sea. Although the ship did not sink, the damage caused by the torpedo's impact put the ship out of commission for several months. Morris was killed in action on 17 May 1942. Beaufort Mk II AW375/AW-Y took off at 5.58 p.m. from Leuchars, Scotland, for another anti-shipping strike. The aircraft was shot down by flak over the Norwegian town of Lista during an attack on the German Battleship *Prinz Eugen*. The pilot and CO of the Squadron, Wg Cdr M. F. D. Williams, was captured, while the rest of the crew was killed. WO A. H. A. Morris (RCAF) and Plt Off. J. F. V. Saunders were buried at the Vanse Churchyard, Norway, while FS J. T. Healey is commemorated on the Runnymede Memorial.

J15080 Squadron Leader Carman Douglas Noble MBE DFC

Born in 16 June 1918 in Durham, Ontario. He first served with No. 40 (B) Squadron RAF. When his tour expired, Noble became an instructor at an OTU. He started his second tour as a member of No. 214 'Federated Malay States' (B) Squadron RAF. Noble failed to return from an operation against Emden, Germany, on the night of 19–20 June 1942. This was his fifty-seventh operation. Stirling Mk I N3762/BU-C took off from Stradishall, Suffolk, and was later shot down on the return leg by a German night fighter. The Stirling crashed at De Driehoek, near Ommen, in the Netherlands. Four crew members—Sqn Ldr P. Nixey DSO, Sgt W. E. Pearson, Sgt D. A. Melville and Sgt A. Buckley—were killed; they are buried at Ommen General Cemetery. The other four men—Fg Off. R. McD. Mitchell, Fg Off. C. D. Noble

(RCAF), WO L. R. Burgin and Sgt J. H. Bailey—became prisoners of war. Noble had been awarded his DFC on 23 October 1945:

> Shortly after leaving the target area, the aircraft was attacked and set on fire by an enemy fighter. All attempts to bring the fire under control having failed, the captain gave the order to abandon the aircraft. All the crew, with the exception of the captain and Flight Lieutenant Noble, had jumped when the aircraft exploded. Flight Lieutenant Noble, who had sustained severe burns to his hands and face in his efforts to fight the fire, was blown clear and landed safely. He left the area of the crashed and burning aircraft after having ascertained that there was nothing he could do to help the captain, and soon met another member of the crew. Together they evaded the German search party who were combing the area of the crash, and after walking a distance of approximately 100 miles in five nights they reached Holland. Here, they were captured by the Germans. Whilst under escort, Flight Lieutenant Noble attacked his captors and succeeded in making good his escape on one of their bicycles. Although the burns on his hands and face had by this time become putreous and extremely painful, Flight Lieutenant Noble covered a further 80 miles before being captured a second time.

However, according to Dutch sources, this sequence of events actually occurred slightly differently. During the night of 22–23 June, two Allied airmen were arrested by two members of the constabulary just south of the village of Wijhe, on the Deventer–Zwolle road in the province of Overijssel. There was a struggle, and both policemen were hit hard. One airman seized a service pistol and bicycle and made off into the dark. During the next night, two members of the local police force at Deventer brought a cyclist to their guard room at Deventer; he was wearing an airman's uniform and was in possession of the stolen bicycle and the pistol. Noble was arrested *en route* to the town of Zutphen. A number of hours after being brought to the police guard room at Deventer, he was given to the German Secret Police based at Arnhem.

Noble was held at the famous Stalag Luft III in Sagan, where he took part in preparations for 'The Great Escape'. On 1 October 1946, he was awarded an MBE for his involvement in several escape attempts:

> Flight Lieutenant Noble was forced to abandon his aircraft on the 18 June 1942 [*sic.*], when it was shot down near the Dutch-German frontier. He and another member of the crew began to walk westward and, on the fourth day, were arrested by two Dutch policemen. After a struggle, Flight Lieutenant Noble succeeded in getting away and continued alone till he reached the outskirts of Arnhem, where he was again arrested and sent to a prisoner of war camp at Sagan in Germany. While there, he himself made three unsuccessful attempts at escape and aided in the escape of many other prisoners. Early in 1943, he attempted to get away in a garbage wagon but was discovered before

it left the camp. Shortly afterwards, he made a similar attempt in a truck loaded with tree branches but was discovered before the truck passed the camp entrance. In June 1943, a mass attempt was made by twenty-six prisoners of whom Flight Lieutenant Noble was one. They planned to escape as they were being marched to the showers, but the attempt was discovered within half an hour and all were recaptured the following day. Between June 1943 and March 1944, Flight Lieutenant Noble took part in various tunnel-digging operations and was also a member of the escape committee. On 25 March 1944, a tunnel was successfully broken and seventy-five officers escaped through it. Flight Lieutenant Noble was immediately apprehended on the discovery of the escape and subsequently sentenced to three weeks' solitary confinement. In January 1945, the camp was evacuated and the prisoners forced to march to Bremen. One extremely cold night, Flight Lieutenant Noble was instrumental in arousing or finding shelter for men who were on the verge of collapse from fatigue or cold. He was responsible on that occasion for saving at least twenty lives. Flight Lieutenant Noble was liberated on 2 May 1945. His enthusiasm and keenness never failed despite the many disappointments and punishments which he had to undergo. Throughout his imprisonment his services were of the highest value to his fellow prisoners.

Noble was repatriated to Canada on 8 July 1945. He remained in the post-war RCAF, serving as an Administrative Officer at several headquarters. Noble was promoted to the rank of Squadron Leader on 1 January 1952. He retired at the beginning of the 1960s, while serving at the RCAF Staff College in Toronto, Ontario.

J2828 Flight Lieutenant James Garvie Pidduck

Born on 3 March 1914 in Montreal, Quebec. He was posted to No. 20 OTU RAF at Lossiemouth, Morayshire, Scotland. Pidduck took off on 4 February 1941 for a cross-country flight and bombing practice in Wellington Mk IC R1367. At 10.40 a.m., after reaching a turn in the circuit, the aircraft overbanked and stalled at low altitude. It crashed and burned half a mile south-east of Lossiemouth. Second pilot Sgt E. G. Morris, wireless operator Sgt S. Summersgill and front gunner Sgt J. K. Blencoe were killed instantly. The skipper, Sgt D. M. Walker (RNZAF), died later that day from his injuries. The deceased airmen were laid to rest in Lossiemouth. Navigator Plt Off. J. G. Pidduck (RCAF) and rear gunner Sgt P. G. Carvenec were the only survivors, but both suffered serious injuries. After his recovery, Pidduck was repatriated to Canada in early 1942.

On 30 January 1942, he began serving as an instructor with the Central Air Navigation School at Rivers, Manitoba. Pidduck later served with No. 1 Initial Training School in Toronto, Ontario, beginning on 14 February. Next he went to No. 1 AOS at Malton, Ontario, where he began serving on 20 September. On 30 April 1943, it was back to operational flying. He was now with No. 117 (BR) Squadron

RCAF, based at Sydney, Nova Scotia. Pidduck flew anti-submarine patrols over the Gulf of Saint Lawrence on Consolidated Catalinas and the Canadian Vickers-built Canso. He was demobbed from the RCAF on 16 April 1945.

J2832 Pilot Officer John Henry Purser

† Age twenty-one, born in Lucknow, Ontario. He was serving with No. 115 (B) Squadron RAF when he failed to return from the raid on Bremen, Germany, on the night of 29–30 June 1941. Wellington Mk II W5459/KO-L took off at 11.14 p.m. from Marham, Norfolk. The aircraft was shot down at 1.52 a.m. by *Hauptmann* Walter Ehle from Stab II./NJG 1. The Wellington crashed in Altenwerder, located 2.5 miles to the south-west of Hamburg. The entire crew—Flt Lt J. A. J. Bailey DFC, Plt Off. G. W. Tetlow, Plt Off. J. H. Purser (RCAF), Sgt E. T. Panes, Sgt F. R. Nichols and FS R. M. Gray DFM—are buried at the Becklingen War Cemetery in Soltau, Niedersachsen, in Germany.

R54910 Sergeant Joseph Harold Campbell Roberts

† Age twenty-four, born in Calgary, Alberta. He served with No. 75 'New Zealand' (B) Squadron RAF. He failed to return from an operation against Duisburg, Germany on the night of 15–16 July 1941. Wellington Mk IC R3171/AA-(?) took off from Feltwell, Norfolk, and is believed to have crashed into the sea near the Dutch coast. Sgt R. E. E. Fotheringham (RNZAF) is buried at Bergen-op-Zoom War Cemetery and Sgt J. H. C. Roberts (RCAF) at the New Eastern Cemetery in Amsterdam. The rest of the crew—Sgt E. V. K. Higgins (RAAF), Sgt S. A. Dyer (RNZAF), Sgt P. E. Hare (RNZAF) and Sgt D. M. MacKinnon (RNZAF)—are commemorated on the Runnymede Memorial.

R56850 Sergeant Thomas Herbert Rose

† Age nineteen, born in Gladstone, Manitoba. He served with No. 40 (B) Squadron RAF. Rose failed to return from his first raid against Boulogne-sur-Mer, France, on the night of 12–13 March 1941. Wellington Mk IC T2515/BL-U took off at 7.50 p.m. from Alconbury. It later crashed near Wimille, 3 miles to the north of Boulogne-sur-Mer. The entire crew—Sgt D. W. Gough (RNZAF), Sgt T. G. Webb (RNZAF), Sgt T. H. Rose (RCAF), Sgt H. Jones, Sgt F. Stones and Sgt W. J. Morgan—are buried at the Wimille Communal Cemetery. They were a very young crew; both pilots and the navigator were only nineteen, while the two air gunners were only twenty-one.

R60002 Sergeant Thomas Scott Royan

† Age twenty-one, born in Calgary, Alberta. He served with No. 22 (TB) Squadron RAF. Royan was killed on 27 August 1941. Beaufort Mk I N1171/OA-H took off at 7.00 p.m. from Thorney Island for a 'Gardening' sortie in vicinity of Brest, France. An SOS was received when the aircraft was supposed to be returning; there was no further contact. The bodies of FS H. Menary DFM and Sgt T. S. Royan (RCAF) were later washed ashore and subsequently buried at St Mary's Old Church Cemetery on the Isles of Scilly. The other two crew members, Sgt F. S. R. Heard and Sgt R. P. S. Grenfell, are commemorated on the Runnymede Memorial.

R63912 Sergeant James Philip Scott

† Age nineteen, born in Toronto, Ontario. He served with the No. 22 (TB) Squadron RAF. Scott failed to return from an anti-shipping strike on 6 April 1941. Beaufort Mk I N1016/OA-X, one of six aircraft, took off at 4.20 p.m. from St Eval, Cornwall, *en route* to attacking the German battleship *Gneisenau*, which was anchored in the French port of Brest. Due to bad weather, his aircraft (piloted by Fg Off. K. Campbell) reached the target alone. After a short period of waiting for other aircraft, Campbell decided to make a lone attack. The crew was able to launch the torpedo from a height of 50 feet while encountering heavy fire from about 1,000 anti-aircraft guns and machine guns of all calibres. They soon received fatal hits from a flak barrage, causing the Beaufort to crash into the harbour. The entire crew—Fg Off. K. Campbell, Sgt J. P. Scott (RCAF), Sgt W. C. Mulliss and FS R. W. Hillman—were killed; they were buried at Kerfautras Cemetery in Brest, France. Fg Off. Campbell posthumously received the Victoria Cross, the highest British order.

R63906 Sergeant John Hodgins Smith

† Age twenty-nine, born in Toronto, Ontario. He served with No. 22 (TB) Squadron RAF. Smith was killed on 24 April 1941. His Beaufort Mk I L9950/OA-L took from St Eval, Cornwall, for a 'Gardening' sortie near Brest, France. No further communication was received from the aircraft. The bodies of the four crewmembers were later recovered. FS S. I. Sanders, Sgt J. H. Smith (RCAF), Sgt C. L. Ginnetta and Sgt H. Burton are interred in four different cemeteries—St Mary's Old Church Cemetery on the Isles of Scilly, St Illogan in Camborne Redruth, and St Peter Churchyard Cemetery and Blaby Cemetery in Leicestershire.

J941 Flying Officer Arthur Evans Snell

† Age thirty, born in Toronto, Ontario. He served with No. 42 (TB) Squadron RAF. Snell failed to return from an operational sortie on 16 October 1941. Beaufort Mk I L9939/AW-W took off at 2.00 p.m. from Leuchars, Scotland, on a 'Rover Patrol' and disappeared without a trace. The entire four-man crew—Plt Off. G. S. Turner, Fg Off. A. E. Snell (RCAF), Flight Sgt R. L. Robinson and Sgt G. G. King—are commemorated on the Runnymede Memorial.

R64120 Sergeant Wilbur Lloyd Waldron

† Age twenty-five, born in Kitchener, Ontario. Waldron served with No. 99 'Madras Presidency' (B) Squadron RAF. He failed to return from an operation against Vegesack, Germany, on the night of 9–10 April 1941. Wellington Mk IC R1440/LN-J took off at 8.20 p.m. from Waterbeach. The NGZ signal 'bombs gone' was received at 11.36 p.m., but shortly afterwards the Wellington was shot down by *Oberfeldwebel* Paul Gildner from IV./NJG 1. The crippled bomber crashed into Lake Ijssel in the Netherlands. Sgt G. W. Brown was buried at the Harderwijk General Cemetery in the Netherlands. The rest of the crew—Plt Off. T. Fairhurst, Sgt H. V. Wansbrough, Sgt H. L. Waldron (RCAF), Sgt W. R. Moore and Sgt C. W. Hall—are commemorated on the Runnymede Memorial.

R64119 Sergeant Gordon Thomas Webb

† Age twenty-two, born in Hamilton, Ontario. Webb was serving with No. 7 (B) Squadron RAF when he went missing on 28 June 1941, during a daylight raid. Six Short Stirling Mk Is from No. 7 (B) Squadron and No. 15 (B) Squadron were dispatched to attack Bremerhaven, Germany. Stirling Mk I N6007/MG-Q took off at 1.58 p.m. from Oakington. *En route* to the target, the bombers were attacked by German fighters about 37 miles to the north of the Dutch island community of Terschelling. According to German records, *Leutnant* Hans-Eberhard Bethke from Stab I./JG 52 claimed a Short Stirling in this area between 4 and 4.10 p.m. Ten minutes later, *Leutnant* Siegfried Mikosek from 1./JG 52 also claimed another four-engine bomber. However, the reality was somewhat different. Stirling N6007 and Stirling Mk I N3663/MG-H (piloted by Fg Off. G. B. Blacklock) survived the initial three-minute dogfight, which ended near sea-level. Five minutes later they were attacked by six Messerschmitt Bf 109s. One of them moved in close enough for the dorsal gunner to score hits on the engine. Shortly afterwards, at 4.15 p.m., *Leutnant* Bethke had to bale out of his Bf 109F-1 W.Nr. 8942. He safely parachuted into the sea, where he was later picked up. The next attack from the German fighters

knocked out the starboard outer engine of N6007. Fg Off. Blacklock started to circle the crippled aircraft in an effort to provide covering fire. The badly shot-up Stirling finally crashed into the sea about 20 miles from Flamborough Head. The fuselage broke into two parts on impact before sinking, taking the entire crew with it. The crew consisted of Flt Lt J. K. Collins, Sgt W. Hardie, Sgt G. T. Webb (RCAF), Sgt C. Kelly, Sgt A. T. Cole, FS D. W. E. Chapple and Sgt F. C. Williams. The entire crew is commemorated on the Runnymede Memorial.

R54909 Sergeant Wilbur Frederick Webber

† Age twenty-three, born in St Stephen, New Brunswick. Webber was serving with No. 218 'Gold Coast' (B) Squadron RAF when killed on 18 May 1941. At 11 a.m., his Rolls-Royce Merlin-powered Wellington Mk II W5448/HA-Z was on a training flight when the dinghy came loose from its storage area in the starboard engine nacelle. It jammed the right rudder. The dinghy eventually broke free and flew away from the aircraft. Shortly afterwards, the aircraft struck the ground at full speed approximately 5 miles south-east of Downham Market, Norfolk. It succumbed to fire and was destroyed. Plt Off. B. E. Lymbery, Sgt K. W. Coates, Sgt W. F. Weber (RCAF), Sgt L. Crawshaw, and Sgt G. L. M. Bayly were killed instantly, while Sgt R. G. Mew died in hospital on 20 May 1941. The crew members are buried at five different cemeteries around England. Sgt Webber and Plt Off. Lymbery were laid to rest at Holy Trinity Churchyard in Marham.

J15295 Flying Officer Melbourne Williams

Born on 15 November 1919 in the USA. He completed his tour of operations with the RAF and later served as an instructor in the United Kingdom. Williams was promoted to the rank of Pilot Officer in March 1942, followed a promotion to Flying Officer on 1 November 1942. He returned to Canada on 26 December 1942. Williams served as an instructor with No. 1 Central Navigation School at Rivers, Manitoba, from 21 January 1943 until 8 February 1944, when he was posted as an instructor to No. 8 AOS at Ancienne Lorette, Quebec. He was then posted to RCAF Headquarters in Ottawa on 5 April 1944. This was a short-lived assignment as on 6 May 1944 he was posted to RCAF Station Mountain View, Ontario. He left the RCAF on 28 February 1945, just before the end of the war.[1]

APPENDIX VI

Pilot Officer Sydney 'Timbertoes' Carlin MC DFC DCM

Sydney Carlin, the son of a drysalter, was born in 1889 in Hull, Yorkshire. He had a brief stint in the Army between 1907 and 1908 as a member of the famed 18th (Queen Mary's Own) Hussars. Young Sydney was working as a farmhand when war broke out. He re-enlisted in his old unit shortly after war was declared, and soon found himself shipped off to Belgium. For his meritorious actions, Sydney was awarded the Distinguished Conduct Medal on 5 August 1915. A commission to Second Lieutenant followed the next month; his promotion to Lieutenant would come the following year, in May 1916.

Sydney now commanded a field company of the Royal Engineers, and he would distinguish himself during the Battle of Delville Wood. His company was taking murderous fire while finishing a new trench, but he and his men were able to stem numerous counter-attacks and drive the Germans back to their own lines. Sydney sustained serious wounds during the battle; his leg was in such a bad shape that the doctors had no choice but to amputate it. *The London Gazette* printed the citation to his Military Cross in the 20 October 1916 edition.

It was impossible for Sydney to return to the trenches with an artificial limb, so he decided he would learn to fly. Sydney trained at own expense, and upon qualifying as a pilot he transferred to the Royal Flying Corps. He had a short tour as a flying instructor at Upavon, Wiltshire, before being told that he would be posted to an operational squadron. On 26 May 1918, he reported for duty with No. 74 (F) Squadron at Clairmarais, France. At that time, the unit was under the command of Maj. Keith Logan Caldwell MC, operating the rugged S.E.5a.

It was here that Capt. Edward Corringham Mannock DSO MC—a Flight Commander with the Squadron and a fighter ace with thirty-eight kills already— gave Sydney the nickname 'Timbertoes'. Sydney claimed ten German kills between 13 July and 15 September 1918; the tally consisted of five balloons, three Fokker C. VIIs, and one DFW C destroyed, alongside the contribution to the demise of a Pfalz D.III that went out of control and crashed while he was chasing it.

Appendix VI

Sydney was also acting as a Flight Commander during this period, being promoted to the rank of Temporary Captain on 9 August 1918. On 5 September, he narrowly escaped death after colliding mid-air with the Squadron's commander, Maj. Caldwell MC. Both managed to get their damaged aircraft down safely.

Sydney's luck finally ran out on 21 September 1918. While flying an S.E.5a (s/n D6958), he was shot down by German fighter pilot *Unteroffizier* Siegfried Westphal, from Jasta 29. This was Westphal's second of an eventual six victories. Sydney's stint as a prisoner of war only lasted for a short period of time, as the First World War ended on 11 November of that year.[1] On 2 November, *The London Gazette* published the citation to his Distinguished Flying Cross:

A gallant and determined pilot, who sets a fine example to his squadron. Though handicapped by the loss of a leg, he is bold and skilful in attack, and has destroyed four balloons and shot down two enemy machines.[2]

Sydney returned to his farm after the war ended, later going overseas to Kenya and finding work on the farm of a German Baron. While there, he would form a friendship with a young Charles Pickard, whom he taught polo.

Sydney was re-enlisted into the British Army at the outbreak of the Second World War. He found himself shipped to Malta in February 1940. Despite his medical handicap, he was able to return to service with the Royal Air Force. Sydney was not permitted to fly as a pilot due to his age, but he steadfastly refused to 'fly a desk'. In July 1940, he returned to the United Kingdom, where he was commissioned with the rank of Pilot Officer under service number 81942.

By the end of August, he was posted as an air gunner to No. 264 'Madras Presidency' (F) Squadron. The Squadron was a night fighter unit under the command of Sqn Ldr George Desmond Garvin, equipped with the two-seat Boulton Paul Defiant Mk I. Sydney carried out his first patrol on the night of 28 August from the Squadron's home at RAF Station Kirton-in-Lindsey, Lincolnshire.

Sydney was sent on a gunnery course at the Central Gunnery School, RAF Station Warmwell, Dorset, on 8 September 1940. After successfully making it through the course, he was posted to RAF Station Wittering, Northamptonshire, home of No. 151 (F) Squadron, on 5 January 1941. This night-fighter unit was under the command of Sqn Ldr Jack Sylvester Adams DFC and equipped with Hawker Hurricane Mk Is and Boulton Paul Defiant Mk Is.

Being cooped up in the rotating turret of the Defiant did not appeal to Sydney, so he made a phone call to his old friend from his days in Kenya, Sqn Ldr Pickard. 'Pick', as he was popularly known, was a Liaison Officer with No. 311 'Czechoslovak' (B) Squadron, based at East Wretham, Norfolk. Sydney was looking for a trip over Germany if possible. He got his wish, and on the night of 18 March 1941 he found himself on a Wellington bound for Bremen. Also on board the aircraft was Plt Off. Gellner.

After they returned from the sortie, they all headed down to a local pub frequented by RAF personnel. While driving back to the station, they were involved in a motor vehicle accident. Sydney was seriously injured, requiring a prolonged stay in hospital. When he was released from hospital on 15 April 1941, he made his way back to Wittering, where he was soon promoted to Acting Flying Officer.

RAF Station Wittering seemed to be attracting more than its fair share of attention from the Luftwaffe. On 8 May 1941, it was attacked twice. An extract from the No. 151 (F) Squadron ORB reads:

> Our efforts were curtailed by a Ju 88 which dropped a stick of eight anti-personnel bombs across 'A' Flight dispersal, writing off two aircraft and damaging four others, also killing Fg Off. Carlin—he was the only casualty. His loss is felt by all.

The RAF Station Wittering ORB stated:

> The first attack was made by a diving aircraft and ten HE and Incendiary bombs were dropped. Plt Off. Carlin, No. 151 Squadron, was killed. Several aircraft were hit and sustained minor damage, one being totally destroyed by fire.[3]

At the age of fifty-two, Sydney was most likely the second-oldest RAF flying aircrew member on active duty killed during the Second World War. The oldest was fifty-six year-old air gunner Plt Off. Sir Arnold Talbot Wilson KCIE CSI CMG DSO (75684). He was killed in action while on board Wellington Mk IC L7791/LF-(?) from No. 37 (B) Squadron. The aircraft crashed near Eringhem, south of the French port of Dunkirk, during an air raid against Nieuwpoort, Belgium, on 31 May 1940.[4]

The notes in Gellner's diary about Fg Off. Carlin's victories as an air gunner with No. 151 (F) Squadron are not supported by any documentation. The Squadron's ORB stated that he mostly flew with pilot Flt Lt D. A. P. McMullen. They flew several night patrols together, but did not make any claims. During the nights of 9–10 and 10–11 April 1941, a number of members of the Squadron (including Flt Lt McMullen) claimed several enemy aircraft shot down, but Fg Off. Carlin was still in hospital, recovering from his automobile accident, at this time.[5]

Endnotes

PART I

Chapter 1

1. The *Duchess of Richmond* was built by John Brown & Co. Shipyard in Glasgow in June 1928. She started her transatlantic voyages on 15 March 1929 by sailing from Liverpool to St John, New Brunswick. During the Second World War, she served as a troopship. On 16 July 1947, she was returned to civil use and re-named as the *Empress of Canada*. The ship made over 186 voyages prior to being lost on 25 January 1953 at Gladstone Dock, Liverpool. A fire broke out and became uncontrollable, resulting in the sinking of the vessel.
2. The SS *Champlain* was a cabin class ocean liner built in 1932 by Chantiers et Ateliers de Saint-Nazaire, Penhoët, for French Line. She was one of the most modern steamers of that time. After the outbreak of the Second World War, she carried many refugees from Europe to North America, including many Jews. The ship sunk near La Pallice when she struck a German sea mine on 17 June 1940.
3. The 6th Canadian Infantry Brigade was formed at Camp Shilo, Manitoba, in May 1940. Two battalions set sail for the United Kingdom on 16 December. Its first camp on the British Isles was near Aldershot, Hampshire. Brigadier David Roy Sargent was the Commanding Officer in 1940–41.
4. Jan Masaryk (1886–1948), son of the first Czechoslovak President, Tomáš Garrigue Masaryk (1850–1937), Czechoslovak envoy in the United Kingdom 1925–38 and Minister of Foreign Affairs for the Czechoslovak government in exile based in London 1940–45.
5. It was the HMS *Formidable*, an Illustrious-class aircraft carrier commissioned on 24 November 1940. Her first task was to escort an Allied convoy sailing to Cape Town, South Africa, between December 1940 and January 1941.

Chapter 2

1. The bombing of Liverpool, an important port in the maritime connection with the USA, began in August 1940. Between then and October 1940, the Luftwaffe carried out 200 air raids against the seaport. In December, the total number of air raids increased to 300. During a three-night period of 20–22 December, 365 citizens were killed.

Chapter 3

1. Manning Depot, the unit every RCAF recruit must pass through immediately after joining up.
2. No. 1 Personnel Dispatch Centre was based at Uxbridge from 1 September 1940 until 28 February 1941, when it was renamed as No. 3 Personnel Reception Centre (PRC).
3. During the bombing in the second half of 1940, Londoners started to look for shelter and safe places to stay overnight in the underground stations. Authorities tried to prohibit this at first, but they finally relented and provided beds, toilets, and catering. Some stations served as official government venues. War Cabinet meetings were held in Downing Street Station until the Cabinet War Rooms were finished.
4. Lady Hardinge, born Helen Gascoyne-Cecil, wife of Maj. Sir Alexander Henry Louis Hardinge, 2nd Baron Hardinge of Penshurst, Private Secretary to the Sovereign between 1936 and 1943.
5. Queen Elizabeth (1900–2002), King George VI's spouse, later the Queen Mother.
6. Princess Margaret Rose (1930–2002), King George VI's younger daughter.
7. Princess Elizabeth, King George VI's older daughter, who became Queen Elizabeth II in 1952.
8. Grosvenor Place is located in the London Borough of Westminster, next to the gardens of Buckingham Palace. The Czechoslovak Embassy was at 8 Grosvenor Place from the end of the First World War until 1956. During the Second World War, 9 Grosvenor Place housed the office of the Czechoslovak President in Exile, Dr Edvard Beneš.

Chapter 5

1. In fact, Maj. Ernest Evelyn Rich DSO of the Royal Horse Artillery was killed in France on 1 December 1917.
2. Maps named after the Flemish cartographer Gerardus Mercator (1512–1594), who in 1569 was the first person to transfer the known world map into a rectangle network of meridians and parallels. *Air Publication 1234: Air Navigation Volume I*—an RAF manual for air navigation instruction.
3. Squadron Navigation Officer—among his main tasks were assisting the Squadron CO with the navigational questions, instructing the crews in new navigational principles and improving the navigation quality of the Squadron, and administering navigation aids, maps, and manuals.
4. Grp Capt. Thomas Williams MC DFC & Bar (08195), a First World War veteran with nine victories, commanded RAF Station Watton between July 1940 and July 1941. He was nineteen years older than his wife.
5. On 13 December 1940, *The Daily Telegraph* printed the following account: 'Three RAF Officers, Wg Cdr J. F. Griffiths DFC, Sqn Ldr H. R. Graham and Flt Lt A. H. S. Browne, were decorated by President Beneš yesterday with the Czech War Cross for service to the Czechoslovak Air Forces. They are the first British officers to receive the newly created award.' Both the diarist and the article are inaccurate, as Flt Lt Browne was awarded the Czechoslovak Gallantry Medal. Both decorations were newly created by an order of Czechoslovak government authorised on 30 August 1940 and officially published on 20 December 1940.
6. No. 311 (B) Squadron was short of flying staff during its earliest days, so some fighter pilots were posted in as second pilots. Some airmen with a sport pilot licence requesting postings into fighter pilot training were quickly retrained as air gunners, W/T operators or navigators. This unpopular solution resulted in a few airmen refusing to serve. First to be posted to the Czechoslovak Depot at Cosford on 22 September 1940 was air gunner Plt Off. Lubomír Úlehla (82644), who was discharged from the RAF on 9 October 1940. Brothers Fg Off. Ludvík Kozák (82611) and Fg Off. Pavel Kozák (82650), both W/T operators in training, arrived at Cosford on 13 November with 'bad character'. They were discharged on 19 December 1940.

Operational pilot Sgt Karel Fák (787620) refused to take part on a sortie after previously taking part in six, and was released on 2 January 1941. On 17 December, pilot-in-training Sgt Karel Novotný (787564) refused to fly on a Wellington; he was discharged on 6 January 1941.

7. The first RAF 'area bombing' raid on a German industrial town as revenge for the bombing of the British towns Coventry and Southampton. There were only 134 bombers taking part in this raid; three aircraft were lost. One hundred and two crews claimed they attacked the primary target. Most of the bombs fell outside the town centre, causing little damage. Thirty-four civilians were killed, while eighty-one were injured.
8. The Pilot's Notes for the Wellington Mk IC describe the flap control (for which the second pilot was responsible) as follows: 'The flap control lever is returned in its neutral position by a spring-loaded catch which is released for operation by depressing the knob.'
9. Plt Off. Vladimír Nedvěd (82624) avoided hospital treatment (he returned to operations on 6 February 1941), so he did not go to the hospital in Bury St Edmunds in an ambulance. However, Plt Off. Josef Doubrava (82595) went to hospital with a cut on the base of his nose and bruised ribs (returning to operations on 23 February 1941) and Sgt Josef Pavelka (787230) went with multiple fractures and an injured spine (not returning to operations until 18 October 1943).
10. MSI was a unique code consisting of five or six characters, of which the first two or three were letters. The letters denoted aircraft taking off from a particular airfield for a particular air raid; the remaining characters denoted their number in the sequence. MSIs were assigned by Flying Control, and aircraft routes and estimated times were logged against the MSI. Later, when the radar station picked up an aircraft track and reported it to the Filter Room, the flying control liaison officer would compare this to the MSIs and advise on whether it is possible hostile, possible friendly, or an unknown aircraft.

Chapter 6

1. Air Raid Precautions was an organisation set up in 1924 to protect civilians from the danger of air raids. ARP members checked that black-out restrictions were enforced, and they were trained to extinguish fires and provide first aid.
2. Sgt Arnošt Havlík (787635, later commissioned Flt Lt 62216) first served with the RAF as an interpreter. He passed a course for accounting clerks between 28 March and 31 May 1941 and then joined No. 311 (B) Squadron as Chief Accountant. From 11 March 1944 until the end of the war, he worked at the Czechoslovak Inspectorate General in London. He owned the chemical and cosmetics factory 'Laboratoires VALDOR', located in the Paris suburb of Argenteuil, before the outbreak of the Second World War.
3. A group of forty Czechoslovak airmen assigned to the sixteen-week Armourers Course arrived at Manby on 29 November 1940, along with two interpreters.
4. Jacques Schneider (1879–1928), a prominent French financier, balloonist and aircraft enthusiast, proposed the Coupe d'Aviation Maritime Jacques Schneider in 1912. It was a contest for seaplanes with the goal of supporting the technical advances of civil aviation.

Chapter 7

1. A few Wellington Mk Is and IAs with dual controls were allotted to No. 311 (B) Squadron for the training of new pilots. On 12 January 1941, only one such type was on strength with the Squadron—Wellington Mk IA L7776/KX-Q.
2. According to the RAF Station Honington ORB, all operations were cancelled at 9.20 p.m.
3. The Pilot's Notes for the Wellington Mk IC stated the stalling speed was between 67 and 72 mph, depending on the aircraft's load.

4. The Bomb Selector Control Panel had sixteen switches in two rows of eight; each would trigger a bomb-release mechanism in the bomb bay. On the right-hand side of the panel there are also two sliding plastic strips protected by a metal safety cover; when pushed to the left, these strips would jettison all the aircraft's bombs in a disarmed state. The jettison function was also used to ensure that all bombs had been released on a final bomb run, when the bomb aimer would call, 'Bombs gone; jettison bars across,' to inform the pilot that all bomb releases had been triggered—whether or not these had been activated when the bomb-release button was pressed.
5. The pilot's bomb-jettison remote-control handle was located above the main instrument panel of the Wellington Mk IC.
6. The whole day-long search was carried out by aircraft from RAF Stations Honington, Feltwell, Watton and East Wretham. The three aircraft from No. 311 (B) Squadron took off between 9.15 and 11.10 a.m. while six aircraft from No. 9 Squadron took off between 12.21 and 12.23 a.m. The aircraft from No. 311 (B) Squadron finished their (unsuccessful) search between 2.40 and 3.10 p.m., while No. 9 (B) Squadron arrived back between 2.04 and 3.53 p.m.
7. *Sokol* (Falcon) is gymnastics organisation that still exists today. It was founded by Miroslav Tyrš and Jindřich Fügner in Prague, in the Czech region of Austria-Hungary, in 1862. The *Pobočka Sokol 311 Peruť* (Falcon Branch 311 Squadron) of *Sokolská župa zahraniční* (The Falcon Abroad District) was founded on 14 January 1941. The first chairman was Plt Off. Jaromír Král, who held the position for just two days before being killed.
8. Flt Lt Thomas Gresham Kirby-Green (39103) served with the OTF of No. 311 (B) Squadron as a Pilot Instructor between October 1940 and June 1941. He was then posted to No. 40 (B) Squadron and promoted to Squadron Leader. His Wellington Mk IC, Z8862/BL-B, failed to return from a raid on Duisburg, Germany, on the night of 16–17 October 1941. He became a prisoner of war in the Stalag Luft III camp in Sagan, Germany. Following the Great Escape, he was one of fifty men executed by the Gestapo in late March and early April 1944.
9. The British Air Ministry, based at Adastral House in Kingsway, London, was the highest RAF authority. As there was no independent Czechoslovak Air Force—as opposed to the Polish Air Force, for example—Czechoslovak airmen and Czechoslovak squadrons were subordinate to this authority. However, in this particular case, it is more likely that the diarist was referring to the Czech government in exile's Ministry of National Defence.
10. Flt Lt Jaroslav Kulhánek (86624) served at the Czechoslovak Inspectorate General in London until 14 July 1941. After a course at No. 57 OTU, he joined No. 124 'Baroda' (F) Squadron on 11 November 1941. On 13 March 1942, Kulhánek failed to return from a bomber escort to Hazebrouck. His Spitfire Mk VB, BL758/ON-L, was shot down by a Focke-Wulf 190 from II./JG 26, crashing near Offrethun in France.
11. Plt Offs Karel Hančil (82600), Karel Kovář (82610), Zdeněk Matuška (82621), František Růžička (82631) and Václav Vaněček (82645) refused to serve in the RAF if they were not to be trained as fighter pilots. They were discharged from the RAF on their own request on 13 January 1941.
12. The rest of the Czechoslovak Army personnel that managed to evacuate France was based at Cholmondeley Park, Cheshire. They were transformed into the 1st Czechoslovak Mixed Brigade on 12 August 1940. This unit moved to Leamington Spa in October 1940, being reorganised into the Czechoslovak Independent Brigade Group in July 1941. From May 1942, this unit was based at Ilminster, Somerset, and assigned to guard duty along the coast. On 1 September 1943, the Czechoslovak Independent Armoured Brigade Group was formed by the consolidation of these forces with Czechoslovak troops from the Middle East. By the end of 1944, the brigade had seen action in France during the siege of Dunkirk.
13. A Small Bomb Container was used for carrying small bombs in the bomb bay. An SBC can take hold of up to 236 4-lb incendiary bombs.
14. The summary of the ORB shows that in fact, a total of ninety-five Czechoslovak airmen took part in the raids—thirty-one pilots, sixteen navigators, sixteen W/T operators, and thirty-two

gunners. This represented nearly sixteen complete crews. With this total, the losses reached 29 per cent. In addition, it is now known that twenty of those twenty-seven missing men were killed, while the rest were captured.

Chapter 8

1. Plt Off. Anthony St Croix Rose (90719), aged twenty-nine, a pilot with No. 615 'County of Surrey' (F) Squadron based at RAF Station Croydon, was killed on the night of 11 September 1939, when his Gloster Gladiator Mk I, K7987 crashed a mile to the north of Bletchingley, Surrey, while carrying out formation-flying training.
2. Canada House was built between 1824 and 1827 at Trafalgar Square in central London. It was designed by architect Sir Robert Smirke. The Canadian government acquired the building in 1923. The RCAF Overseas Headquarters were based at 20 Lincoln's Inn Fields, Holborn.
3. Horace Hume van Wart (1892–1951) had served as an officer with the Canadian Siberian Expeditionary Force as part of the Allied intervention forces in Vladivostok, Russia, in 1919. While he was there, he liaised with officers from the Czechoslovak Legions. Van Wart formed a strong bond with the Czechs and remained in contact with a number of them in his later years. He opened his own law firm after graduating from the Faculty of Law, and he later became Honorary Consul of the Czechoslovak Republic in Toronto, Ontario, on 22 August 1936.
4. Ernest Bevin (1881–1951) was a British trade union leader and member of the Labour Party. He became Minister of Labour and National Service in 1940, filling the role of Foreign Secretary from 1945 until his death.
5. *Polskie Siły Powietrzne* (The Polish Air Force) was recognised by the British government as a sovereign entity force on 5 August 1940. Polish airmen wore RAF uniforms but with their own Polish insignia and ranks. Polish squadrons formally operated under the supervision of the Air Ministry, but they were commanded by the Polish Inspectorate General in London. There were two serving Administrative Officers with the surname Janik—Plt Off. Julian Jan Andrzej Janik (P-2514) and Fg Off. Stanisław Janik (P-2048).

Chapter 9

1. Sgt Vilém Bufka (787572) was recovering from a frostbitten legs that he suffered during an operational flight on 16 January 1941. Sgt František Kráčmer (787244) was in hospital for an unknown reason (unconnected with operational duty); he did not begin operations until 26 February 1941.
2. The RAF also used the 'Q Code', which comprised several tens of three-letter codes starting with 'Q', for both questions and answers, each having a specific meaning. The 'QDM' code meant, 'What is the magnetic course to steer to reach you?'
3. The crew in Wellington Mk IC L7842/KX-T lost their bearings when returning from Boulogne-sur-Mer; due to incorrect navigation, they accidentally landed at a German-occupied French airfield near Flers, south of Caen. They were made prisoners of war. The German-marked Wellington was used on test flights by 2./*Versuchsverband Staffel* of the *Erprobungsstelle der Luftwaffe* at Rechlin. The Wellington's fate is uncertain, but it is thought that it was destroyed in an Allied air raid.
4. During an air raid against Hanover, Germany, on the night of 10–11 February 1941, RAF Bomber Command lost eight aircraft. One of them was Wellington Mk IC T2610/PM-(?) from No. 103 (B) Squadron, which ditched into the sea. All six crew members were injured, but they managed to get to a dinghy. They were rescued two days later by the Danish merchant ship SS *Tovelil*.
5. A German expression for 'chaos'.

6. Wg Cdr William Stephen Pomeroy Simonds (32131) and Wg Cdr Karel Toman-Mareš (82579).
7. Wellington Mk IC R1022/KX-K was crewed by Sgt Alois Šedivý, Sgt Josef Čapka, Plt Off. Lubomír Svátek, Plt Off. Jaroslav Liška, Sgt Pavel Babáček, and Sgt Vladimír Cupák. Due to fog and empty fuel tanks, the pilot crash-landed at 1.05 a.m. on a field at Wheatley Farm, near RAF Station Swinderby. The aircraft's propellers, flaps, front turret, and belly were damaged, but the crew escaped uninjured.
8. Gellner's use of the term 'our' refers to the whole of RAF Bomber Command, not just No. 311 (B) Squadron.
9. Brigadier Sir Archibald Fraser Home CB CMG DSO (1874–1953) served in the British Army from 1895. He served as a Staff Officer between 1905 and 1919, later becoming His Majesty's Bodyguard of the Honourable Corps of Gentlemen-at-Arms until 1938.
10. The British Empire Services League (BESL) was founded in 1921 by Field Marshal Lord Douglas Haig and South African Prime Minister Field Marshal Jan Christiaan Smuts. It was formed to bring together individual veteran's organisations and associations from all across the British Empire.
11. The French card game '*Vingt-et-un*' ('Twenty-one') was introduced in French casinos in around 1700; it was the precursor to blackjack.
12. The Bomb Disposal Squad was a mobile pyrotechnic RAF unit that was responsible for the digging out and disposal of unexploded bombs of both German and British origin. During first two years of the war, they disposed of 1,512 bombs.
13. The following aircraft went missing during a raid on Wilhelmshaven. Wellington Mk IC T2503/AA-(?) from No. 75 'New Zealand' (B) Squadron, based at RAF Station Feltwell, was probably lost over the North Sea. Its crew comprised Plt Off. A. J. Falconer, Sqn Ldr E. U. G. Solbe, Plt Off. A. V. Muir, Sgt W. D. Morrison, Sgt H. T. Hellier and Sgt A. M. Brodie. Only two of their bodies were recovered, both washed ashore on the German coast. Wellington Mk IC R1045/OJ-M from No. 149 (B) Squadron, RAF Station Mildenhall, was lost without trace along with its crew—Fg Off. I. S. Henderson, Sgt W. P. Jinks, Sgt W. H. MacLeod, Sgt F. May, Sgt J. P. Redmond and Sgt J. Stewart.
14. The ORB of No. 75 'New Zealand' (B) Squadron, based at RAF Station Feltwell, noted eight Wellington Mk ICs taking off between 6.50 and 7.10 p.m. All of them returned to their home base between 9.40 and 11.05 p.m. The Wellington, therefore, probably flew back to the home base after landing in East Wretham. The No. 21 (B) Squadron ORB records Blenheim Mk IV Z5875 taking off at 6.50 p.m. and landing at 10.10 p.m., but according to the diarist, the crew—Flt Lt Barker, Sgt Meanwell and Sgt Spriggs—stayed overnight in East Wretham.
15. The debriefing after a raid on Cologne was recorded by Fg Off. Arnošt Fantl, while the summary for No. 3 Group HQ was prepared by Plt Off. John Gellner.
16. This accident occurred on 23 February 1941 aboard Avro Anson Mk I R9648, crewed by Flt Lt Michael John Earle, Sgt Adolf Musálek, Plt Off. Jiří Engel, Plt Off. Otakar Černý and Plt Off. Jaroslav Zafouk. Plt Off. Engel was slightly injured on landing near Aldford, Cheshire. The incident was caused by the Perspex cover in the middle of the cockpit's ceiling, which served as an emergency exit in case of a crash-landing. It was only fixed in position by a narrow fabric strip, which could be cut in an emergency by pulling a loop of thin steel wire.
17. Leo Joseph John Judson (628731/47205) was attached to No. 311 (B) Squadron from No. 9 (B) Squadron and served as a W/T instructor between September 1940 and May 1941. During this time, he flew two sorties. Judson was awarded the Czechoslovak Gallantry Medal in May 1941 and the honorary Czechoslovak Pilot Badge. He was awarded the DFM on 23 September 1941, and he was commissioned as a Plt Off. in November 1941. He received a DFC while serving with No. 161 (SD) Squadron on 20 April 1943. He reached the rank of Sqn Ldr in November 1943.
18. Wellington Mk IC T2620/WS-G (crewed by Sgt Donnelly, Sgt Peatfield, Sgt Lennard, Sgt Lang, Sgt Church and Sgt Clarice) struck Blenheim Mk IV N3618 from No. 21 (B) Squadron while taxiing for take-off at 11.30 p.m. The crew was unhurt. Wellington T2620 returned to service after repairs, but it was later damaged again. Blenheim N3618 was scrapped.

19. Armstrong Whitworth Whitley Mk V P5027/MH-(?), crewed by Plt Off. Keeling, Sgt Mossley, Sgt Wilson, Sgt Barnes and Sgt Humble.
20. The ORB for 2 March 1941 stated: 'Sqn Ldr Ocelka tests T2372 in the afternoon on a two-hour cross-country flight'. There was no Wellington serving with No. 311 Squadron with this serial number. It is possible that the aircraft was in fact T2972/KX-G or N2772/KX-K from the Training Flight.
21. The ORB recorded the enemy raid as follows: 'At 9.30 p.m. an enemy aircraft attacked the aerodrome and dropped about twenty bombs in one stick along the north side of the aerodrome. The first bomb fell about 5 yards from S 7841 [Wellington Mk IC L7841/KX-S], the others more to the middle of aerodrome. Slight damage from pieces of earth and splinters to the fabric of one aircraft. There were no casualties.'
22. Sqn Ldr Percy Charles Pickard (39392) was awarded the DSO on 7 March 1941 for his service with No. 311 Squadron: 'Since joining the squadron in July 1940, this officer has invariably taken out the new Czech crews on their initial operation or first long-distance mission. On such occasions, he has been the only British member amongst the crews, who have been inspired by his splendid leadership and example. On one occasion it was undoubtedly due to his determined efforts that one Czech crew were rescued after being adrift in the North Sea for over thirteen hours. On another occasion when a crew was forced down in the North Sea, his persistence and good airmanship in failing light, and his sound use of recognition signals enabled surface craft to affect a rescue. His complete disregard for danger was particularly shown on one occasion when a fully loaded bomber crashed and caught fire. He led a rescue party and personally extricated two members of the crew and succeeded in eventually conveying them to safety, although compelled to remain prone in the danger area during the explosion of some of the bombs. He has displayed coolness and courage of a high order and by his magnificent work has contributed largely to the present efficiency of the squadron.'
23. Plt Off. Paul Adair Gilbertson (J3709) joined the RCAF on 24 June 1940. After pilot training at No. 7 EFTS in Windsor and No.1 SFTS in Camp Borden (both in Ontario), he sailed to the United Kingdom in February 1941. After the end of his operational tour with the RCAF's No. 403 'Wolf' (F) Squadron, he served as an instructor at No. 52 OTU. In April 1942 he returned to Canada, where he was active in the formation of Nos 126, 127 and 129 (F) Squadrons. As a Sqn Ldr, he commanded the Hurricane-equipped Nos 125, 126, 127 and 129 (F) Squadrons. Gilbertson went on to achieve the rank of Wg Cdr.
24. Wellington Mk IC R1013/BL-B from No. 40 (B) Squadron based at RAF Station Alconbury. The last message to be received from the aircraft was the wireless operator confirming that the bombs had been dropped. The crew comprised Sqn Ldr E. H. Lynch-Blosse, Plt Off. H. Heaton, Fg Off. S. H. Palmer, Sgt D. R. Clay, Sgt A. Hammond and Sgt H. Caldicott. They all survived and became prisoners of war.
25. Wellington Mk IC R1326/HA-G, No. 218 'Gold Coast' (B) Squadron from RAF Station Marham. Shot down by *Oberfeldwebel* Hans Rasper, flying Messerschmitt Bf 110 'G9+BM' from 4./NJG 1. The Wellington crashed at Opperdoes, in the Netherlands. Fg Off. W. P. Crosse, Sgt J. H. Collopy, Sgt W. J. Chamberlain, and Sgt E. J. Coult were killed, while Sgt A. E. Binnie and Sgt A. Parfitt were captured. Wellington Mk IC N2744/WS-U, No. 9 (B) Squadron, RAF Station Honington, crashed at Versen, about 3 miles to the north-west of Meppen, in Germany. Sgt B. P. Hall, Sgt W. J. Manger, Sgt W. L. Smith and Sgt J. W. Hammond were killed, while Sgt J. R. Brown and Sgt E. Collins were captured.
26. Wittering was the home base for the following units: No. 266 'Rhodesia' (F) Squadron—Spitfire Mk I, IIA, IIB & VB (May 1940 to September 1941); No. 25 (NF) Squadron—Beaufighter Mk IF (November 1940 to January 1942); and No. 151 (NF) Squadron—Hawker Hurricane Mk I (December 1938 to June 1941), Boulton Paul Defiant Mk I (December 1940 to October 1941), Hawker Hurricane Mk IIC (April 1941 to January 1942) and Boulton Paul Defiant Mk II (September 1941 to July 1942).

27. A single Junkers Ju 88 attacked RAF Station Wittering with a load of six 500-lb high-explosives and around 100 incendiary bombs. These damaged or destroyed several buildings, including a hangar housing aircraft from No. 25 (NF) Squadron. Seventeen airmen were killed.
28. Wellington Mk IC R1371/KX-F was originally assigned to the crew of Plt Off. Jindřich Breitcetl, Sgt Josef Bernát, Plt Off. Jindřich Vnouček, Sgt Rudolf Hearing, Sgt Vladimír Kováč and Sgt Jindřich Beneš. Sqn Ldr Percy Charles Pickard, Sgt Benedikt Blatný, Plt Off. Alois Kirchstein, Sgt Vladimír Slánský, Sgt Miroslav Čtvrtlík and Sgt Vilém Jakš were on reserve with Wellington Mk IC R1410/KX-M. Plt Off. Carlin's visit probably led to the change to Sqn Ldr Pickard's crew and the exchange of aircraft.
29. Wellington Mk IC R1378/KX-K was seriously damaged, and four of the crew sustained various injuries. Sgt Leo Anderle was uninjured; Fg Off. Josef Šejbl suffered abrasions to his nose, lower lip, and hand; Plt Off. Vilém Konštacký suffered abrasions to his forehead and thumb and bruising on his right leg; Sgt Jan Plzák was uninjured; Plt Off. Josef Horák suffered slight cuts to his forehead and knee; and Sgt Karel Valach suffered bruising on his back and a suspected fractured vertebrae.
30. Details about the accident are described in the Grp Capt. Pickard's biography, *Wings of Night*: 'Returning along the main road to Thetford, Dorothy in the front saw some lights ahead. The car did not appear to be slowing down. She glanced across at the driver, Wing Commander Toman, and noticed that he was sound asleep! In a flash, Dorothy reached over and swung the steering wheel to the right. The estate car was much too close and with a screech of grinding metal, they hit the obstacle ahead. It was a large pantechnicon furniture lorry. Toman was instantly awake, applied the brakes automatically, but the car hit the ditch on the right hand side, throwing Sidney Carlin out. Everywhere was broken glass, rent metal, and blood.'
31. The RAF Station Honington ORB stated: 'Honington told to have eight aircraft and if possible ten aircraft loaded with 5 × 500 SAP bombs ready and standing by 8 a.m. for operations against Capital ships.' The Capital ships were thought be the German battleships *Gneisenau* and *Scharnhorst*, which were returning from Operation Berlin in the North Atlantic. Since 21 January 1941, the ships had sunk a total of twenty-two Allied ships. On 20 March, they were sighted approximately 600 miles to the west of Spanish Cape Finisterre by the crew of a Fairey Fulmar Mk II from HMS *Ark Royal*. The aircraft's wireless equipment failed, so the crew was unable to relay this information until they landed. Both the *Gneisenau* and *Scharnhorst* escaped under the cover of fog, anchoring in the French port of Brest on 22 March.
32. As Fg Off. František Pohlodek was taxiing Wellington Mk IA P9224/KX-T, the aircraft struck a hole. The starboard propeller was damaged.
33. No. 3 Photographic Reconnaissance Unit was equipped with Spitfire PR Mk IIIs, IVs and Vs for day reconnaissance. The unit also operated two Wellington Mk ICs for night-reconnaissance flights.
34. Wellington Mk IA P9230/KX-X, captained by Plt Off. Jan Hrnčíř, was attacked at 10.50 p.m. by a Junkers Ju 88 most likely piloted by *Hauptmann* Karl Hülshoff from Stab I./NJG 2.
35. The first Liberator Mk Is and IIs were only delivered to the United Kingdom in the first half of 1941. Plt Off. Charles Pears Davidson (J3113) was killed aboard Catalina Mk II AM265/BN-A from No. 240 (GR) Squadron. After taking off on an operational flight on 21 March 1941, the Catalina crashed at Aunagh Hill, Leitrim, Northern Ireland.
36. 'Dimi' was the nickname for another Czech, Fg Off. Vladimír Viktor Havlíček (J3112), who passed his training in the second air observers' course in the BCATP. On the night of 23 December 1941, while serving with No. 240 (GR) Squadron, he was posted as missing after Catalina Mk I W8418/BN-U failed in attempt to land at Pembroke Dock, Pembrokeshire.
37. FS Jan Kaucký (787976) was an instructor at No. 52 OTU from 7 March 1941 until 1 January 1943. Between March and May 1941, the following Czechs also served in Debden: Sgt Bohumír Fürst (787556), WO Miroslav Kopecký (787984), and Sgt Rudolf Zima (787978). They were all former Battle of Britain fighter pilots from No. 310 (F) Squadron.

Endnotes

38. LAC Vítězslav Roth (788002) was the manager of a sugar refinery before the war. He served as a maintenance assistant with No. 311 Squadron from 19 November 1940 until 19 February 1945, when he was transferred to the Czechoslovak Depot at Cosford.
39. Sgt Oldřich Helma (787190) suffered frostbite during an air raid on Braunschweig on 9 April 1941. He returned to active duty on 16 May, as the skipper of a freshman crew attacking Boulogne-sur-Mer.
40. Several of the Czechoslovak ministries resided in the extensive Fursecroft office complex on George Street during the war, including the Ministry of Foreign Affairs.
41. Bohuš František Beneš (1904–1969) was a poet, journalist, and editor. He was the editor-in-chief of *Čechoslovák*, the semi-official magazine of the Czechoslovak government in exile based in London. It was published between 1940 and 1945.
42. No. 310 (Czechoslovak) Fighter Squadron was formed on 12 July 1940 as the first of the Czechoslovak squadrons within the RAF. The Squadron was equipped with Hawker Hurricane Mk Is, IIAs, and IIBs, and operated from Duxford until 26 June 1941. Sqn Ldr František Weber (82584) became the second CO; he served in this role from 28 February 1941 to 7 April 1942.
43. The raid on London lasted nearly seven hours. It was carried out by 685 Luftwaffe bombers; the bomb loads they dropped started approximately 2,000 fires. Over 1,000 people were killed and many historic buildings suffered irreparable damage.
44. Wellington Mk IC R1021/KX-W had flown a previous sortie on 2 March 1941.
45. In fact, there were no survivors from Sgt František Kráčmer's crew; they were flying in Wellington Mk IC R1599/KX-J.
46. No. 9 (B) Squadron's Wellington Mk IC T2900/WS-L (based at RAF Station Honington) sent an SOS message at 12.58 a.m. Their last known position was 30 miles to the east of Lowestoft. The crew comprised Sgt R. D. C. Stark, Sgt F. W. Baker, Sgt J. W. Nightingarl, Sgt G. Gibb, Sgt J. E. Johnson and Sgt H. F. Hurt; their remains were never found.
47. On the night of 17–18 April 1941, RAF Bomber Command sent a total of 118 bombers to Berlin. Eight failed to return—one Wellington Mk IC, two Hampden Mk Is, and five Whitley Mk Vs.
48. William John Woodhouse (1866–1937) was a British university professor and the author of many books about Ancient Rome and Ancient Greece.
49. No. 1 Initial Training School's base was at the Eglinton Hunt Club, Toronto.
50. On the night of 23–24 April 1941, a total of 120 Luftwaffe bombers raided Plymouth. They caused extensive fires—especially in Devonport, in the south-western part of town.
51. Wellington Mk IC R1015/KX-L was crewed by Sgt Jaroslav Doktor, Sgt Miroslav Styblík, Fg Off. František Machálek, Sgt Bedřich Procházka, Sgt Karel Truxa, and Sgt Karel Janšta. At 3.45 a.m., after running out of fuel, they made a wheels-down landing in the countryside approximately 2 miles to the north-west of Wetherby, Yorkshire. The aircraft ended up on its nose during the landing, damaging the fuselage belly under the front gunner's turret. After being partially disassembled by the salvage team, the Wellington was sent for repairs.
52. There were five Czechoslovak pilots serving with No. 46 'Uganda' (F) Squadron during this period—Plt Off. Karel Mrázek (82561), Sgt Prokop Brázda (787673), Sgt Josef Gutvald (787349), Sgt Jiří Řezníček (787691) and Sgt Vladislav Uher (782405).
53. Grp Capt. Clement Flegg Horsley MC (05071) was the CO of RAF Station Church Fenton from June 1940 until June 1941.
54. The Potez 63 was a French multi-purpose aircraft. The bomber version was designated as the Potez 633B.2. The *Groupe de Bombardement d'Assault* II/54, with whom Lt Karel Vildomec served from 8–18 June 1940, was equipped with this type.
55. Sgt Leo Anderle (787563) had, in fact, completed only twenty operations by this date.
56. The basic pay for an operational aircrew member (a pilot with the rank of Sergeant) was 12s 6d per day, plus an extra war pay of 6d. A fine of £11 was therefore equivalent to seventeen days' pay.

Chapter 10

1. Ernest Zucker (born 4 February 1923 in Vienna, Austria) joined the Czechoslovak forces at the beginning of 1942. On 28 February, he was accepted for service with the RAF at the Czechoslovak Depot. He enlisted with the rank of AC2 and the service number 788281. Zucker served as an Electrician I with No. 312 (Czechoslovak) Fighter Squadron until the end of war, reaching the rank of LAC.
2. The Czechoslovak Depot was formed on 12 July 1940 at RAF Station Cosford, and it was based at RAF Station Wilmslow between 19 December 1940 and 13 February 1942. Its purpose was to induct new members of the Czechoslovak Air Force into the RAF and release unsuitable airmen. It also served as a holding unit for airmen between training stages, for airmen waiting for a posting to an operational unit, or for those who had ended their tour of operations.
3. Tollemache Brewery expanded during the 1930s, becoming incorporated into Cobbold Brewery in 1957 as the 'Tolly Cobbold' brand. This brand, in turn, was bought by Ridley's Brewery in 2002.
4. Walter Tschuppik (1899–1955), a Czech-German journalist of Jewish origin, was the editor of *Prager Tagblatt* from 1914 to 1926 and the editor-in-chief of *Süddeutsche Sonntagspost* in Munich from 1926 to 1933. From March to November 1933, he was held as a political prisoner. After he was released from prison, he lived in Czechoslovakia until 1938, when he moved to Switzerland. He moved on to the United Kingdom in 1940.
5. Over 500 Luftwaffe bombers descended on London, killing 1,364 people and injuring 1,616 others. Many significant buildings were destroyed or severely damaged: the roof of the central part of Westminster Abbey and the Deanery were destroyed; the Palace of Westminster and Victoria Tower complex in parliament's Lower House were destroyed; the British Museum's roof burned off, as did that of Lambeth Palace; the Old Bailey was seriously damaged; St Mary-le-Bow church was partially demolished, and its famous bells were totally destroyed; and St James's Palace and St Joseph Catholic Elementary School suffered varying degrees of damage.

Chapter 11

1. Wellington Mk IC R1532/KX-R was crewed by Sgt Josef Bernát, Sgt Václav Ryba, Plt Off. Jindřich Vnouček, Sgt Rudolf Haering, Sgt Vladimír Kováč and Sgt Jindřich Beneš. The combat report was recorded by Squadron Gunnery Leader Fg Off. Jan Fürbach: 'On the way to Hamburg an aircraft from this Squadron (skipper Sgt Bernát, front gunner Sgt Kováč, rear gunner Sgt Beneš) was crossing the English coast at Orford Ness and met an enemy aircraft identified as a Ju 88 at 50 miles from the coast over sea. The aircraft was first seen by the rear gunner at 600 yards on red quarter half up and opened fire from not less than four machine guns (probably three from nose and two from wings). This enemy burst was short and under our aircraft. Our rear gunner replied with two bursts, first at 400 yards. After that attack the enemy aircraft disappeared at green low below. The enemy aircraft repeated his attack from red quarters. Our rear gunner opened fire the first at 200 yards. The enemy aircraft replied with short burst which was seen above the port engine of our aircraft. Our pilot made a dive manoeuvre and dropped all bombs. The enemy aircraft made the same manoeuvre and continued to fire. The rear gunner replied with the third burst. … All attacks were made from the remote side of the moon. Our front gunner had not seen the enemy aircraft at all. The rear gunner fired about 200 rounds.'
2. Wellington Mk IC T2971/KX-H, crewed by Sgt Benedikt Blatný, Sgt Adolf Musálek, Plt Off. Karel Bečvář, Plt Off. Josef Doubrava, Sgt Miloslav Mikulík and Sgt Karel Janšta.
3. On the night of 10–11 May 1941, Czechoslovak pilots serving with No. 1 (NF) Squadron at Redhill airfield were scrambled to intercept a force of 520 Luftwaffe bombers sent to hit

Endnotes

London. They claimed a total of five kills: one He 111 by Plt Off. František Běhal (83221); two He 111s and one Ju 88 by Sgt Josef Dygrýn (787678); one He 111 and one damaged by Sgt Bedřich Krátkoruký (787703); and one Ju 88 by Sgt Jaroslav Novák (787704). Hurricane IIB Z2921/JX-(?), flown by Plt Off. Běhal, crashed at 12.50 a.m. at Addington Road School in Selsdon Park, Sanderstead, near Croydon. Plt Off. Běhal was killed. It was initially thought that he was shot down by return fire from an He 111 he was attacking. However, it now appears that this was a case of friendly fire from the crew of Beaufighter Mk IF R2098, which was being flown by Fg Off. E. D. Crew and Sgt N. Guthrie from No. 604 'County of Middlesex' (NF) Squadron. The Squadron's ORB incorrectly stated: 'Fg Off. E. D. Crew engaged an aircraft and shot it down but it was later ascertained to be a Hurricane. The pilot of this aircraft made a successful parachute descent and is in hospital.'

4. Flt Lt Jindřich Breitcetl's (82537) operational tour began on 8 October 1940. By 18 April 1941, he had only completed sixteen sorties.
5. Grp Capt. Josef Berounský (86313), aged forty-six, served as a Liaison Officer with RAF Bomber Command's No. 3 (B) Group. Administratively, however, he was a member of the Czechoslovak Inspectorate General in London. He also flew three sorties with No. 311 (B) Squadron as an air gunner. Berounský was later released from the RAF and became a member of the Czechoslovak Military Mission in Moscow. On 12 March 1942, he was awarded the CBE. Berounský was returning to the United Kingdom aboard the Town-class light cruiser HMS *Edinburgh* on 30 April 1942. At 3.10 p.m. the ship was torpedoed by German submarine U-456 in the Barents Sea. At the time of the attack, he was sleeping in his cabin; he was never seen again.
6. The following aircraft did not return from the raid on Hanover: Hampden Mk I AD841/PL-Q from No. 144 (B) Squadron, No. 5 Group; Wellington Mk IC R1494/PM-(?) from No. 103 (B) Squadron, No. 1 Group; and Wellington Mk IC R1167/BL-N from No. 40 (B) Squadron, No. 3 Group.
7. 'NGZ' was a code used to indicate 'bombs gone'.
8. Cloudiness, in meteorological terms, is expressed in tenths of sky coverage in the range from 0/10 to 10/10, where 0/10 means clear sky and 10/10 means complete overcast.
9. According to Middlebrook-Everitt's 1996 book *The Bomber Command War Diaries: An Operational Reference Book 1939–1945* (p. 155), it was, in fact, eleven Wellingtons.
10. The port engine of Wellington Mk IC R1410/KX-M (crewed by Flt Lt Josef Šnajdr, Sgt Jaroslav Nýč, Plt Off. Jaroslav Zafouk, Plt Off. Otakar Černý, Sgt František Knap and Sgt Jiří Mareš) caught fire at 2.00 a.m., 14,000 feet above the German town of Nienburg. The pilot was able to extinguish the fire and then fly the aircraft the rest of the way on the starboard engine. At 6.00 a.m., totally out of fuel, Flt Lt Šnajdr had to make a forced landing in a field near Little Bromley, a village approximately 1.5 miles south of Manningtree.
11. Wellington Mk IC R1466/KX-D (crewed by Sgt František Fencl, Sgt Václav Ryba, Fg Off. Stanislav Dvorský, Sgt Emil Mikulenka, Sgt Vojtěch Kubalík and Sgt Vincenc Kocman) had to crash land due to lack of fuel; this was the result of three hits to their petrol tanks. Sgt Fencl put the Wellington down at Thurton, near Great Yarmouth.
12. The Court of Inquiry blamed the pilot, Plt Off. Zeinert: 'Pilot failed to correct initial swing and attempted to take-off cross wind. Pulled aircraft off ground steeply to clear the hedge, stalled and hit trees. Had exceptionally long take-off run of 1,100 yards in which he had more than sufficient space to stop.' Sgt František Dušek and Sgt Maxmilián Stoček died instantly, while the remaining crew members were taken to hospital in Cromer. Plt Off. Stanislav Zeinert died the next day. Plt Off. Miloslav Švic died on 4 June, and the next day he was buried beside his comrades in the St Ethelbert churchyard in East Wretham. The British mechanic who was always listed as 'Cpl Litterland' should also be among the dead, but the Commonwealth War Graves Commission does not record his death on this day, nor for the following few days. It is therefore believed that the mechanic was actually Cpl T. E. Litherland, who appeared in the 17 July 1941 edition of *Flight* under the heading 'Wounded or Injured on Active Service'.

13. Wellington Mk IC W5720/NZ-Q was from the Polish-manned No. 304 'Silesian' (B) Squadron and crewed by Sqn Ldr Beill, Sgt Witkowski, Fg Off. Sokolowski, Sgt Mackula, Sgt Salamon and Plt Off. Krano. It landed at East Wretham at 3.45 a.m. They returned home to Syerston, Nottinghamshire, at 3.30 p.m. No. 304 'Silesian' (B) Squadron (or '*304 Dywizjon Bombowy Ziemi Śląskiej im. Ks. Józefa Poniatowskiego*' in Polish) was formed at Bramcote, Warwickshire, on 22 August 1940. Its first combat sorties were carried out by two Wellington Mk ICs against petrol and fuel oil storage tanks in Rotterdam, the Netherlands, on the night of 24–25 April 1941. The Squadron lost two crews on training and another three on operations during May 1941.

Chapter 12

1. The book *Wings in Exile* was published in English in 1942; the Czech edition, *Křídla ve vyhnanství*, was published simultaneously. Both editions contain a foreword by AVM RNDr Karel Janoušek KCB (86312) without his photograph.
2. No. 5 Maintenance Unit was based at RAF Station Kemble from June 1938 until March 1983. It would go on to be the longest existing unit of this type in the RAF.
3. The bomb bay of a Wellington Mk IC can hold various combinations of additional fuel tanks. In this case, the bomb bay included two tanks with a capacity of 140 gallons each.
4. The Air Transport Auxiliary was a British civil organisation ferrying aircraft around to operational airfields, maintenance units, and aircraft factories. A total of 1,318 ATA pilots (1,152 men and 166 women) delivered over 300,000 aircraft between February 1940 and November 1945.
5. James Allan 'Jim' Mollison (1905–1959) was a Scottish aviation pioneer and the holder of many flying records. He was also the husband of Amy Johnson (1903–1941), a pioneering English aviator. Both served as pilots with the ATA during the Second World War. Sadly, Amy perished while ferrying an Airspeed Oxford on 5 January 1941.
6. Vincent Justus Burnelli (1895–1964) was an American aircraft engineer and designer who conceived and designed the flying wing. The only British-built version by Cunliffe-Owen is known by a number of names, including the Cunliffe-Owen OA Mk I Flying Wing and the OA-1 Clyde Clipper. In 1941 it was requisitioned by the RAF, who established that there was no use for the aircraft; it was then transferred to the Free French Air Force and used in North Africa.
7. No. 41 (Maintenance) Group was formed on 1 January 1939 within RAF Maintenance Command. It was responsible for aircraft allocation and delivery to operational units. The unit was disbanded on 21 July 1961.
8. This was an honorary badge given to Allied airmen to show appreciation for their work with Czechoslovak airmen. Plt Off. Gellner—listed as British—is named amongst Allied airmen in the official document of the Czechoslovak Inspectorate General 'Nominal Roll of British and Allied Personnel Awarded the Czechoslovak Pilot's Brevet'.
9. The diarist mixed up the two places: Port Albert, Ontario, the location of No. 31 Air Navigation School, and Prince Albert, Saskatchewan, the location of No. 6 Air Observer School.
10. The name of the protected moorings located in front of the main harbour, *Port de Commerce*, in Brest.

Chapter 13

1. Two aircraft from No. 9 (B) Squadron did not return from the armed reconnaissance over the French coast on 9 June 1941. Wellington Mk IC R1758/WS-(?) was shot down into the sea at the Belgian port of Zeebrugge by a group of Messerschmitt Bf 109s. The crew—Sgt J. M. Pinkham, Fg Off. D. Bruce, Sgt H. A. Wink, Sgt R. H. Barratt and Fg Off. T. A. Bax—was

captured. The Squadron's CO, Wg Cdr R. G. C. Arnold, flying as the second pilot, was killed. Wellington Mk IC T2620/WS-G also ended up in the sea after combat with a Bf 109. Fg Off. D. F. Lamb DFC, Sgt J. C. Partington, Sgt D. J. Mansfield, Sgt D. A. Humphrey and Sgt R. S. Bunce were killed. The sole survivor, Sgt W. A. Eccles, was captured.
2. However, FS Josef Filler (787473) finished his operational tour on 27 November 1941, after thirty-five bombing sorties lasting 200 hours and thirty-seven minutes in total. Between April and May 1942, he served as an instructor with No. 1429 Czech Operational Training Flight. He later served with No. 1 Signals School at Cranwell and Central Gunnery School at Sutton Bridge. He returned to No. 311 (B) Squadron on 1 February 1943, only to be posted to the Czechoslovak Depot at St Athan on 16 April. While there, his rank was reduced to AC2; from 15 May 1944 until the end of the war, he acted as a member of the ground staff with No 6312 Servicing Echelon.
3. French expression for 'unwillingly'.
4. There was only an emergency airfield at Aalter; the nearest big airfield, Ursel, is located west of Ghent and few miles to the north of Aalter. According to the crew debriefing record, the bombs were dropped at position 51°5'N and 3°22'E—i.e. approximately 16 miles to the south-west of Ursel airfield.
5. The diarist gives an inaccurate number of raids. On 19 June 1941, Wellington Mk IC T2972/KX-G flew only its twenty-ninth sortie.
6. Wellington Mk IC T2990/KX-T was shot down by *Oberleutnant* Egmont Prinz zur Lippe-Weissenfeld of 4./NJG 1. The aircraft crashed near Nieuwe Niedorp, in the Netherlands. The sole survivor from the crew of six was the skipper, FS Vilém Bufka (787572), who baled out and was captured. This information reached the Squadron a few weeks afterwards (as the diarist will later mention).

Chapter 14

1. In 1876, Wilhelm and Jakob Bellak founded a factory that produced cloth and fashion goods from fleece in Krnov, Upper Silesia. From the early part of the twentieth century, the company was directed by Otto and Emil, both sons of Jakob. Before Krnov's occupation by the Germans in 1939, they relocated to Brno; this was followed by a later move to the United Kingdom. Their company was confiscated by the Germans; after the war, it was nationalised and incorporated into the national enterprise Karnola Krnov.
2. Lt Alfred Kitchin (159573) studied piano at the Conservatory in Leipzig during the 1930s. He lived in Vienna and performed in most of the European capitals. In December 1938, Kitchin returned to London and joined the Directorate of Military Intelligence (MI6). He began touring again in 1948. In 1961, Kitchin was head of Trinity College of Music, London.
3. The Czechs provided six pilots and five wireless operators to RAF Ferry Command, which was responsible for the transatlantic ferrying of aircraft in 1942. Under the command of Flt Lt Václav Korda, this small group made forty-one delivery flights over the Atlantic. Throughout the war, only a handful of other Czechs would serve with Ferry Command and its successor, Transport Command. One of them was Flt Lt Joseph Vladimir Sopuck (J24247), an RCAF navigator of Czech origin. Flt Lt Sopuck was killed in the crash of a Canadian-built de Havilland Mosquito FB Mk 26 (s/n KA316) on 1 July 1945. The port Merlin engine failed and was feathered. The RAF pilot, WO Sidney George Witherspoon (1393612), made a turn to port to line the aircraft up for a landing approach; however, he lost altitude in the turn and crashed. The Mosquito burned out after crashing 6 miles south-west of RCAF Station Mont Joli, Quebec.
4. A Latin expression meaning 'I tell as I was told'.
5. *Brünner Ruderverein* (as it is known in German) was the oldest rowing club in Brno, having been founded in 1869.

Chapter 15

1. Tantalus was a figure in Greek mythology who was famous for his eternal punishment; he was made to stand in a pool of water beneath a fruit tree with low branches, with the fruit ever eluding his grasp and the water always receding before he could take a drink. The expression 'Tantalus' work' is used to signify never-ending work.
2. The targets for bombing were codenamed in orders; from 1940–41, the codes consisted of one or two letters in addition to up to three numbers. For example, Wilhelmshaven was 'D5' and Boulougne-sur-Mer was 'CC29'. Therefore, 'Z3C' meant 'aiming point C' in Rotterdam (which was 'Z3').
3. The actions of Plt Off. Jaroslav Kula (82615) are not surprising as they had saved him in an earlier accident. Kula met his fate on 12 March 1942; he was reported as missing while returning from an operation against Kiel, Germany, while part of Sgt Jiří Fína's (787403) crew, on board Wellington Mk IC R1802/KX-P.
4. In fact, Sgt Oldřich Helma (787190) flew seventeen sorties—including eleven as the skipper. The raid on Cherbourg with the freshman crew was his eighteenth.
5. The unfortunate fighter pilot who shot down Wellington Mk IC R1516/KX-U was Wg Cdr Charles Henry Appleton DSO DFC (24139), CO of No. 604 'County of Middlesex' (NF) Squadron. The Squadron ORB stated: 'A friendly bomber was intercepted and shot down.' His number of victories, as stated by the diarist, is inaccurate. The citation for his DSO award from 5 August 1941 reads: 'He has personally destroyed two and damaged two enemy aircraft.'
6. Wellington Mk IC T2561/KX-A was crewed by Fg Off. František Pohlodek, Sgt Oldřich Jambor, Plt Off. Antonín Macenauer, Plt Off. Josef Simet, Sgt Miloslav Mikulík and Sgt František Chmura. The aircraft's wing tip struck a barrage balloon cable, but Pohlodek was able to successfully regain control. Due to lack of fuel and a misfiring engine, he landed at RAF Station Grantham, approximately 63 miles to the north-west of East Wretham. The aircraft was handed over to No. 43 (Maintenance) Group for repairs. It was returned to the Squadron on 9 July 1941 (for more details, see Appendix III).
7. In the face of harsh criticism, Flt Lt Antonín Macenauer (82619) was able to complete an operational tour of thirty-four operations on 7 December 1941. He completed his pilot training in 1942. Between 15 August and 7 December 1943, Macenauer flew operations with No. 312 'Czechoslovak' (F) Squadron. He later flew with several non-operational units, ending the war as a Liaison Officer.
8. Between 1934 and 1944, the Deschimag Werke AG shipyard in Bremen built the following ships: two heavy cruisers (the *Lützow* and *Seydlitz*) forty-one destroyers, one mine-layer, and two submarines.
9. Robert John Graham Boothby (66070) was a British Conservative politician who held a junior ministerial office (Parliamentary Secretary to the Ministry of Food) in 1940–41. He repeatedly tried to persuade the British government to release the frozen accounts of Czechoslovak banks. It later became clear that the American industrialist Richard Weisenger offered Boothby 10 per cent of the amount that would be returned to Weisenger from his investments in Czechoslovakia. Boothby was forced to resign after the affair became public. He joined the RAF and reached the rank of Flt Lt.
10. This course lasted several days and was held at No. 3 (B) Group Target Towing Flight in Newmarket, Suffolk. The purpose of the course was to refresh gunnery skills by shooting at ground targets and towed aerial drogues. Each gunner flew as many as fifteen hours of training.
11. The diminutive form of the first name of the skipper, Plt Off. Václav Korda.
12. The Commanding Officer at RAF Station Honington received the following complaint on 2 June 1941: 'On 1 June 1941 at 18.10 Wellington 'N' of No. 311 Squadron was spotted at a height between 25 and 30 feet above the roofs of houses in Bury St Edmunds.' On 10 June 1940, Sgt Jaroslav Nýč (787166), the pilot of the particular aircraft on this day, testified: 'When returning

Endnotes

from a training navigational flight on 1 June 1941 I made a dive with Wellington N 1718 [R1718/KX-N] to a height of about 200 feet above Bury St Edmunds. I did two circuits at low altitude and went to the satellite airfield in East Wretham. The plane landed perfectly. Now I am aware that I violated aviation rules and I regret my offence very much.'

13. This was a searchlight used for runway lighting to help make night landings easier. It was named after its manufacturer, the Chance Brothers. Their glassworks had been well-known producers of optical glasses for watch lights and other lighting equipment since the nineteenth century.
14. Enemy raids were briefly recorded in the Squadron ORB. The following entry was made for the night of 17–18 July: 'At 00.40 an enemy aircraft dropped a stick of bombs across the aerodrome, causing little damage but rendering the aerodrome unserviceable for a short period.' On the night of 18–19 July: 'The aerodrome was attacked at 00.21 by an enemy aircraft and bombs were dropped amongst dispersal at the south-east corner of the aerodrome.' Attacks on training aircraft in the air were apparently unsuccessful as there is no record of such an incident.
15. Wellington Mk IC R1804/KX-D was crewed by Fg Off. Josef Stránský, Sgt František Vaníček, and Sgt Oldřich Šiška. During take-off, they struck a splinter from a bomb dropped during previous night's air raid. The tire on the right undercarriage leg burst, causing the aircraft to turn directly towards the steamroller in the distance. All the airmen escaped from the burning plane. The civilian driver of the steamroller—Mr George Potter from Sudbury, Suffolk, working for the building company E. J. Doe—was killed instantly.
16. The crew skippered by Sgt Jaroslav Nýč (787166), who were lost on the night of 16-17 July 1941, are missing from this list.
17. Those forged ration coupons were dropped by the British in effort to paralyse the German economy, which was short of many commodities. Ration coupons for food were introduced in Germany and other occupied countries during the first stage of the war. Later, ration coupons for clothing and footwear were also issued.
18. The Heinkel He 113 never existed—it was just a myth created by German propaganda. When the Germans published a few photographs of several fighters in 1940, the He 113 turned out to be a Heinkel He 100D-1 photographed on different airfields and painted with different markings of non-existing fighter units. It is probable that the aircraft referred to in the diary was a misidentified Messerschmitt Bf 109.
19. According to the official documents, the medals were handed over to him on 2 August 1941 at the Czechoslovak Inspectorate General in London, but his participation in the air raid on the date shown is unlikely. For more details, see Appendix II.
20. Deutsche Werke AG was formed in 1925 by the consolidation of Kaiserliche Werft Kiel and other engineering and armament companies. Merchant ships were initially supposed to be built there, but when the Nazi regime came to power in 1933, the production was changed to *Kriegsmarine* ships. Amongst the most famous ships built there were the battleship *Gneisenau* and heavy cruiser *Blücher*. From 1935, the company also started to produce submarines, and they were still in production at the end of the war. Damaged ships were also repaired there—one example was the battleship *Scharnhorst* in 1942.
21. Wellington Mk IC X3221/KX-O was crewed by Fg Off. František Pohlodek, Sgt Oldřich Jambor, Plt Off. Antonín Macenauer, Plt Off. Josef Simet, Sgt Karel Truxa and Fg Off. Jan Fürbach. According to the debriefing record, they flew on track from North Walsham to 53°55'N 4°00'E, to 53°50'N 6°20'E, and then on to Wilhelmshaven, where bombs were dropped at 1.40 a.m. The bombs were dropped here instead of Hamburg (53°47'N 6°02'E) due to engine trouble. On the way back, the crew became lost in clouds over the Zuiderzee area. Several courses were obtained for QDMs—185°, 242°, 250° and 203°. The aircraft went back and forth several times before the crew discovered they were over Schiphol Airport, Amsterdam. At 5.05 a.m., while flying over the sea near Ijmuiden, the rear gunner reported a Messerschmitt Bf 110 at a distance of 300 yards. It did not attack. Over the English coast,

they crossed to the south of Southwold. According to the graphics schedule of the air raid, the D/F station at Honington sent the following courses for the aircraft's QDMs: 242° at 3.57 a.m.; 203° at 4.09 a.m.; 250° at 4.23 a.m.; 219° at 4.32 a.m.; and 294° at 5.50 a.m. The aircraft landed at 6.10 a.m. In fact, the first course of 185° had been sent by an unknown German-controlled station in an effort to persuade the crew to fly into an area where German night fighters were operating. The Germans most likely wanted to fool the crew into believing that they were actually back over England rather than still over the Netherlands.

22. Seven months was the average time it took for most of No. 311 Squadron's members to finish a 200-hour operational tour. This represented thirty-five to forty operational sorties over a six- or seven-month period. However, there were also occasions when an airman needed approximately a year to finish his tour. Only a few were able to complete their tour in just five months.
23. No. 3 Blind Approach Training Flight was formed on 9 December 1940 at Mildenhall, Suffolk, to train airmen in instrument flying. On 31 October 1941, it was reorganised as No. 1503 Beam Approach Training Flight.

Part II: Biography

1. Hubený, D., The National Archives, Czech Republic, Police Headquarters, ref. 42/G-7/187, letter to the author on 6 March 2009.
2. Library and Archives Canada (LAC), Military Service File, RG 24, Volume 10827, John Gellner 19540; Masaryk University Archive, Faculty of Law—Books: A5/13, A5/21, A5/118, A5/127, A5/135, A5/142, Rectorate—Books: A1/19; Pajer, M., letter to the author on 2 April 2008.
3. Gellner, L., letter to the author on 25 May 2009; Kober, *Advocacy in the Czech Lands 1884-1994* (1994), p. 106.
4. The National Archives, Czech Republic, The Czechoslovak Ministry of Internal Affairs—London, ref. 2-90/3431-3432g; Pajer, M., letter to the author on 2 April 2008.
5. VÚA Praha, 24, ref. 24-8/9; Gellner, L., letter to the author on 23 November 2008.
6. Kober, *Advocacy in the Czech Lands 1884-1994* (1994), p. 106.
7. Gellner, J., *A Life that Might Seem like One Long Adventure Holiday* (2005), p. 25.
8. The National Archives, Czech Republic, The Czechoslovak Ministry of Internal Affairs—London, ref. 2-90/3431-3432g.
9. LAC, Military Service File, RG 24, Volume 10827, John Gellner 19540.
10. VÚA Praha, ČSL VB, 687/BI/1/183, No. 311 Squadron Operations Record Book, 1940.
11. LAC, Military Service File, RG 24, Volume 10827, John Gellner 19540; VÚA Praha, ČSL VB, ref. 254/C-V/1/240, Writings: C 850/6/P2, Plt Off. Gellner—air observer 1941-1942.
12. VÚA Praha, ČSL VB, ref. 502/CIII-3a/5/271, No. 311 Squadron establishment on 18 July 1944.
13. VÚA Praha, ČSL VB, ref. 835/C-II/1/212, Writings: S 41/Air, Bombing Leaders 1940–1943; ČSL VB, ref. 42/A-4/1/3, Volume of Confidential Issues and Orders 1941; VKPR, ref. 26/3/1/4, General writings 1941, čj. 801—1000.
14. Gellner, *A Life that Might Seem like One Long Adventure Holiday* (2005), p. 21.
15. LAC, Military Service File, RG 24, Volume 10827, John Gellner 19540; http://www.convoyweb.org.uk.
16. Hull, A. C., via Gates, M., letter to the author on 29 March 2008.
17. The oldest British Regular Army regiment in continuous active service since 1650. In addition to its famous involvement on many battlefields, No. 7 Company guards the Royal Palaces.
18. LAC, Military Service File, RG 24, Volume 10827, John Gellner 19540.
19. Hull, A. C., letter to the author on 2 March 2009.
20. LAC, Military Service File, RG 24, Volume 10827, John Gellner 19540; Accident Record Card Tiger Moth s/n 8872; Charland, C., letter to the author on 30 March 2009; Aircraft History Card Tiger Moth s/n 8872; Walker, R. B., letter to the author on 30 March 2009.
21. LAC, Military Service File, RG 24, Volume 10827, John Gellner 19540; Accident Record Card

Endnotes

Avro Anson s/n 6360; Charland, C., letter to the author on 30 March 2009; Aircraft History Card Avro Anson s/n 6360; Walker, R. B., letter to the author on 30 March 2009.

22. LAC, Military Service File, RG 24, Volume 10827, John Gellner 19540; Canadian Armed Forces Directorate of History and Heritage (DHH), Document 84/44-3.
23. Gellner, *A Life that Might Seem like One Long Adventure Holiday* (2005), pp. 35-36.
24. The National Archives, Czech Republic, The Czechoslovak Ministry of Internal Affairs—London, ref. 2-90/3431-3432g.
25. RAF Museum Hendon, Flying Accident Card, AM Form 1180, Marauder FB457; The National Archives (TNA), AIR 26/647, ORB No. 45 (Atlantic Transport) Group, Appendices, 1 April 1943–31 May 1944.
26. LAC, Military Service File, RG 24, Volume 10827, John Gellner 19540; DHH, Document 84/44-3; TNA, AIR 29/668 ORB No. 24 OTU; Sheerin, D. P., letter to the author on 12 October 2008.
27. LAC, Military Service File, RG 24, Volume 10827, John Gellner 19540; TNA, AIR 29/754 ORB No. 6 Group Battle School, Dalton; Moyes, *Bomber Squadrons of the RAF and their Aircraft* (1964), pp. 248–249.
28. Malayney, N., ORB No. 429 Squadron RCAF, letter to the author on 2 July 2008.
29. RAF Museum Hendon, Aircraft Movement Card, AM Form 78, Halifax LW694; TNA, AIR 28/451 ORB RAF Leeming, January 1943–December 1944.
30. Millare-Adolfo, M. J., RAF Museum Hendon, letter to the author on 7 August 2008.
31. Fahey, *Britain 1939–1945: The Economic Cost Of Strategic Bombing* (2006), p. 199.
32. Hull, A. C., letter to the author on 2 March 2009.
33. Malayney, N., ORB No. 429 Squadron RCAF, letter to the author on 2 July 2008.
34. Gellner, *A Life that Might Seem like One Long Adventure Holiday* (2005), p. 36.
35. Sedláková, M., Terezín Initiative Institute database via the Jewish Museum in Prague; letter to the author on 18 April 2008; Němcová. E., and Langhamerová, M., The National Archives (Czech Republic), Torso of Pankrác prison books of the Prague Gestapo from 1941–1942; letters to the author on 15 and 29 April 2009; Hubený, D., The National Archives, Czech Republic, Occupational Prison Records, Catalogue of Czechoslovak and Foreign Prisoners from the Terezín Ghetto Cremated in the Terezín Crematorium, letter to the author on 6 March 2009; *Death Books from Auschwitz, Index of Names A–L Vol. II* (1995), p. 342; http://en.auschwitz.org.pl.
36. LAC, Military Service File, RG 24, Volume 10827, John Gellner 19540; Gellner, *A Life that Might Seem like One Long Adventure Holiday* (2005), pp. 40–43.
37. LAC, Military Service File, RG 24, Volume 10827, John Gellner 19540; Hull, B., letter to the author on 24 May 2009.
38. Gellner, *A Life that Might Seem like One Long Adventure Holiday* (2005), pp. 44-50; Gellner, L., letter to the author on 28 November 2008.

Appendix I

1. VÚA Praha, VKPR, ref. 26/2/1/4, General writings 1941, čj. 501-800; VKPR, ref. 26/3/1/4, General writings 1941, čj. 801-1000; ČSL VB, ref. 42/A-4/1/3, Volume of Confidential Issues and Orders 1941; LAC, Military Service File, RG 24, Volume 10827, John Gellner 19540; http://rcafassociation.ca/uploads/airforce/2009/07/ALPHA-GA.GE.html.
2. LAC, Military Service File, RG 24, Volume 10827, John Gellner 19540.
3. TNA, AIR 2/9334, Non-immediate awards week ending 1 Nov 1941: Bomber Command and Fighter Command Allied personnel.
4. LAC, Military Service File, RG 24, Volume 10827, John Gellner 19540; http://www.veterans.gc.ca/eng/remembrance/medals-decorations/campaign-stars-medals-1939-1954/cvsm.
5. Ford, C., Veterans Affairs Canada, letter to the author on 21 May 2009.

6. Carter, F., letter to the author on 30 December 2008; Halliday, H. A., letter to the author on 2 January 2009.
7. LAC, Military Service File, RG 24, Volume 10827, John Gellner 19540; Ford, C., Veterans Affairs Canada, letter to the author on 21 May 2009.
8. http://www.gg.ca/honour.aspx?id=620&t=12&ln=Gellner.

Appendix II

1. Although this is an official letter from the highest Czechoslovak authorities, it refers to the Czechoslovak Gallantry Medal by the wrong name.
2. TNA, AIR 2/6123, Decorations, Medals, Honours and Awards (Code B, 30): Award of Czechoslovak Decorations to RAF Personnel; VÚA Praha, ČSL VB, ref. 254/C-V/1/240, Writings: C 850/6/P2, Plt Off. Gellner—air observer 1941-1942; VKPR, ref. 26/3/1/4, General writings 1941.

Appendix III

1. TNA, AIR 20/4377, RAF offensive against *Scharnhorst, Gneisenau* and *Prince Eugen*; AIR 20/6018, *Scharnhorst, Gneisenau* and *Prince Eugen*: interim report of offensive by the RAF.
2. Busch, *The Story of the Prince Eugen* (1960), p. 96.
3. TNA, AIR 24/233, ORB Bomber Command, July 1941; AIR 25/52, ORB No. 3 Group, January 1941–December 1943; AIR 41/47, The RAF in Maritime War; The Atlantic and Home Waters Vol. III: The Preparative Phase July 1941–February 1943; Smith, S., letter to the author on 25 December 2008.
4. TNA, AIR 27/789, ORB No. 99 Squadron; AIR 27/801, ORB No. 101 Squadron; AIR 27/1001, ORB No. 149 Squadron; AIR 27/126, ORB No. 9 Squadron.
5. VÚA Praha, ČSL VB, ref. 470/CIII-1/65/264, Operations over Cherbourg and Brest on 1 July 1941.
6. Busch, *The Story of the Prince Eugen* (1960), pp. 97-103.
7. Schmalenbach, *Cruiser Prinz Eugen: Under Three Flags* (1985), pp. 141-142; Fuller, T., letter to the author on 23 March 2009.
8. TNA, AIR 20/4377, RAF offensive against *Scharnhorst, Gneisenau* and *Prince Eugen*.
9. VÚA Praha, ČSL VB, 687/BI/2/183, No. 311 Squadron Operations Record Book, 1941 (RAF Form 540); Middlebrook-Everitt, *The Bomber Command War Diaries: An Operational Reference Book 1939–1945* (1996), p. 170.
10. Huguen, *Brittany in the Battle of the Atlantic* (2003), p. 109.
11. Murray, E., letter to the author on 24 April 2008.
12. VÚA Praha, ČSL VB, ref. 470/CIII-1/65/264, Operations over Cherbourg and Brest on 1 July 1941; ČSL VB, ref. 208/C-III-1/2/109, Air accident reports April—July 1941; Log Book of Antonín Macenauer; Vacek, M., letter to the author on 20 February 2009; Vacek, P., letter to the author on 14 April 2009.
13. RAF Museum Hendon, Flying Accident Card, AM Form 1180, Wellington T2561.
14. TNA, AIR 24/233, ORB Bomber Command, July 1941.
15. TNA, AIR 20/4377, RAF offensive against *Scharnhorst, Gneisenau* and *Prince Eugen*.

Appendix IV

1. RAF Museum Hendon, Aircraft Movement Card, AM Form 78, Wellington T2972.
2. TNA, AIR 27/2134, ORB No. 620 Squadron; RAF Museum Hendon, Aircraft Movement Card, AM Form 78, Halifax LW694; Malayney, N., ORB No. 429 Squadron RCAF, letter to the author on 2 July 2008.

3. RAF Museum Hendon, Aircraft Movement Card, AM Form 78, Marauder FB424.
4. TNA, AIR 27/352, ORB No. 31 Squadron; RAF Museum Hendon, Aircraft Movement Card, AM Form 78, Dakota FL541; Pajer, *The Wings for Victory and Post-War Renewal* (2004), pp. 225-228.
5. RAF Museum Hendon, Aircraft Movement Card, AM Form 78, Mitchell FW119.

Appendix V

1. Chorley, W. R., letter to the author on 21 May 2009; Halliday, H. A., letters to the author on 12 August 2008, 18 August 2008, 2 October 2008 and 7 April 2009; Welting, H., letter to the author on 5 April 2008; http://rcafassociation.ca/heritage/1914-1945.

Appendix VI

1. Franks, *SE 5/5a Aces of World War I* (2007), pp. 68–69; Hamilton, *Wings of Night: Secret Missions of Group Captain Pickard, DSO and Two Bars, DFC* (1977); http://www.theaerodrome.com/aces/england/carlin.php; http://www.bbm.org.uk/Carlin2.htm.
2. Supplement to *The London Gazette*, 2 November 1918, (30989/12963), http://www.thegazette.co.uk.
3. TNA, AIR 27/1019 ORB No. 151 Squadron; AIR 28/950 ORB RAF Station Wittering. There was not much damage, and neither, in fact, was a Defiant Mk I from No. 151 Squadron destroyed during the raid. Three Defiant Mk Is (s/nos N1790, N3459, and T3916) were damaged, while a single Hurricane Mk II Z2890 was destroyed by fire.
4. http://ww2talk.com/forums/topic/17612-po-sir-arnold-talbot-wilson-kia-31-may-1940.
5. TNA, AIR 27/1019 ORB No. 151 Squadron; AIR 28/1515 ORB RAF Station Wittering.

Bibliography and References

Archival Sources

Central Military Archive, Prague (VÚA):
  The Czechoslovak Air Force in the United Kingdom (ČSL VB)
  The President's Military Office (VKPR)

The Canadian Armed Forces Directorate of History and Heritage (DHH)
The Canadian Virtual War Memorial (CVWM)
Library and Archives Canada (LAC)
Masaryk University Archive, Brno
The National Archives, Czech Republic:
  Police Headquarters
  The Prague Police Office
  Occupational Prison Records
  The Czechoslovak Ministry of Internal Affairs—London

The National Archives (TNA), Kew:
  Air Ministry Registered Files (AIR 2)
  Air Ministry, Department of the Chief of the Air Staff Registered Files (AIR 8)
  Bomber Command Registered Files (Air 14), Fighter Command Registered Files (AIR 16)
  Air Ministry and Ministry of Defence, Air Department, Private Office Papers (AIR 19)
  Air Ministry and Ministry of Defence, Papers accumulated by the Air Historical Branch (AIR 20)
  Operations Record Books, Squadrons (AIR 27)
  Operations Record Books, RAF Stations (AIR 28)
  Operations Record Books, Miscellaneous Units (AIR 29)

The National Defence Imagery Library
RAF Museum Hendon:
  Aircraft Movement Cards
  Flying Accident Cards

Terezín Initiative Institute, Prague
The Terezín Memorial
Veterans Affairs Canada

Selected Books

Ailsby, C., *Allied Combat Medals of World War Two Vol. I: Britain, the Commonwealth and Western European Nations* (Sparkford: Patrik Stephens, 1989)

Allison, L., and Hazard, H., *They Shall Grow Not Old* (Brandon: Commonwealth Air Training Museum Inc., 1995)

Beneš, B. (ed.), *Wings in Exile* (London: Čechoslovák, 1942)

Busch, F. O., *The Story of the Prince Eugen* (Robert Hale: London, 1960)

Chisholm, D., *Their Names Live On: Remembering Saskatchewan's Fallen in World War II* (Regina: Canadian Plains Research Center, University of Regina, 2001)

Chorley, W. R., *Royal Air Force Bomber Command Losses of the Second World War Vol. II–V: Aircraft and Crew Losses 1941–1944* (Leicester: Midland Counties Publications, 1993–1997); *Royal Air Force Bomber Command Losses of the Second World War Vol. VII: Operational Training Units 1940–1947* (Leicester: Midland Counties Publications, 2003)

Coughlin, T., *The Dangerous Sky: Canadian Airmen in World War II* (London: William Kimber & Co., 1968)

Death Books from Auschwitz, Index of Names A–L Vol. II (Sterbebücher von Auschwitz, Namenverzeichnis A–L Vol. II) (Munich-New Providence-London-Paris: Herausgegeben Staatlichen Museum Auschwitz-Birkenau, 1995)

Delve, K., *Vickers-Armstrongs Wellington* (Ramsbury: The Crowood Press, 1998)

Earl, D. W., *Hell on High Ground. Vol. II* (Ramsbury: The Crowood Press, 1999)

Fahey, J., *Britain 1939–1945: The Economic Cost of Strategic Bombing* (Sydney: University of Sydney, 2006)

Falconer, J., *Bomber Command Handbook 1939–1945* (Stroud: Sutton Publishing, 2003)

Foreman, J., *Air War 1941: The Turning Point Part I: From the Battle of Britain to the Blitz* (Walton on Thames: Air Research Publications, 1994); *Air War 1941: The Turning Point Part II: From the Blitz to the Non-Stop Offensive* (Walton on Thames: Air Research Publications, 1994)

Franks, N., and VanWyngarden, G., *Fokker D VII Aces of World War I Part II* (Oxford: Osprey Publishing, 2003)

Franks, N., *Royal Air Force Fighter Command Losses of the Second World War Vol. II: Operational Losses: Aircraft and Crews 1942–1943* (Leicester: Midland Publishing, 1998); *SE 5/5a Aces of World War I* (Oxford: Osprey Publishing, 2007)

Gellner, J., *A Life that Might Seem like One Long Adventure Holiday* (Toronto: Ernest Zucker, 2005)

Hamilton, A., *Wings of Night: The Secret Missions of Group Captain Charles Pickard, DSO and Two Bars, DFC* (London: William Kimber & Co., 1977)

Hammerton, J., *ABC of the RAF* (London: The Amalgamated Press)

Hatch, F. J., *Aerodrome of Democracy: Canada and the British Commonwealth Air*

Huguen, R., *Brittany in the Battle of the Atlantic (La Bretagne dans la bataille de l'Atlantique)* (Spézet: Coop Breizh, 2003)

Kober, J., *Advocacy in the Czech Lands 1884-1994 (Advokacie v Českých zemích v létech 1884-1994)* (Praha: Česká advokátní komora, 1994)

Konarski, M., *304 Squadron* (Sandomierz: Stratus, 2005)

Korda, V., *The RAF Pilot (Pilotem RAF)* (Praha: Mladá fronta, 1992)

Krzystek, T. J., *Polish Air Force Personnel in Great Britain 1940-1947 (Personel polskich sił powietrznych w Wielkiej Brytanii w latach 1940-1947)* (Warszawa: Altair, 2007)

Martyn, E., *For Your Tomorrow: A Record of New Zealanders Who Have Died while Serving with the RNZAF and Allied Air Services since 1915 Vol. I (Fates 1915–1942)* (Christchurch: Volplane Press, 1998)

McNeill, R., *Royal Air Force Coastal Command Losses of the Second World War Vol. I: 1939–1941* (Hickley: Midland Publishing, 2003)

Meekcoms, K., *The British Air Commission and Lend-Lease* (Tonbridge: Air Britain Historians, 2000)

Middlebrook, M., and Everitt, C., *The Bomber Command War Diaries: An Operational Reference Book 1939–1945* (Leicester: Midland Counties Publications, 1996)

Miller, W. H., *Pictorial Encyclopaedia of Ocean Liners 1860–1994* (New York: Dover Publications, 1995)

Moyes, P. J. R., *Bomber Squadrons of the RAF and their Aircraft* (London: Macdonald & Co., 1964)
Pajer, M., *The Wings are Heading Over Germany* (*Křídla míří nad Německo*) (Cheb: Svět křídel, 1994); *The Wings for Victory and Post-War Renewal* (*Křídla pro vítězství a poválečnou obnovu*) (Cheb: Svět křídel, 2004)
Pilot's Notes for Wellington I, IA & IC (London: Air Ministry, 1941)
Rajlich, J., *On the Skies of the Proud Albion Vol. II-VII* (*Na nebi hrdého Albionu Vol. II-VII*) (Cheb: Svět křídel, 2000-2005)
Rawlings, J. D. R., *Coastal, Support and Special Squadrons of the RAF and their Aircraft* (London: Jane's Publishing Co., 1982)
Royal Air Force Wittering: The First Ninety Years 1916-2006 (Peterborough: RAF Wittering, 2006)
Schmalenbach, P., *Cruiser Prinz Eugen: Under Three Flags* (*Kreuzer Prinz Eugen: Unter Drei Flaggen*) (Herford: Koehler Verlag, 1985)
Shores, C., Franks, N., and Guest R., *Above the Trenches: A Complete Record of the Fighter Aces and Units of the British Empire Air Forces, 1915-1920* (London: Grub Street Publishing, 1990)
Sturtivant, R., and Hamlin, J., *RAF Flying Training and Support Units since 1912* (Tonbridge: Air Britain Historians, 2007)
The King's Regulations & Air Council Instructions for the Royal Air Force with Appendices and Index 1942 (London: HMSO, 1942)
The RCAF Overseas: The First Four Years (Toronto: Oxford University Press, 1944)
Training Plan 1939-1945 (Ottawa: Directorate of History Department of National Defence, 1983)
Váňa, J., and Rail, J., *Czechoslovak Airmen in France 1939-1940* (*Českoslovenští letci ve Francii 1939-1940*) (Praha: AVIS, 2005)
Váňa, J., Sigmund, J., and Padior, E., *Czechoslovak Air Force Personnel in the RAF* (*Příslušníci československého letectva v RAF*) (Praha: AVIS, 1999)
Vančata, P., *311 Squadron* (Sandomierz: Stratus, 2013)
Ward, C., and Smith, S., *3 Group Bomber Command: An Operational Record* (Barnsley: Pen & Sword Books, 2008)

Magazines and Periodicals

Flight Magazine 1940-45
The Globe and Mail 1939-45
The Hamilton Spectator 1939-43
The Toronto Telegram 1940-41
The Toronto Daily Star 1940-41

RAF Log Books

Jaroslav Doktor, Antonín Macenauer, Miroslav Vild, and Karel Vildomec

Selected Websites

http://aces.safarikovi.org
http://forum.12oclockhigh.net
http://forum.keypublishing.co.uk
http://www.cairdpublications.com
http://www.convoyweb.org.uk
http://www.cwgc.org
http://www.thegazette.co.uk
http://www.polishsquadronsremembered.com
http://www.prinzeugen.com
http://www.rafcommands.com
http://www.rafweb.org